ANCIENT ROME
INFOGRAPHICS

NICOLAS GUILLERAT x JOHN SCHEID x MILAN MELOCCO

ANCIENT ROME INFOGRAPHICS

WITH A FOREWORD BY PHILIP MATYSZAK

Nicolas Guillerat is a data designer and graphic artist.

John Scheid is Emeritus Professor at the Collège de France, as well being the author of *An Introduction to Roman Religion*, *The Craft of Zeus* and *The Gods, the State and the Individual*.

Milan Melocco has a doctorate in history from the Sorbonne Univerity.

Philip Matyszak has a doctorate in Roman history from St John's College, Oxford. He is the author of many books on classical civilization, including *Chronicle of the Roman Republic*, *The Enemies of Rome*, *Ancient Rome on Five Denarii a Day*, *Ancient Athens on Five Drachmas a Day*, *Lives of the Romans* (with Joanne Berry) and *Legionary*.

On the front cover: Graphic illustrating the standard equipment issued to a Roman legionary (see page 91).

Translated from the French *Infographie de la Rome antique* by Matthew Clarke

First published in the United Kingdom in 2021 by
Thames & Hudson Ltd, 181A High Holborn, London WC1V 7QX

First published in 2021 in the United States of America
by Thames & Hudson Inc., 500 Fifth Avenue, New York, New York 10110

Reprinted in 2023

Original edition © 2020 Passés Composés/Humensis, Paris
This edition © 2021 Thames & Hudson Ltd, London

British Library Cataloguing-in-Publication Data
A catalogue record for this book is available from the British Library

Library of Congress Control Number 2021934197

ISBN: 978-0-500-25262-8

Printed and bound in Slovenia by DZS-Grafik d.o.o

Be the first to know about our new releases,
exclusive content and author events by visiting
thamesandhudson.com
thamesandhudsonusa.com
thamesandhudson.com.au

CONTENTS

FOREWORD

The Roman empire was both huge and diverse, yet in this the empire was not unique even among ancient empires. A few centuries previously, the heirs of Alexander the Great had ruled an empire so vast that it stretched from the Mediterranean to Afghanistan, and contemporary empires in India and China were even more populous. Yet the Roman Empire deserves our special attention, for no other state has so affected the later development of modern Europe, and for better or worse, Europe has changed the world.

Yet the Roman empire was not only a European empire – the Levant, the Maghreb, and Egypt were all integral parts of the empire – arguably even more so than peripheral states such as Britain. Indeed, parts of Asia Minor still called themselves 'Roman' in 1297, when William Wallace was defending Scottish independence against the English at Stirling Bridge.

At its peak, the Roman Empire stretched from the Atlantic shores of Britain and Spain, along the Atlas Mountains of North Africa, and down to the second cataract of the Nile. From there it encompassed Saudi Arabia (conquered by Trajan) and east of the ruins of Babylon on the banks of the river Euphrates. In Europe, the northern border of Rome's empire was the Danube – with the province of Dacia to the north – and the Rhine, the two rivers forming a combined frontier of some 4,000 kilometres.

To control this massive empire and withstand barbarian attacks from beyond the frontiers, Rome had an army which, at the most generous estimates, numbered half a million men including legionaries, auxiliaries and naval forces – that is, about the size of the army that currently defends Egypt alone.

Because Rome's population and economy could not support a larger army (indeed, Rome could not really afford the army that it had), Rome's forces were stretched to an almost impossible extent. The only way that Rome could hold down so extensive an empire against internal and external threats was with not just the acquiescence of the population, but its enthusiastic support. How Rome gained and maintained such support is one of the great, and largely unlearned, lessons we can take from the history of the empire.

The Roman empire was never a static entity. When Rome's first emperor, Augustus, brought the state under his control in 31 BCE, Rome already ruled an extensive empire that included Greece, Gaul, Spain and a good portion of North Africa. This was an empire of various foreign peoples who were ruled by Rome. These subjects did not even think of themselves in national terms such as Spaniards or Gauls, but as Atrebates, Celtiberians or Athenians. It was a tribute to the Roman genius for government that by the 5th century CE, the empire ruled by Rome had become an empire of Romans, in which free citizens from Egypt to Wales all considered themselves Romans, members of the same body politic.

This achievement should not be underestimated. At about the time that tradition ascribes to the foundation of Rome, another empire in Mesopotamia had come crashing down. This was the Assyrian empire, whose domains were ruled by Assyrians for Assyrians. The subjects of the empire were there to serve the Assyrian nation, and any who protested at the empire's ever-increasing exactions were mercilessly crushed. So when, at the end of the 7th century BCE, Assyria showed signs of weakness, a coalition of the empire's former subjects arose in rebellion and destroyed the Assyrian empire so comprehensively that archaeologists are still searching for the remains of some former Assyrian cities.

Contrast this with the end of the Roman Empire, when even after the political and military structures that supported the empire had crumbled away in the west, the peoples once ruled by Rome desperately insisted that they were still Roman and clung to whatever bits of Roman law and culture that they could maintain.

There was one major reason for this – as the biographer Plutarch remarked: 'More than anything else this is what gave increase to Rome – that the state always united those whom it conquered and incorporated them within itself.' Even in the earliest days of the city, those conquered by Rome discovered that they were not subjects, but fellow citizens of the victors. When the city of Rome ran out of room for its new citizens, the Romans came up with a groundbreaking new concept: namely that people could become Roman citizens while simultaneously remaining citizens of their own community.

The concept of dual citizenship had never been previously tried in the ancient world, where citizenship was invariably confined to just one city and jealously guarded by those who had it. Rome's new strategy of allowing members of other communities to become Roman citizens (even freed Roman slaves became Romans) was a huge success. So much so that when Rome did try restricting the growth of the citizenship, the peoples of Italy went to war with Rome to obtain it. This was the so-called Social War of 90 BCE, which is perhaps the only known opposite to a war of independence.

Through absorbing new communities into the citizen body and by placing colonies of citizens at strategic points in conquered lands, Rome's domains grew as a mosaic of city-states, each with its own culture and character, yet all also Roman. In consequence, the Roman Republic saw some of its greatest citizens – men such as Marius and Cicero – come from places such as Arpinum, which was captured by Rome in 305 BCE. This record of inclusiveness continued into the empire, which saw emperors such as Philip the Arab, and Maximinus Thrax (the Thracian). Septimius Severus was of North African stock, the emperor Trajan was born in Spain and Constantine the Great in what is today Serbia.

In short, not only did one not have to be born in Rome to be a Roman emperor, but by the 5th century, Rome was not even the capital of its own empire, that role having been taken over first by Milan, then by Ravenna in the west and Constantinople in the east. This shows that not only was Rome open to talent – consider Publius Ventidius, who saw his first Roman triumphal parade as a captive in that parade, and his second as the conquering general being honoured – but the Romans were themselves also extraordinarily open to new ideas.

In the crisis of the 3rd century, barbarian invasions and plague shook Roman faith in their gods, and left the populace open to the idea of Christianity, which became the established faith of the empire by the 5th century. In the 3rd century of its existence, Rome's domains had about as many Christians as did the Sasanian Persian empire to the east. By the fall of Rome in the 5th century, Europe was solidly Christian – a religious change that had profound effects for later generations.

When talking of the Roman Empire, historians usually break their subject into several different eras. There is the Republican Empire, when Rome had no emperor but was ruled by magistrates elected by an (admittedly very limited) democracy. While it is often claimed that the Roman Republic collapsed due to its inability to manage its new domains, the issue is more complex than that. Firstly, there is no evidence that autocracies are better at administration than democracies, and secondly, the administrative structure of the Republican Empire was adopted almost intact by the first emperors, and this worked reasonably well for them.

The Roman Empire itself was basically a well-disguised military dictatorship. The artful Augustus did most of the disguising, and indeed he claimed to be merely the 'first citizen' of the empire. The word for 'first citizen' – *princeps* – has given us the modern word 'prince' and the name for Augustus's form of government, which is today called the Principate. Later, when the rule of the emperors became more accepted and emperors became more despotic, their form of government was known as the Dominate. This latter form of government lasted into the Late Roman Empire, which is the period usually counted from the rule of Constantine the Great in 306 CE till the fall of the Western Empire in 470.

There are historians who argue that the end of imperial government in the west did not mean that Rome had fallen. Socially, linguistically and culturally, the Roman empire underwent huge changes but lived on. Today we elect a candidate because Romans standing for office wore the chalk-whitened *toga candida*. Brides are carried over the threshold, because that is how they were transported in Roman times. A Roman temple was not a temple until a priest called an augur had performed the rites, as even today we inaugurate buildings and enterprises. These and countless other examples show that we are not merely the successors to the Roman empire – in very many ways we are still Romans.

Philip Matyszak

INTRODUCTION

The history of Rome is very long. Over 2,000 years passed from its foundation (probably in 753 BCE) to the fall of Constantinople in 1453, and the Roman Empire covered a vast area, stretching from the Scottish borders to the Sahara, from Gibraltar to the Black Sea. This enormous scale explains why this book must necessarily confine itself to the history of the Western Empire, which came to an end in 476 CE. This is still a long period, even though our knowledge of its earliest centuries is relatively impoverished due to a lack of sources. Furthermore, the final century of the Western Empire was tumultuous, as it was dominated by invasions, making it too complex for the purposes of this work. Moreover, as the Roman Empire was not a single centralized territory but rather a mosaic of extremely diverse institutional and cultural elements, with each city-state operating according to its own logic, it is impossible to do justice to all these parallel histories. It therefore seemed more appropriate to basically devote our attention to the Roman state, the *res publica* of the Roman people, the political centre of this sprawling ensemble – and the highest authority over it. To see how the inhabitants of the Roman world defined themselves in these circumstances, we begin with a brief section on the provinces and cities.

The study of this (already long) period running from the 5th century BCE to the 4th century CE gives rise to another problem: the amount and quality of the sources available to us, and the limitations that these impose on an undertaking of this kind, especially as regards hard data. The closer we get to the Empire's foundation, the fewer the sources, and the less useful they become. Although more and more archaeological findings from the early centuries are being unearthed (including some that are truly spectacular), these are mute witnesses that cannot be invoked without close examination of the historical and mythological texts in which they are mentioned, a long time after the event. Who were the Roman kings? Do we really know their names, or are these the fruit of subsequent legends? Was Servius a slave – hence his name – or did that very name happen to serve as the basis for the creation of his legend? What were the institutions of royal Rome, and what was their history? There are so many questions that have to go unanswered. It is true that some very ancient inscriptions have survived but unfortunately, they do not really help us very much. One of these, found inside the Roman Forum, in a sacred area under a marble slab known as the Black Stone (*Lapis Niger*), has been dated to the 6th or 5th century BCE. It tells us that there was once a king (*rex*), who was accompanied by a herald or usher (*calator*), and that a particular event gave rise to a punishment (*sacratio*, an exclusion from the civic community and 'return' to the gods, as well as the seizure of livestock). The details of this inscription are fragmentary but they have been subject to numerous interpretations; even if we favour one particular explanation, it would provide us with very little worthwhile information. This paucity of solid facts means that it has little more than chronological significance. Our examination of Roman history will therefore be brief during the early centuries, only coming into its own when useful historical documents, texts, inscriptions and city plans become available. Broadly speaking, this takes us to the 4th century BCE.

After that time, we can place greater trust in ancient historians, particularly those of the last three centuries of the Republic and the first three centuries of the Empire. From the 4th century CE onwards, however, we encounter a dearth of reliable chroniclers, and history once again becomes an arduous critical exercise, even though the sources are abundant and there is greater access to inscriptions, particularly after the 1st century CE. Even though we are able to use the available documents to reconstruct the institutions, the social, political, military and economic life and, indeed, the very history of Rome, we often lack one essential element: reliable and serviceable hard data. The manuscripts that are available to us often feature inaccurate transcriptions from older texts, and most fail to quantify their data at all, or at best do so haphazardly. We cannot expect to amass data to match the sources available to modern and contemporary historians. We must always be aware that data from ancient history is dependent on calculations and reconstructions that are sometimes sketchy and may be undermined by subsequent archaeological findings. Moreover, historians of the ancient world are often handling the only documents of their kind in existence. In these circumstances, there are no alternative sources, and this circumstance is what separates their research from that of their colleagues studying modern and contemporary history.

Despite these limitations, however, enough data is available to create a history of the Roman world in infographics, divided into three sections. Chapter I, 'The Lands and People of the Empire', focuses on the expansion of the Roman world and its power from its original roots on the banks of the Tiber. It goes on to describe the general features, development and social structure of the Roman people. Particular attention is given to the evolution of the everyday lives of Roman citizens and other inhabitants of the Empire, revolving around the city-states of Italy and the provinces, all with their equivalent but still very specific institutions. It would be perfectly possible to devote an entire book to the Roman cities and colonies, which were never constituted in exactly the same way, and the 'peregrine' (non-Roman) cities, which developed countless different systems for organizing political, judicial and institutional life. Such a work would undoubtedly demonstrate the enormous diversity of the Roman world but would do little to further the reader's understanding of its structure.

Chapter II, 'Government, Worship and Social Needs', explains how this vast ensemble worked, starting with the institutions of Rome under the Republic and the Empire, and of course the distinctive figure of the emperor himself. It would be impossible to adequately summarize the Greco-Roman culture that marked the thousand years covered in this book – that would once again require a whole book of its own – so we have instead focused on one of the most outstanding aspects of Roman culture: its jurisprudence, which is still shaping the Western world today. There follows a section on the highly specific development of religion in Rome, from public and private cults to the revolution engendered by the emergence of Christianity. Among other social issues, considerable space is devoted to the Roman economy. This topic can be confusing for the modern reader, largely because it is a subject of hot debate between 'modernists' and 'primitivists', who are both often driven by the scarcity of sources, or indeed their own personal bias, to invoke theories that allow them to create a synthesis.

Chapter III analyses Rome's military might by presenting the Roman army and highlighting its main strength as its soldiers, which enabled it to wear down most of its opponents. The military history of Rome ground to a halt when its last enemy, the Germanic barbarians, managed to take the place of battle-fatigued Roman soldiers and therefore appropriate imperial power from the inside.

As pointed out above, we have been unable to discuss certain topics in depth owing to the specificity of our approach and the scale of the documentation required. We therefore decided to exclude most of the culture of the Roman world. This cannot be adequately explored without a survey of Greek and Roman poets, philosophers, storytellers, historians and sages who were active over a period of six centuries, not to mention the Roman intellectuals who prompted a renewed interest in the Greek thinkers of the 5th century BCE and were largely responsible for the subsequent transmission of their ideas to future generations. Similarly, the Romans were inspired by the achievements of Hellenic architecture but developed them by applying their own architectural and decorative skills, with their own distinctive character, and providing, in their turn, inspiration for future architects (even today). We have avoided any extensive discussion of this topic, although in passing we refer to temples, basilicas, triumphal arches and luxurious houses, as well as public monuments built to house spectacles and performances, such as theatres, circuses and amphitheatres. These buildings are also featured on our maps but we do not describe them in detail, partly because they are very similar to each other (the main differences being those of size). Circuses are mentioned in their most common context: the conclusion of and accompaniment to a major religious festival. Similarly, the imposing amphitheatres were not used on an everyday basis – and the performances presented there were usually closer to bullfights and wrestling matches than the gladiatorial massacres so beloved of Hollywood. In this case, as in all the subject areas covered in these pages, we have striven to describe and contextualize the basic structural elements of the Roman world.

I. THE LANDS AND PEOPLE OF THE EMPIRE

FROM CITY TO EMPIRE

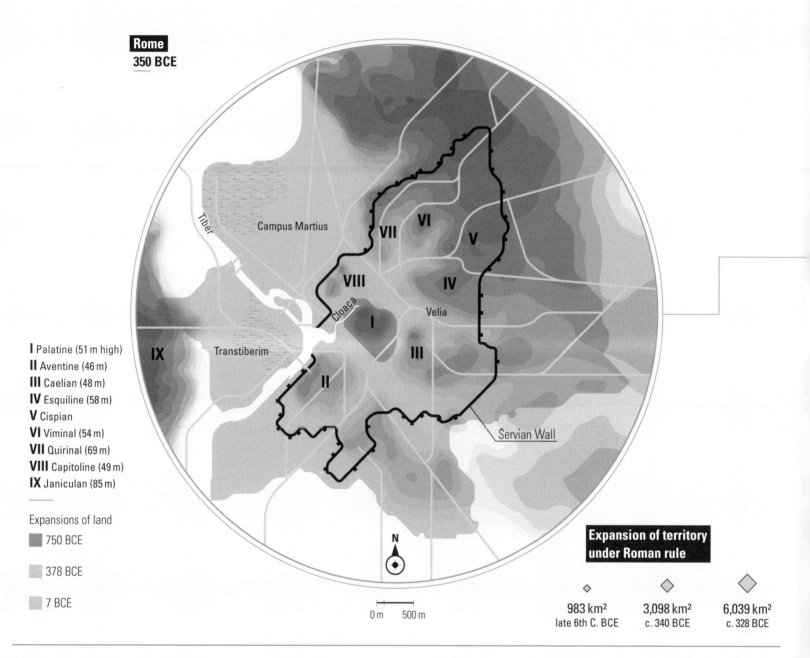

Rome
350 BCE

Tiber

Campus Martius

VII

VI

V

VIII

IV

Cloaca

Velia

I

Transtiberim

IX

III

II

Servian Wall

I Palatine (51 m high)
II Aventine (46 m)
III Caelian (48 m)
IV Esquiline (58 m)
V Cispian
VI Viminal (54 m)
VII Quirinal (69 m)
VIII Capitoline (49 m)
IX Janiculan (85 m)

Expansions of land

750 BCE

378 BCE

7 BCE

N

Expansion of territory under Roman rule

0 m 500 m

983 km²
late 6th C. BCE

3,098 km²
c. 340 BCE

6,039 km²
c. 328 BCE

The long history of Rome spans more than two thousand years, if the Byzantine period is taken into account. According to legend, Rome was founded in 753 BCE, but, be that as it may, the site was definitely occupied by at least the 10th century BCE. Rome lost control over its Western territories in 476 CE, but in its Greek domains, which were the richest and easiest to defend, the Empire, governed from Constantinople, endured until that city's fall in 1453.

The alliances that Rome built up with its neighbouring cities allowed it to gain control over central Italy within a few hundred years. From that time on, there was no holding back. Looking southwards, Rome attacked Abruzzi (then held by the fearsome Samnite people) and the Greeks' southern colonies, but it soon found itself confronted by another imperialistic power, the city of Carthage,

whose empire stretched from present-day Tunisia to the Spanish coast. Carthage's dominions included Sicily and Sardinia, both of which were also of interest to Rome. This led to three wars, known as the Punic Wars, which took place between 260 and 146 BCE, and eventually resulted in the destruction of Carthage. This positive outcome notwithstanding, Rome was often severely challenged over the course of these conflicts, not least by the Carthaginian military genius Hannibal, who invaded Italy in 218 BCE. Despite his brilliance and the skill of his troops, Hannibal was eventually overcome by the sheer numbers of Rome's allied forces. From then on, the cities in the Mediterranean recognized that Rome was almost invincible, as the alliances that it had been consolidating since the 5th century BCE allowed it to quickly mobilize new troops to replace any losses. A formidable military machine had thus emerged.

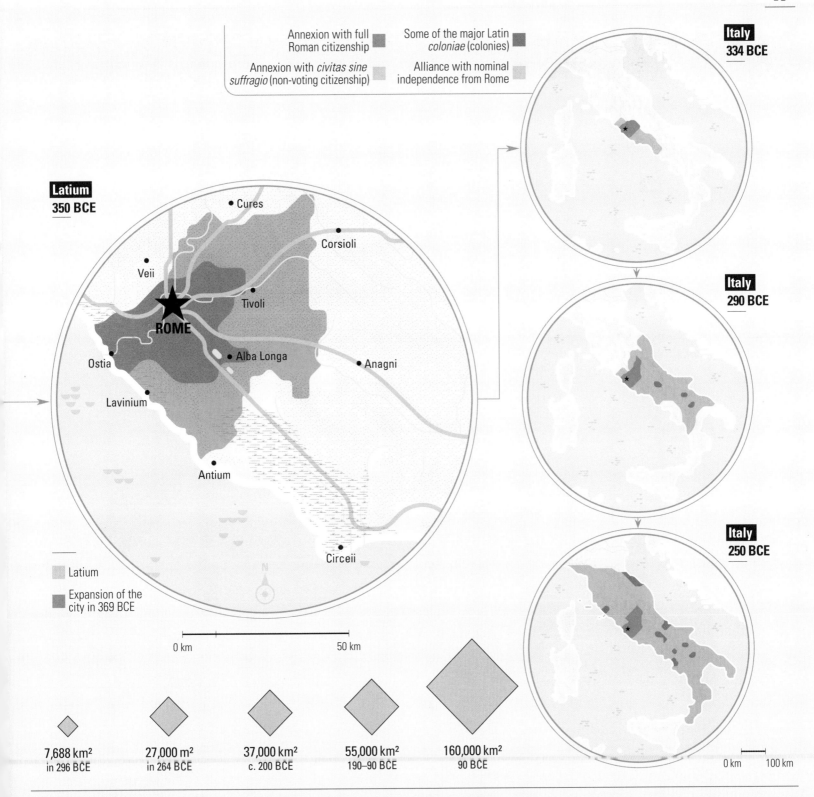

Italy 334 BCE

Italy 290 BCE

Italy 250 BCE

Annexion with full Roman citizenship

Annexion with *civitas sine suffragio* (non-voting citizenship)

Some of the major Latin *coloniae* (colonies)

Alliance with nominal independence from Rome

Latium 350 BCE

Cures

Corsioli

Veii

Tivoli

ROME

Ostia

Alba Longa

Anagni

Lavinium

Antium

Circeii

N

Latium

Expansion of the city in 369 BCE

0 km — 50 km

7,688 km² in 296 BCE

27,000 m² in 264 BCE

37,000 km² c. 200 BCE

55,000 km² 190–90 BCE

160,000 km² 90 BCE

0 km — 100 km

The Roman power base was not slow to take advantage of this, and Rome swiftly occupied the parts of Spain that had formerly been under Carthaginian rule, as well as Sicily, Sardinia, and, finally, the territory of Carthage itself. It meddled in the affairs of the Greek cities, destroyed the remains of the Macedonian empire in Greece and Asia Minor and put down lasting roots in that part of the world. During the 1st century BCE, Egypt and the kingdoms in the interior of Asia Minor likewise fell under its sway, as Rome astutely took sides in the civil wars and uprisings that sprung up in the region. At the start of the modern era, therefore, the known world was virtually unified: Rome's empire stretched from Gibraltar to the Black Sea, from the English Channel in the north to the Sahara and the Euphrates in the south. In the 1st century CE, the Romans went on to conquer parts of western Germany,

Austria and Romania, as well as Britain (stretching as far north as the Scottish border) and the southeastern section of Arabia.

In around 120 CE, this empire achieved its fullest extent and approached the natural limits of its power. The Romans were never able to permanently establish themselves on the far side of the Lower Rhine and Lower Danube, or beyond the Antonine Wall in Britain, while, to the south, the Euphrates would always prove an unbreachable barrier, even though some of the kingdoms to the east did fleetingly become Roman vassals. Within these boundaries, however, Rome and its allies were able to introduce a process of globalization that would last more than three centuries and generate major trade contacts between all parts of the Western world. This conglomeration would only start to fragment under the pressure of regular invasions by barbarian peoples.

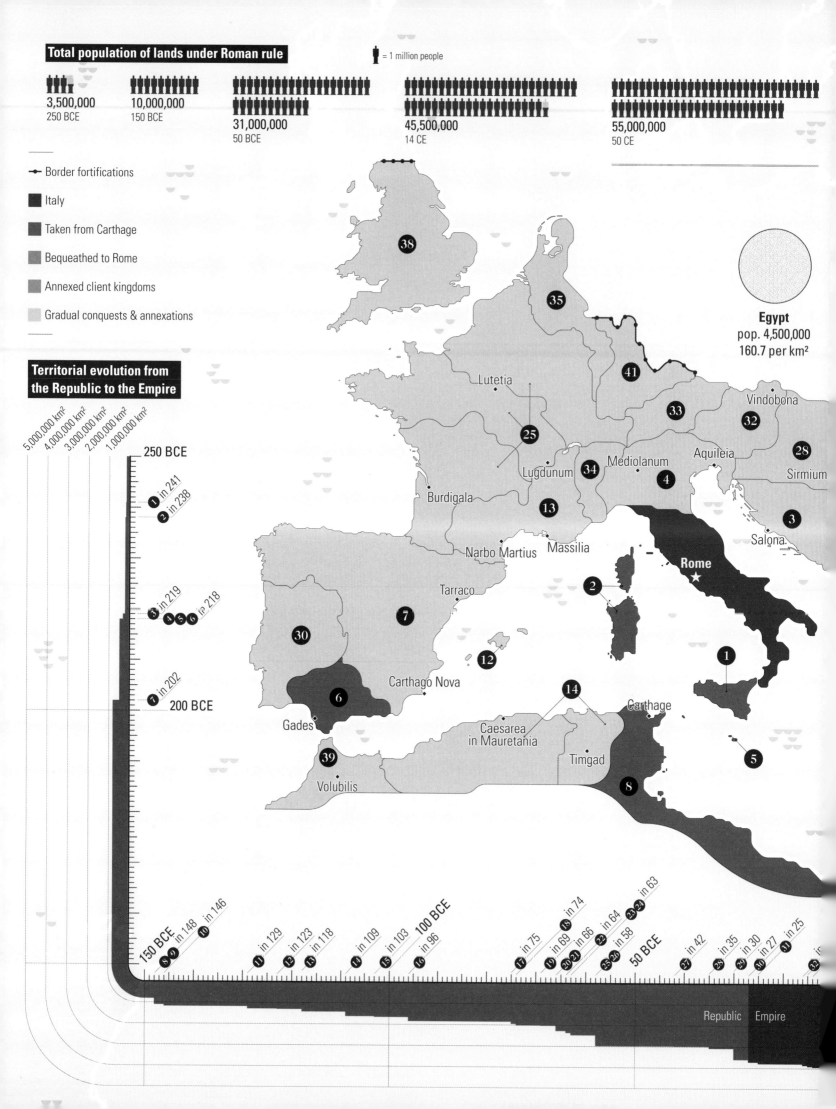

Total population of lands under Roman rule

= 1 million people

3,500,000
250 BCE

10,000,000
150 BCE

31,000,000
50 BCE

45,500,000
14 CE

55,000,000
50 CE

Border fortifications

Italy

Taken from Carthage

Bequeathed to Rome

Annexed client kingdoms

Gradual conquests & annexations

Egypt
pop. 4,500,000
160.7 per km²

Territorial evolution from the Republic to the Empire

5,000,000 km²
4,000,000 km²
3,000,000 km²
2,000,000 km²
1,000,000 km²

250 BCE

1 in 241
2 in 238

3 in 219
4 5 6 in 218

7 in 202
200 BCE

150 BCE
8 9 in 148
10 in 146

in 129
in 123
in 118

in 109
in 103
100 BCE
in 96

in 75
in 74
in 69
in 66
in 64
in 63
in 58
50 BCE

in 42
in 35
in 30
in 27
in 25

Republic Empire

Map labels

Lutetia
Vindobona
Lugdunum
Mediolanum
Aquileia
Sirmium
Burdigala
Salona
Narbo Martius
Massilia
Rome
Tarraco
Carthago Nova
Gades
Carthage
Caesarea in Mauretania
Timgad
Volubilis

70,000,000
165 CE

46,000,000
200 CE

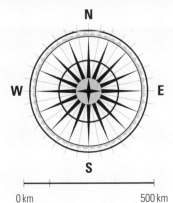

N

W   E

S

0 km   500 km

Population density and distribution in the Roman empire in 14 CE

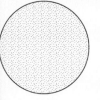

Italy
7,000,000
28 per km²

Sicily
600,000
23 per km²

Sardinia & Corsica
500,000
1 per km²

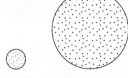

Hispania
5,000,000
8.5 per km²

Transalpine Gaul
1,500,000
15 per km²

Gaul
3,400,000
6.3 per km²

Danube
2,000,000
4.7 per km²

Greece
3,000,000
11.2 per km²

1 Sicily
2 Sardinia & Corsica
3 Illyria & Dalmatia
4 Cisalpine Gaul
5 Malta
6 Baetica
7 Hispania
8 Africa Proconsularis
9 Peloponnese
10 Thrace
11 Asia
12 Balearic Islands
13 Transalpine Gaul
14 Numidia
15 Cilicia
16 Cyrenaica
17 Moesia
18 Bithynia
19 Crete
20 Armenia
21 Colchis
22 Syria & Phoenicia
23 Judea
24 Bosporan Kingdom (client)
25 Gaul (Gallia)
26 Cyprus
27 Rhodes
28 Pannonia
29 Egypt
30 Lusitania
31 Galatia
32 Noricum
33 Rhaetia
34 Alpes Maritimae
35 Germania Inferior
36 Cappadocia
37 Lycia
38 Britain
39 Mauretania
40 Tyras & Olbia
41 Germania Superior
42 Dacia
43 Arabia
44 Mesopotamia & Assyria

Olbia
Tanais

Pergamon
Byzantium
Ephesus
Corinth
Athens
Cyrene
Alexandria
Jerusalem
Damascus
Tyr
Palmyra

in 17
in 43
in 44
in 45
in 56
50 CE
in 81
100 CE
in 106
in 115
150 CE

1,000,000 km²
2,000,000 km²
3,000,000 km²
4,000,000 km²
5,000,000 km²

I. THE CITY

Until the 4th century CE, Rome was almost entirely located on the left bank of the Tiber, with the exception of the Transtiberim (Trastevere) district on the right bank. The Rome of legends was confined to the Palatine Hill and the Valley of the Forum, but from the 6th century BCE onwards the Servian Wall enclosed a much more substantial area. Rome's civil space was defined by the *pomerium*, a legal and religious boundary that, according to the city's founding myth, had been drawn in the ground by a plough steered by Romulus. Within the limits of the pomerium, the magistrates were allowed to take auspices and inaugurate a sacred space (*templum*) that could be used for political and religious ceremonies. The pomerium was enlarged on several occasions. In the 2nd century BCE, for instance, it was extended by a mile, along with the privileges and obligations associated with it. The city continued to expand, however, and in around 270 CE, the Aurelian Walls were built to surround all the urban space that had been consolidated up to that point.

The political heart of the city lay in the Roman Forum, the Forum Boarium and the Campus Martius ('Field of Mars'). The magistrates were based in the buildings in the Roman Forum, which was also the home of the Senate (Curia) and the Tribal Assembly (*comitia tributa*). The Campus Martius was located outside of the pomerium and was used for military exercises and meetings of the Centuriate Assembly (*comitia centuriata*), made up of men eligible for military service. The Forum Boarium, which was traditionally a cattle market, was an important trading area and river dock for the port of Rome.

These neighbourhoods continued to evolve under the Empire. The house built by Augustus on the Palatine grew, in only a few decades, into an enormous imperial palace, and for some 15 years it was the site of Nero's sumptuous palace, the Domus Aurea ('Golden House'). The original Forum acquired a series of monuments and eventually became too small, so it was expanded with five additional fora. In the reign of Augustus, the military and political areas of the Campus Martius were augmented by parks, baths, temples, public altars, the Mausoleum of Augustus and spaces devoted to food distribution. The area stretching from the Aventine to the Aurelian Walls was given over to docks and storehouses. The Transtiberim district was primarily a residential area based around a large park, and successive Emperors gradually endowed it with more public baths and other civic spaces.

Rome also boasted the Circus Maximus, where chariot races and staged hunts were held during major festivals. Other circuses were built on the Campus Martius and, in late antiquity, on the right bank of the river, on the future site of St Peter's Basilica. During the Republic period, the central area of the old Roman Forum was used for gladiatorial games held as part of funeral rituals. In 70 CE, the Flavians built a huge amphitheatre, the Colosseum, on the former site of Nero's Domus Aurea, both to mark the latter's demolition and to provide a venue for staged hunts and gladiatorial games. Domitian added a further group of buildings, including the Odeon of Domitian and a stadium, which housed the Saecular Games of 88 CE.

The necropolises or cemeteries of Rome were traditionally located on the Esquiline Hill and by the sides of the main roads leading out of the city. Under the Empire, however, underground catacombs began to be built.

Pomerium

- - - legal boundary of the city of Rome, marking a civil space within which political, religious and public rites could be performed.

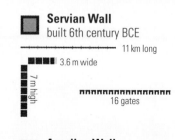

Servian Wall
built 6th century BCE

11 km long

3.6 m wide

7 m high

16 gates

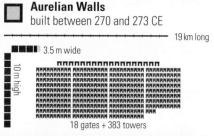

Aurelian Walls
built between 270 and 273 CE

19 km long

3.5 m wide

10 m high

18 gates + 383 towers

1. Aqua Appia aqueduct
2. Aqua Anio Vetus aqueduct
3. Aqua Marcia aqueduct
4. Aqua Tepula aqueduct
5. Aqua Julia aqueduct
6. Aqua Virgo aqueduct
7. Aqua Alsietina aqueduct
8. Aqua Claudia aqueduct
9. Aqua Anio Novus aqueduct
10. Aqua Neroniana aqueduct
11. Aqua Trajana aqueduct
12. Aqua Antoniniana aqueduct

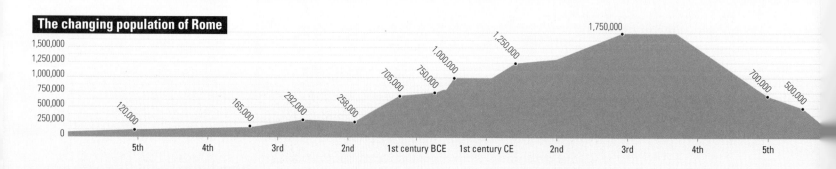

The changing population of Rome

1,500,000
1,250,000
1,000,000
750,000
500,000
250,000
0

120,000
165,000
292,000
258,000
705,000
750,000
1,000,000
1,250,000
1,750,000
700,000
500,000

5th | 4th | 3rd | 2nd | 1st century BCE | 1st century CE | 2nd | 3rd | 4th | 5th

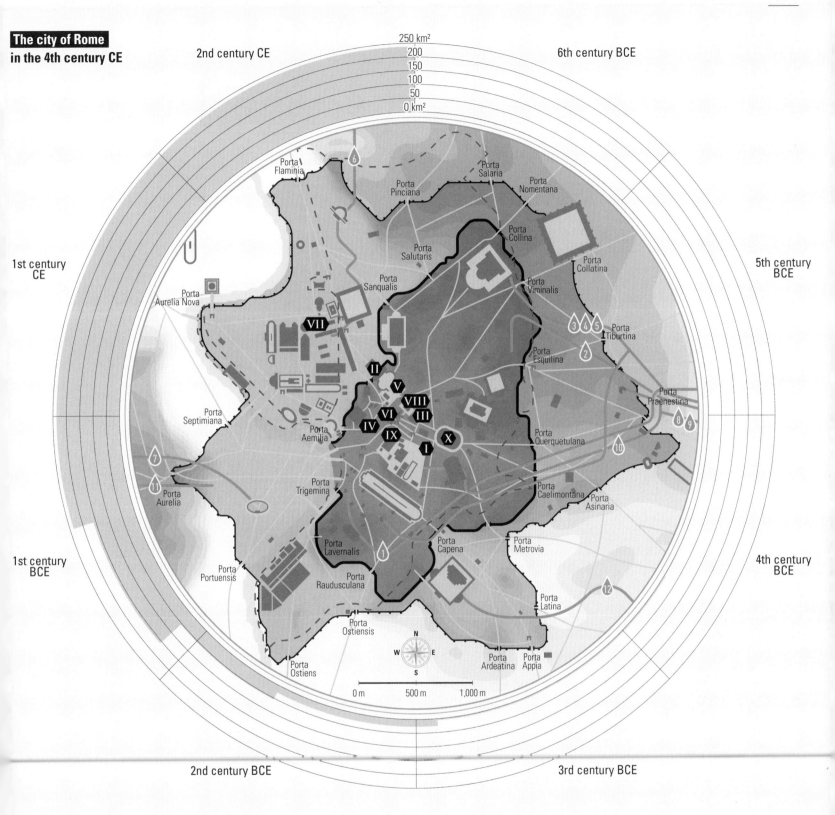

The city of Rome
in the 4th century CE

2nd century CE

6th century BCE

250 km²
200
150
100
50
0 km²

1st century CE

5th century BCE

Porta Flaminia
Porta Salaria
Porta Pinciana
Porta Nomentana
Porta Collina
Porta Salutaris
Porta Collatina
Porta Viminalis
Porta Sanqualis
VII
Porta Tiburtina
Porta Esquilina
II
V
Porta Aurelia Nova
VIII
III
Porta Praenestina
VI
IV
IX
X
I
Porta Septimiana
Porta Aemilia
Porta Querquetulana
Porta Trigemina
Porta Caelimontana
Porta Asinaria
Porta Aurelia
Porta Capena
Porta Metrovia
Porta Lavernalis
Porta Portuensis
Porta Raudusculana
Porta Latina
Porta Ostiensis
Porta Ardeatina
Porta Appia
Porta Ostiens

1st century BCE

4th century BCE

N W E S

0 m   500 m   1,000 m

2nd century BCE

3rd century BCE

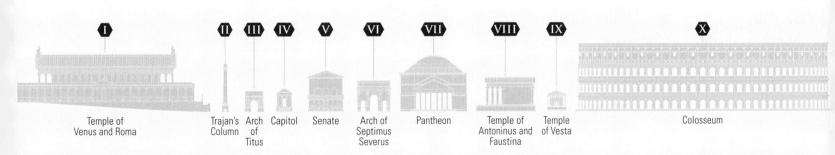

I — Temple of Venus and Roma
II — Trajan's Column
III — Arch of Titus
IV — Capitol
V — Senate
VI — Arch of Septimus Severus
VII — Pantheon
VIII — Temple of Antoninus and Faustina
IX — Temple of Vesta
X — Colosseum

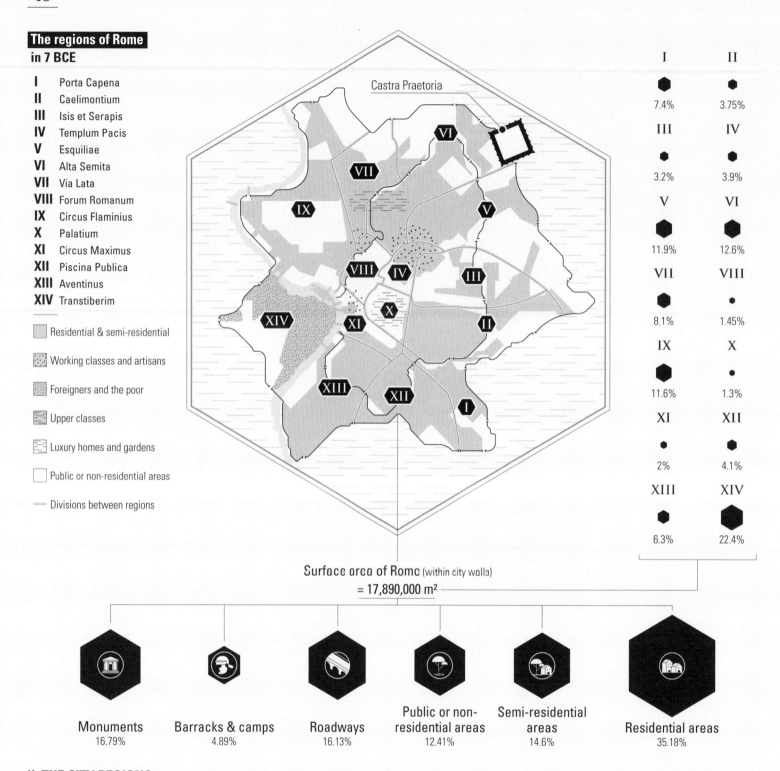

The regions of Rome
in 7 BCE

I	Porta Capena
II	Caelimontium
III	Isis et Serapis
IV	Templum Pacis
V	Esquiliae
VI	Alta Semita
VII	Via Lata
VIII	Forum Romanum
IX	Circus Flaminius
X	Palatium
XI	Circus Maximus
XII	Piscina Publica
XIII	Aventinus
XIV	Transtiberim

Residential & semi-residential

Working classes and artisans

Foreigners and the poor

Upper classes

Luxury homes and gardens

Public or non-residential areas

Divisions between regions

Castra Praetoria

I	II
7.4%	3.75%
III	IV
3.2%	3.9%
V	VI
11.9%	12.6%
VII	VIII
8.1%	1.45%
IX	X
11.6%	1.3%
XI	XII
2%	4.1%
XIII	XIV
6.3%	22.4%

Surface area of Rome (within city walls)
= 17,890,000 m²

Monuments	Barracks & camps	Roadways	Public or non-residential areas	Semi-residential areas	Residential areas
16.79%	4.89%	16.13%	12.41%	14.6%	35.18%

II. THE CITY REGIONS

Republican Rome was divided into four large regions or districts (I: Suburana; II: Esquilina; III: Collina; IV: Palatina). Between the years 12 and 7 BCE, Augustus divided the increasingly sprawling city into 14 regions, which were subdivided into neighbourhoods, or *vici* (265 under the Flavians and at least 324 under Constantine). Each *vicus* had a *compitum*, a shrine located at a crossroads, which was used for collective worship and other gatherings. Every vicus was presided over by four annually appointed *magistri*, mostly recruited from freed slaves.

Since accessible transport was rare, poor people crammed into the centre of Rome in order to take advantage of its political life and grain dole. All the city's important sites were effectively located in regions IV, VIII, IX and XI, and here the 150,000 to 200,000 men with the status of *paterfamilias* (head of household)

who were entitled to food handouts would receive wheat and oil every month. Commoners could also take part in political events and religious festivals, particularly banquets and the distribution of sacrificed meat, as well as watching the games that were traditionally held to bring events of this kind to a conclusion. The elite, meanwhile, had not only residences in the centre of Rome but also large houses and gardens on the city outskirts.

Under Augustus, public baths were confined to the centre but over time they were installed in all parts of the city. Bathhouses thus became communal facilities, along with public fountains and bakeries. Security within the city was entrusted to watchmen (who also put out fires), with one squad of around 600 men for every two city regions, and three urban cohorts (the equivalent of a police force), whose barracks were on the Campus Martius.

Urban planning in the city regions of Rome in the 4th century CE (in figures and %)

Legend: ■ Housing ■ State ■ Business ■ Hygiene ■ Leisure ■ Religious and commemorative

Scale: 50% / 25% / 10% / 5%

	I	II	III	IV	V	VI	VII	VIII	IX	X	XI	XII	XIII	XIV
Houses 1,782	120/6.7%	127/7.2%	160/9%	88/4.9%	180/10.1%	146/8.2%	120/6.7%	130/7.3%	140/7.9%	89/5%	89/5%	113/6.3%	130/7.3%	150/8.4%
Apartment blocks 44,300	3,250/7.3%	3,600/8.1%	2,757/6.2%	2,757/6.2%	3,850/8.7%	3,403/7.7%	3,805/8.6%	3,480/7.9%	2,777/6.3%	2,642/6%	2,600/5.9%	2,487/5.6%	2,487/5.6%	4,405/9.9%
Streets/districts 305	10/3.3%	7/2.3%	12/3.9%	8/2.6%	15/4.9%	17/5.6%	15/4.9%	34/11.1%	35/11.5%	20/6.6%	19/6.2%	17/5.6%	18/5.9%	78/25.6%
Administrative & public buildings 67	1/1.5%	2/3%		5/7.5%	4/6%		1/1.5%	30/44.8%	14/20.9%	8/11.9%	1/1.5%		1/1.5%	
Barracks 17		3/17.6%	1/5.9%		1/5.9%	2/11.8%	3/17.6%	1/5.9%			1/5.9%		2/11.8%	3/17.6%
Schools and libraries 18		1/5.6%	1/5.6%	1/5.6%				8/44.2%	3/16.76%		1/5.6%	1/5.6%	1/5.6%	1/5.6%
Fora 15				1/6.7%			1/6.7%	8/53.3%	2/13.3%				2/13.3%	1/6.7%
Porticoes 35	2/5.7%		1/2.9%	1/2.9%			3/8.6%	4/11.4%	18/51.4%	1/2.9%	2/5.7%		3/8.6%	
Granaries 334	16/4.8%	27/8.1%	17/5.1%	18/5.4%	22/6.6%	18/5.4%	25/7.5%	18/5.4%	25/7.5%	48/14.4%	16/4.8%	27/8.1%	35/10.5%	22/6.6%
Bakeries 263	20/7.6%	15/5.7%	16/6.1%	15/5.7%	15/5.7%	16/6.1%	15/5.7%	20/7.6%	20/7.6%	20/7.6%	16/6.1%	20/7.6%	20/7.6%	24/9.1%
Balneae (small bathhouses) 951	86/9%	85/8.9%	80/8.4%	75/7.9%	75/7.9%	75/7.9%	75/7.9%	85/8.9%	63/6.6%	44/4.6%	15/1.6%	63/6.6%	44/4.6%	86/9%
Public fountains 1,217	87/7.15%	65/5.35%	65/5.35%	78/6.4%	74/6.1%	73/6%	76/6.25%	120/9.9%	120/9.9%	89/7.3%	20/1.6%	81/6.7%	89/7.3%	180/14.8%
Thermae (bath complexes) 9	2/18.2%		2/18.2%		2/18.2%				2/18.2%			1/9%	2/18.2%	
Circuses, theatres, amphitheatres 24		3/12.5%	3/12.5%		2/8.3%				11/45.8%	1/4.2%	1/4.2%			3/12.5%
Triumphal arches & obelisks 48	7/14.6%	1/2.1%		1/2.1%	2/4.2%	1/2.1%	1/2.1%	10/20.8%	5/10.4%	3/6.2%	16/33.3%			1/2.1%
Shrines 305	10/3.3%	7/2.3%	12/3.9%	8/2.6%	15/4.9%	17/5.6%	15/4.9%	34/11.1%	35/11.5%	20/6.6%	19/6.2%	17/5.6%	18/5.9%	78/25.6%
Temples & altars 194	3/1.55%	4/2.1%	3/1.55%	19/9.8%	4/2.1%	10/5.15%	5/2.6%	48/24.7%	32/16.5%	22/11.3%	25/13%	2/1%	11/5.7%	6/3.1%

III. THE FORA

The political heart of Rome would remain in the Valley of the Forum right until the end, even though political power was exercised from the 1st century CE by a combination of the Imperial Palace, the Curia and the imperial prefectures. The magistrates continued to administer justice here from their official headquarters, and the area played host to many political and religious rituals, both old and new, either in the open air or inside temples.

By the end of the Republic, the old Forum had become too small and so it was supplemented by additional fora. To the north, there was Caesar's Forum, followed by those of Augustus, Nerva, Vespasian (the Forum of Peace) and Trajan. The semi-circular halls of the new porticoes were used for institutional purposes, as law courts, archives (those of the Prefect of Rome were in the Forum of Peace), Latin and Greek libraries (in Trajan's Forum, on either side of the column) and educational establishments (in the Forums of Augustus and Trajan). Later constructions included the enormous Temple of Venus and Roma (under Hadrian) and the Basilica of Maxentius and Constantine (4th century), which, like all buildings of this type, was covered.

The fora could be accessed via the major Roman roads, from the Campus Martius to the north, from the Imperial Palace and the Circus Maximus to the west and from the Colosseum to the south, and so were connected to all other major political and civic institutions.

Timeline of the construction of Roman buildings ● State buildings ● Porticoes ● Public venues ● Triumphal arches ● Fora ● Baths ● Temples ● =1

— Fires — Floods — Earthquakes — Sacking

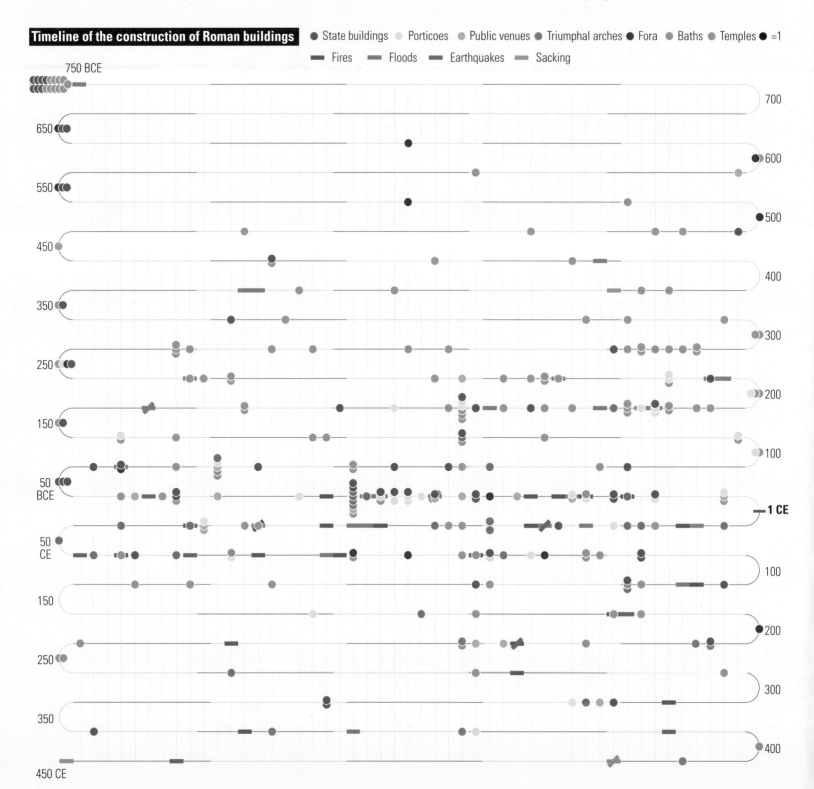

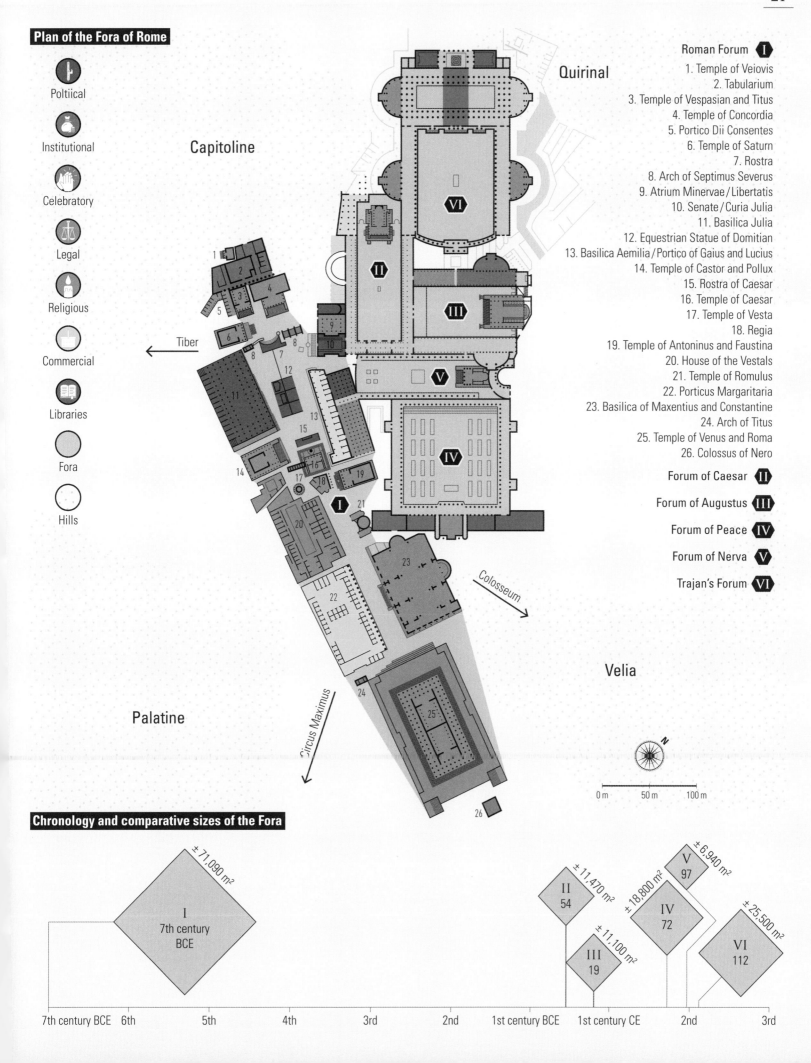

Plan of the Fora of Rome

- Poltiical
- Institutional
- Celebratory
- Legal
- Religious
- Commercial
- Libraries
- Fora
- Hills

Capitoline

Quirinal

Tiber

Palatine

Velia

Colosseum

Circus Maximus

Roman Forum **I**

1. Temple of Veiovis
2. Tabularium
3. Temple of Vespasian and Titus
4. Temple of Concordia
5. Portico Dii Consentes
6. Temple of Saturn
7. Rostra
8. Arch of Septimus Severus
9. Atrium Minervae / Libertatis
10. Senate / Curia Julia
11. Basilica Julia
12. Equestrian Statue of Domitian
13. Basilica Aemilia / Portico of Gaius and Lucius
14. Temple of Castor and Pollux
15. Rostra of Caesar
16. Temple of Caesar
17. Temple of Vesta
18. Regia
19. Temple of Antoninus and Faustina
20. House of the Vestals
21. Temple of Romulus
22. Porticus Margaritaria
23. Basilica of Maxentius and Constantine
24. Arch of Titus
25. Temple of Venus and Roma
26. Colossus of Nero

Forum of Caesar **II**

Forum of Augustus **III**

Forum of Peace **IV**

Forum of Nerva **V**

Trajan's Forum **VI**

0 m   50 m   100 m

Chronology and comparative sizes of the Fora

I — 7th century BCE — ± 71.090 m²

II — 54 — ± 11.470 m²

III — 19 — ± 11.100 m²

IV — 72 — ± 18,800 m²

V — 97 — ± 6.940 m²

VI — 112 — ± 25,500 m²

7th century BCE   6th   5th   4th   3rd   2nd   1st century BCE   1st century CE   2nd   3rd

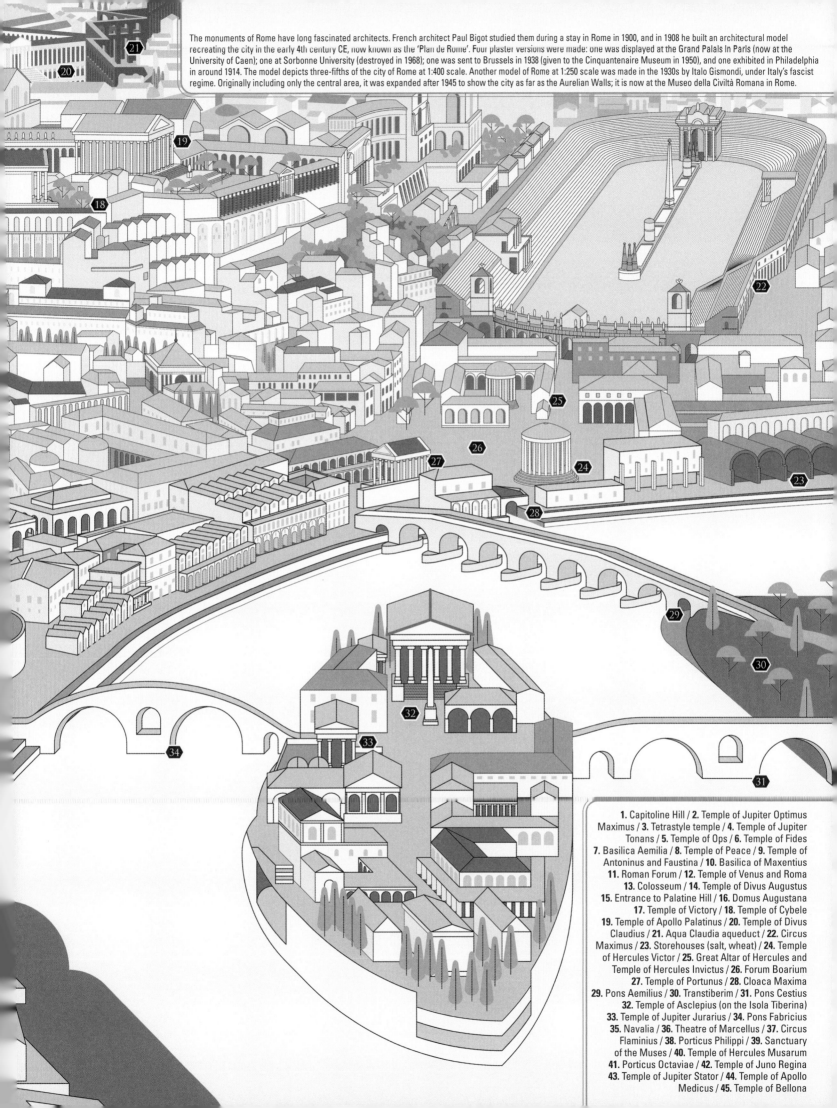

The monuments of Rome have long fascinated architects. French architect Paul Bigot studied them during a stay in Rome in 1900, and in 1908 he built an architectural model recreating the city in the early 4th century CE, now known as the 'Plan de Rome'. Four plaster versions were made: one was displayed at the Grand Palais In Paris (now at the University of Caen); one at Sorbonne University (destroyed in 1968); one was sent to Brussels in 1938 (given to the Cinquantenaire Museum in 1950), and one exhibited in Philadelphia in around 1914. The model depicts three-fifths of the city of Rome at 1:400 scale. Another model of Rome at 1:250 scale was made in the 1930s by Italo Gismondi, under Italy's fascist regime. Originally including only the central area, it was expanded after 1945 to show the city as far as the Aurelian Walls; it is now at the Museo della Civiltà Romana in Rome.

1. Capitoline Hill / 2. Temple of Jupiter Optimus Maximus / 3. Tetrastyle temple / 4. Temple of Jupiter Tonans / 5. Temple of Ops / 6. Temple of Fides 7. Basilica Aemilia / 8. Temple of Peace / 9. Temple of Antoninus and Faustina / 10. Basilica of Maxentius 11. Roman Forum / 12. Temple of Venus and Roma 13. Colosseum / 14. Temple of Divus Augustus 15. Entrance to Palatine Hill / 16. Domus Augustana 17. Temple of Victory / 18. Temple of Cybele 19. Temple of Apollo Palatinus / 20. Temple of Divus Claudius / 21. Aqua Claudia aqueduct / 22. Circus Maximus / 23. Storehouses (salt, wheat) / 24. Temple of Hercules Victor / 25. Great Altar of Hercules and Temple of Hercules Invictus / 26. Forum Boarium 27. Temple of Portunus / 28. Cloaca Maxima 29. Pons Aemilius / 30. Transtiberim / 31. Pons Cestius 32. Temple of Asclepius (on the Isola Tiberina) 33. Temple of Jupiter Jurarius / 34. Pons Fabricius 35. Navalia / 36. Theatre of Marcellus / 37. Circus Flaminius / 38. Porticus Philippi / 39. Sanctuary of the Muses / 40. Temple of Hercules Musarum 41. Porticus Octaviae / 42. Temple of Juno Regina 43. Temple of Jupiter Stator / 44. Temple of Apollo Medicus / 45. Temple of Bellona

THE ROMAN PEOPLE

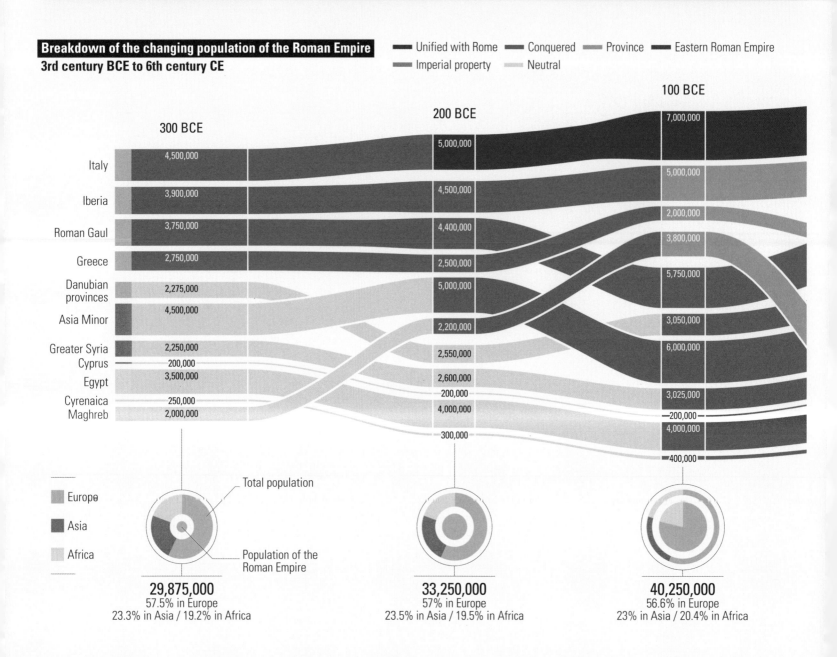

Legend: Unified with Rome ■ Conquered ■ Province ■ Eastern Roman Empire ■ Imperial property ■ Neutral

300 BCE

Region	Population
Italy	4,500,000
Iberia	3,900,000
Roman Gaul	3,750,000
Greece	2,750,000
Danubian provinces	2,275,000
Asia Minor	4,500,000
Greater Syria	2,250,000
Cyprus	200,000
Egypt	3,500,000
Cyrenaica	250,000
Maghreb	2,000,000

200 BCE: 5,000,000 · 4,500,000 · 4,400,000 · 2,500,000 · 5,000,000 · 2,200,000 · 2,550,000 · 2,600,000 · 200,000 · 4,000,000 · 300,000

100 BCE: 7,000,000 · 5,000,000 · 2,000,000 · 3,800,000 · 5,750,000 · 3,050,000 · 6,000,000 · 3,025,000 · 200,000 · 4,000,000 · 400,000

■ Europe
■ Asia
■ Africa

Total population
Population of the Roman Empire

29,875,000
57.5% in Europe
23.3% in Asia / 19.2% in Africa

33,250,000
57% in Europe
23.5% in Asia / 19.5% in Africa

40,250,000
56.6% in Europe
23% in Asia / 20.4% in Africa

I. THE CHANGING POPULATION

The demographics of the ancient world are a complex matter. The available information is scattered, often contradictory or incomplete, and rarely continuous. Global statistics can only be assembled by extrapolating information from a variety of sources. In the case of Rome, the available information often specifies numbers of citizens, and sometimes (but not always) their families as well. Other sources provide general figures for the population of the Mediterranean or the Roman world but these are often unreliable, as they come from literary texts that have been copied dozens of times. These circumstances demand a critical examination of data, as they cannot be easily extrapolated to our own times.

There is a further problem, however, regarding population distribution. The realities of the Roman era mean that the major demographic sources (often censuses) generally record only free men: i.e. male Roman citizens. Broader information about women and slaves (current or freed) only emerges gradually with the advent of the Empire, but even then, the available sources frequently leave many questions unanswered. Slave status, for example, was not necessarily synonymous with poverty and destitution. Although we do know that some slaves were forced to labour in quarries and mines, or on large agricultural estates, we have very little solid information about them. Far more is known, however, about slaves and freedmen in cities, who sometimes enjoyed a standard of living that would be the envy of some free citizens. It is essential, therefore, to evaluate all the data with care – even more so when it is patchy.

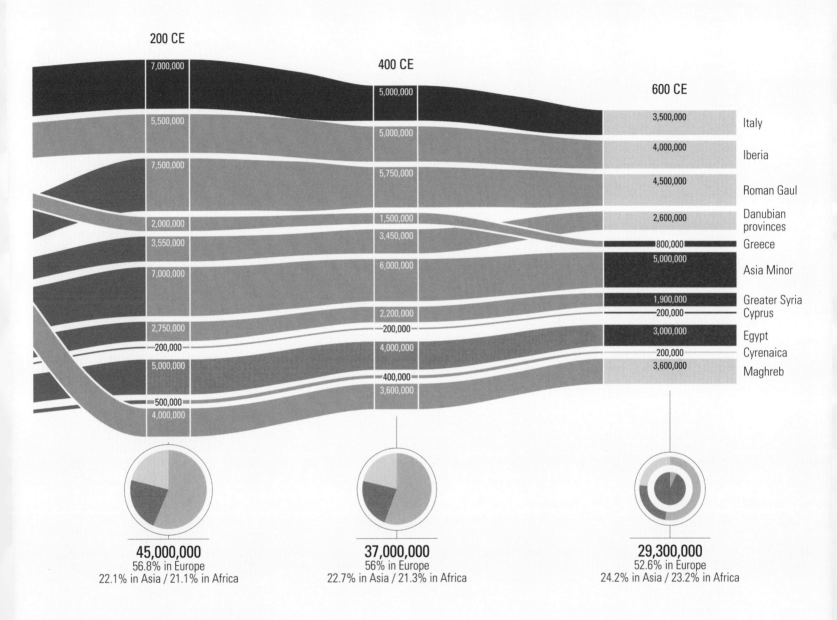

200 CE
7,000,000
5,500,000
7,500,000
2,000,000
3,550,000
7,000,000
2,750,000
200,000
5,000,000
500,000
4,000,000

400 CE
5,000,000
5,000,000
5,750,000
1,500,000
3,450,000
6,000,000
2,200,000
200,000
4,000,000
400,000
3,600,000

600 CE
3,500,000
4,000,000
4,500,000
2,600,000
800,000
5,000,000
1,900,000
200,000
3,000,000
200,000
3,600,000

Italy
Iberia
Roman Gaul
Danubian provinces
Greece
Asia Minor
Greater Syria
Cyprus
Egypt
Cyrenaica
Maghreb

45,000,000
56.8% in Europe
22.1% in Asia / 21.1% in Africa

37,000,000
56% in Europe
22.7% in Asia / 21.3% in Africa

29,300,000
52.6% in Europe
24.2% in Asia / 23.2% in Africa

Breakdown of population by social status in 14 CE

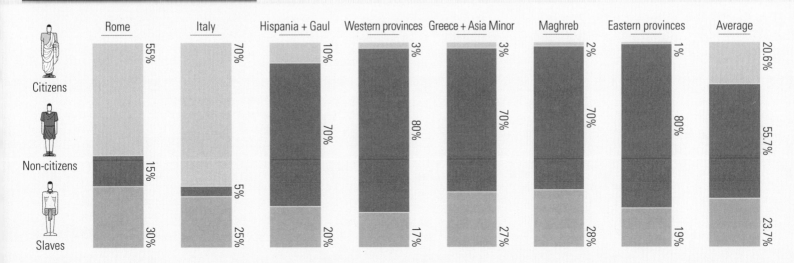

Citizens

Non-citizens

Slaves

Rome
55%
15%
30%

Italy
70%
5%
25%

Hispania + Gaul
10%
70%
20%

Western provinces
3%
80%
17%

Greece + Asia Minor
3%
70%
27%

Maghreb
2%
70%
28%

Eastern provinces
1%
80%
19%

Average
20.6%
55.7%
23.7%

II. LEGAL STATUS

The Mediterranean societies of the ancient world experienced great changes between the 4th century BCE and the 3rd century CE. All of them were founded and remained based on a specific set of legal rights, either before or after being conquered by Rome. The extraordinary longevity of Rome's power over the Western world had a profound impact on its social system, but its defining characteristic was the right to citizenship (the bedrock of legal status), which could be granted by law to *peregrini* (non-Romans or foreigners) and freed slaves, which set Rome apart from virtually all other political entities. Individual status in the Roman world was defined in two ways. People were rooted in their city of origin, remaining a citizen of that place until death. They could also become a Roman citizen, however, and even – if they had the financial means and wherewithal (in other words, if they came from a distinguished local family) – pursue a political career in Rome as a Roman equestrian (*eques*) or senator. This two-pronged mechanism meant that, from the 2nd century onwards, and more specifically after the Edict of Caracalla in 212 CE, all free men in the Roman empire became Roman citizens, provided that they were not convicted of any serious crime, and so they all benefitted from dual citizenship. This status was extremely difficult to modify, as only the emperor had the power to change a person's citizenship of origin.

The increasing prominence of *peregrini* in the Roman world was partly a reflection of Roman conquests, but it was also a result of the aforementioned decree of 212 CE, which boosted the total number of Roman citizens to around 40,000,000 people – or almost the entire free population of the Western world. The degree of access to Roman citizenship had already been exceptional ever since the 3rd century BCE, but this further extension of its privileges is still unparalleled in Western history. From that point on, all free men from the Mediterranean world (in the broadest sense) enjoyed the same legal privileges as Romans from Italy or the city of Rome itself, and they were all subject not only to the laws of their city of origin but also to Roman civil law. This situation had repercussions on the emergence of modern rights. The right to appeal to the emperor himself (as opposed to earlier appeals to the Roman people) was open to any free citizen under sentence (or in fear of being so) from a local or Roman magistrate. Finally, although the status of citizen was granted to fathers and their sons, women would by the same measure indirectly receive rights that were denied to their counterparts in other parts of the Mediterranean world.

Slavery was another fundamental fact of the ancient world – and one that never went away. For a long time, slaves outnumbered citizens (not to mention the high numbers of foreigners, about whom very little is known). Nevertheless, Roman law included processes through which slaves could be freed, and citizens made such heavy use of these that, in the early years of the Empire, the authorities tried to introduce further checks to prevent it. The primary beneficiaries of emancipation were urban slaves who had daily contact with a family; once freed, they would become, to some degree, part of the family of the owner who had freed them and adopt his name. They would remain subject, like a child, to the domestic power of the paterfamilias (their 'patron'), and their possessions would revert to the latter on their death. The stain of slavery would bar the route to a political career for one or two generations but, as a general rule, freed slaves were among the most dynamic elements of society. The slaves of the city of Rome, the imperial cities and, indeed, the emperor himself could also be granted their freedom, and under the Empire, former imperial slaves came to hold important administrative roles.

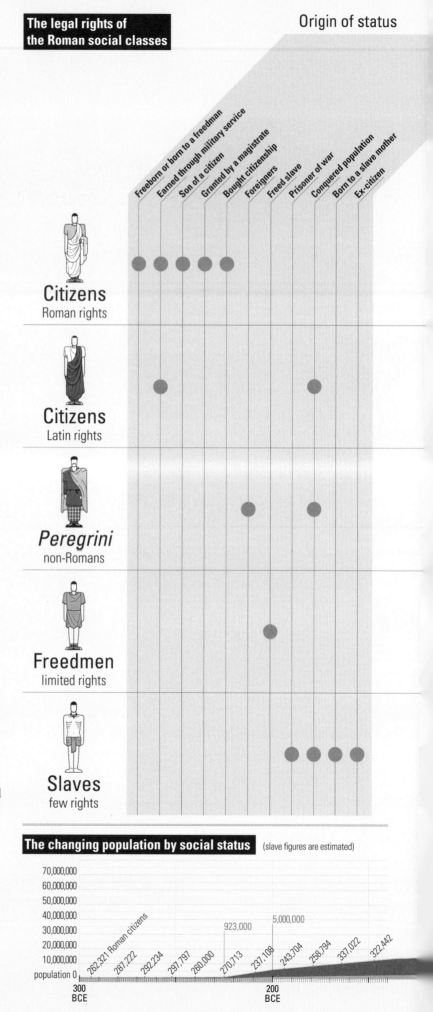

The legal rights of the Roman social classes — Origin of status

The changing population by social status (slave figures are estimated)

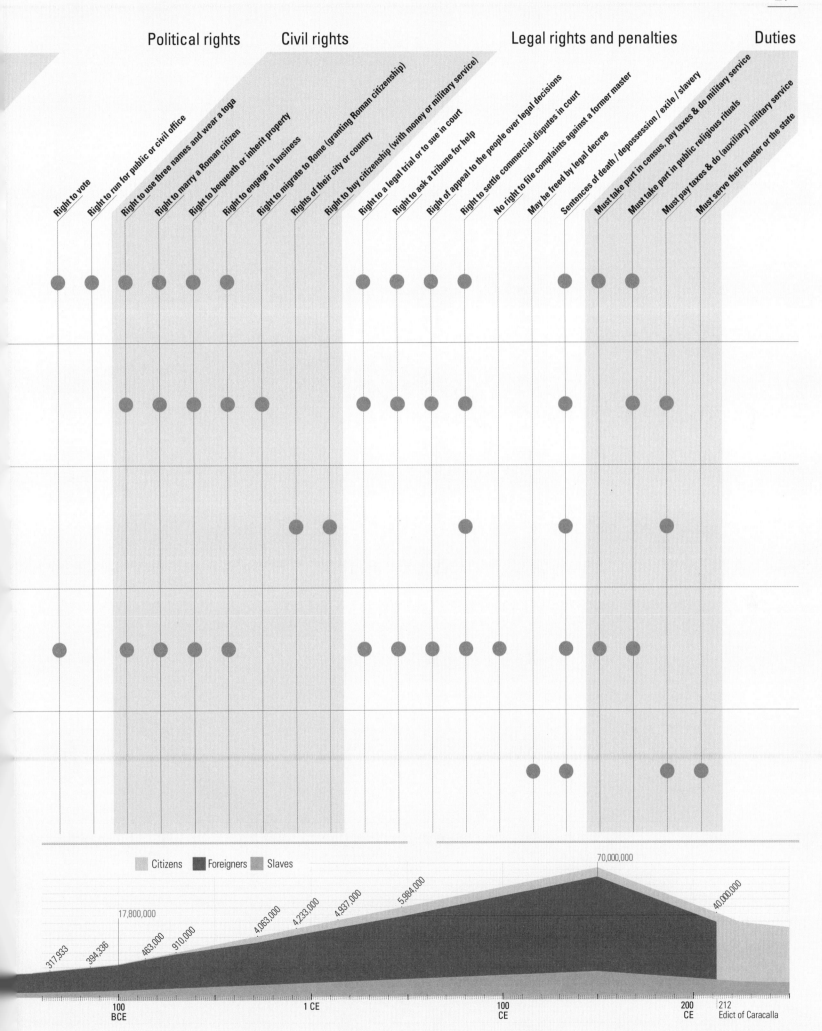

III. SOCIAL AND POLITICAL PATRONAGE

Roman social status was based on the family background of its citizens, which was recorded every five years by two censors and then, from Domitian's reign onwards, by more bureaucratic means. During the Republic, the upper echelons of society were wealthy senators and the equestrian class (*equites*). The senators were usually equestrians in pursuit of a career in politics, and they often spent part of their fortune on electoral handouts for their supporters. Senators were not allowed to get involved in commerce and their fortunes could be severely depleted by electoral campaigns. In order to replenish their coffers, after their service as praetors or consuls they would lobby for an appointment as the governor of a rich province or, better still, a province involved in a war. The equestrians, for their part, would often serve as centurions or tribunes in the army before boosting their assets by collecting taxes in a province or distributing public provisions. They were not barred from commercial activities.

This hierarchy was complemented by the plebeians. Their status did not necessarily imply poverty, although some plebs were indeed very poor, especially in the cities. Many, however, were small-scale traders and property owners, and some were even quite well-off. The

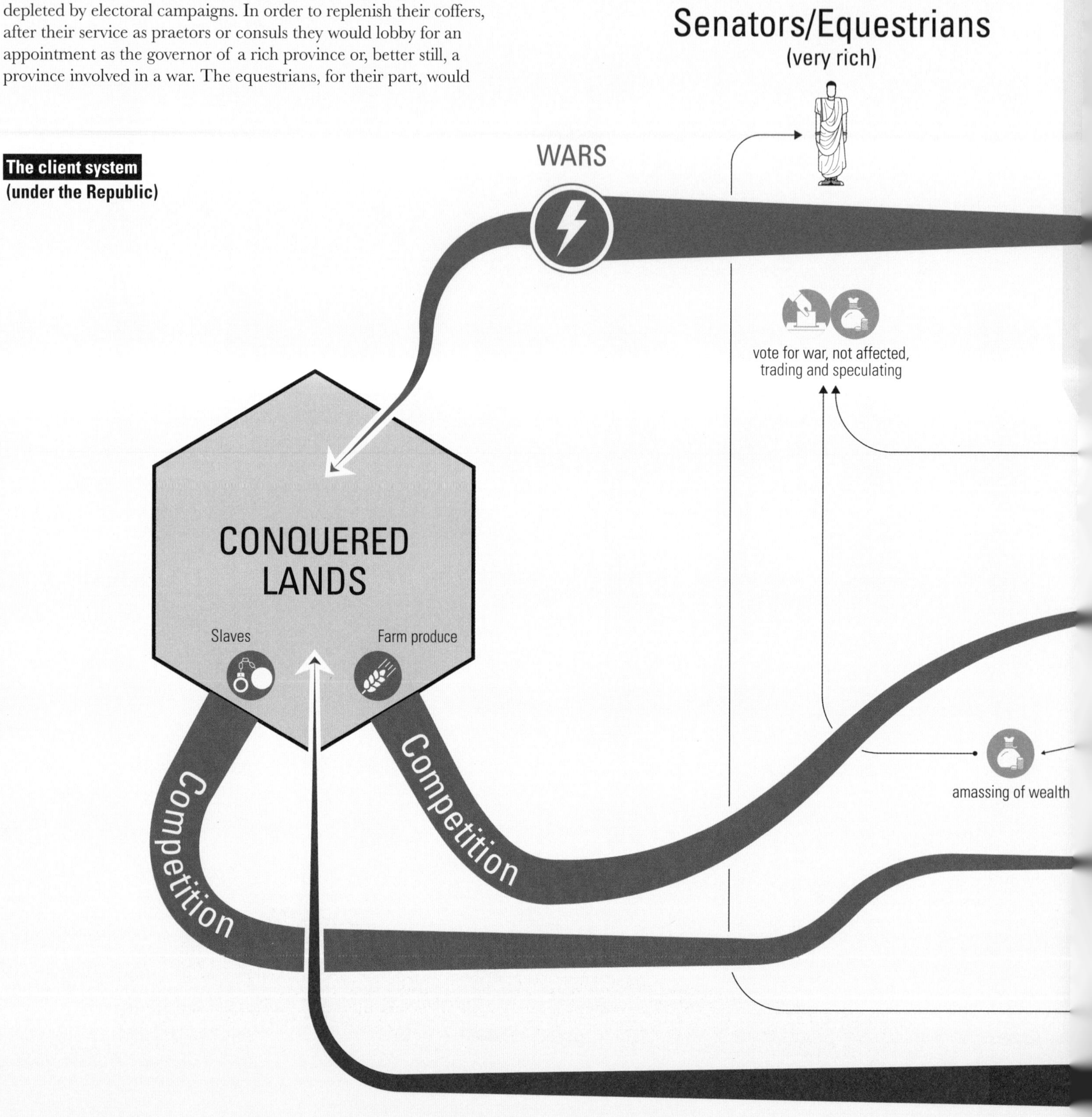

The client system
(under the Republic)

WARS

Senators/Equestrians
(very rich)

vote for war, not affected,
trading and speculating

amassing of wealth

CONQUERED
LANDS

Slaves

Farm produce

Competition

Competition

bulk of the legions comprised plebs with sufficient funds for military service, while the upper ranks came from the equestrian and senatorial orders. Financial or military setbacks could endanger this system by pushing the lower strata of the plebs into the patronage of senatorial families, who would thus bolster their influence and their capacity to play a role in political affairs. An upheaval of this kind was responsible for a regime change during the last century of the Republic and,

in more general terms, such disruptions to the system were one of the underlying causes of wars of conquest and civil conflicts.

Although the system persisted under the Empire, provincial governments largely ceased to provide opportunities for personal enrichment and the army was exclusively dependent on the emperor. Furthermore, it must not be forgotten that most manual labour was performed not by free citizens but by slaves.

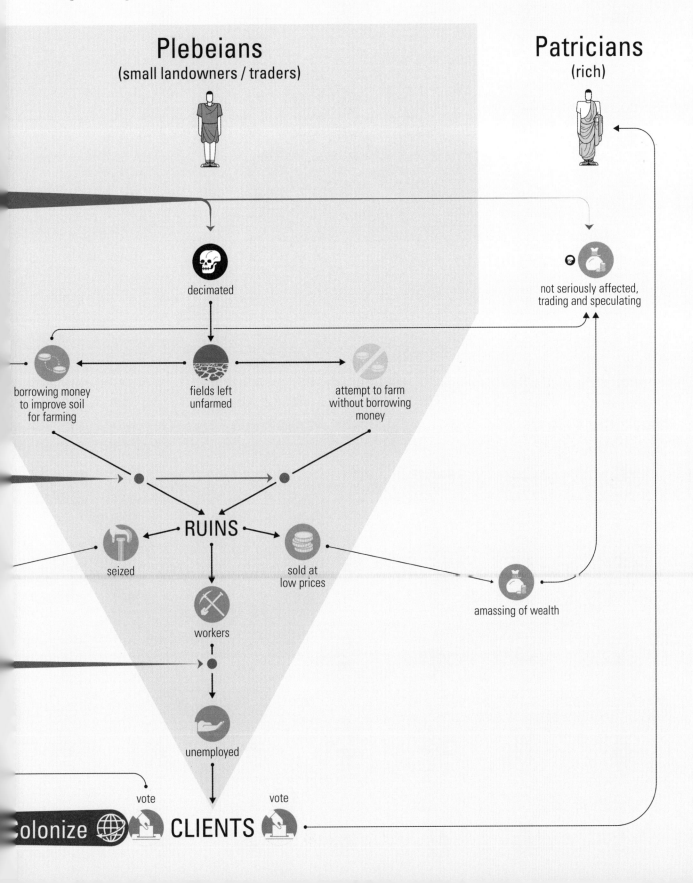

Social status and distribution of wealth

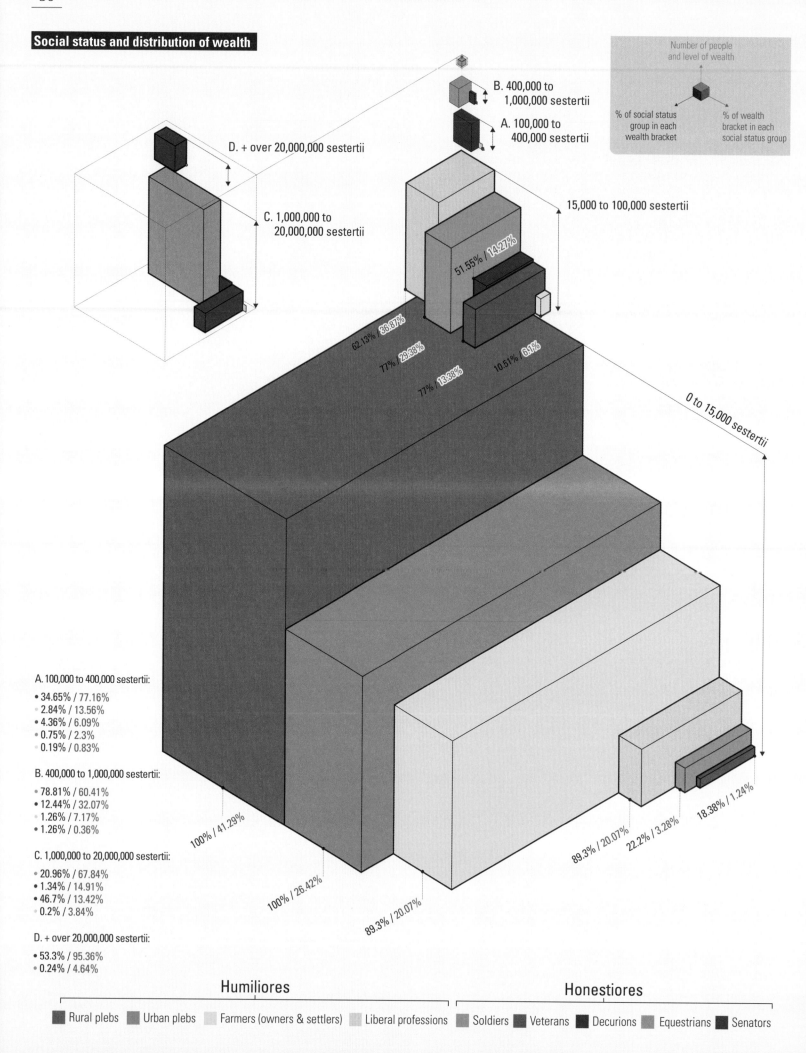

Number of people and level of wealth

% of social status group in each wealth bracket

% of wealth bracket in each social status group

B. 400,000 to 1,000,000 sestertii

A. 100,000 to 400,000 sestertii

D. + over 20,000,000 sestertii

C. 1,000,000 to 20,000,000 sestertii

15,000 to 100,000 sestertii

0 to 15,000 sestertii

51.55% / 14.27%

62.13% / 36.87%

77% / 29.38%

77% / 13.38%

10.51% / 6.1%

89.3% / 20.07%

22.2% / 3.28%

18.38% / 1.24%

100% / 41.29%

100% / 26.42%

89.3% / 20.07%

A. 100,000 to 400,000 sestertii:

- 34.65% / 77.16%
- 2.84% / 13.56%
- 4.36% / 6.09%
- 0.75% / 2.3%
- 0.19% / 0.83%

B. 400,000 to 1,000,000 sestertii:

- 78.81% / 60.41%
- 12.44% / 32.07%
- 1.26% / 7.17%
- 1.26% / 0.36%

C. 1,000,000 to 20,000,000 sestertii:

- 20.96% / 67.84%
- 1.34% / 14.91%
- 46.7% / 13.42%
- 0.2% / 3.84%

D. + over 20,000,000 sestertii:

- 53.3% / 95.36%
- 0.24% / 4.64%

Humiliores

Honestiores

■ Rural plebs ■ Urban plebs ■ Farmers (owners & settlers) ■ Liberal professions   ■ Soldiers ■ Veterans ■ Decurions ■ Equestrians ■ Senators

IV. SOCIAL STRUCTURES

This illustration represents a family in Rome itself, but from the 3rd century onwards, similar family structures were found across the Western world, including in Greece (although the status of women was somewhat different there). Nevertheless, the structure outlined here includes some rights that applied only to Roman citizens and their families.

The *paterfamilias* or head of the household had all the rights, at least until the time of Augustus, when the courts could intervene in cases of adultery and married women with three children could gain emancipation from male tutelage. Other than that, all members of the family – the *domus*, meaning 'house' – were under the control of the paterfamilias, and freed slaves were still subject to his authority, even after obtaining citizenship. Slaves and domestic servants constituted

the *familia*, in its original sense: the word is derived from *famulus*, meaning slave or servant. Some very large families, known as *gentes*, were groupings of descendants of a common ancestor, such as the *gens* Julia, Claudia, Cornelia, etc. In these patrician families, the paterfamilias had close relationships with 'clients', people connected to him for economic and political reasons, or by friendship. His clients might be poor plebs from Rome who looked to him to improve their finances, but might also be equestrians or senators who needed his support. This client base could even encompass entire cities, provinces or regions of Italy, such as Umbria in the case of the Pompeys. The patron-client relationship was enshrined in formal agreements: clients counted on the support of their patron, who in his turn expected political, and sometimes military, support from his clients.

Roman family structure and social relationships

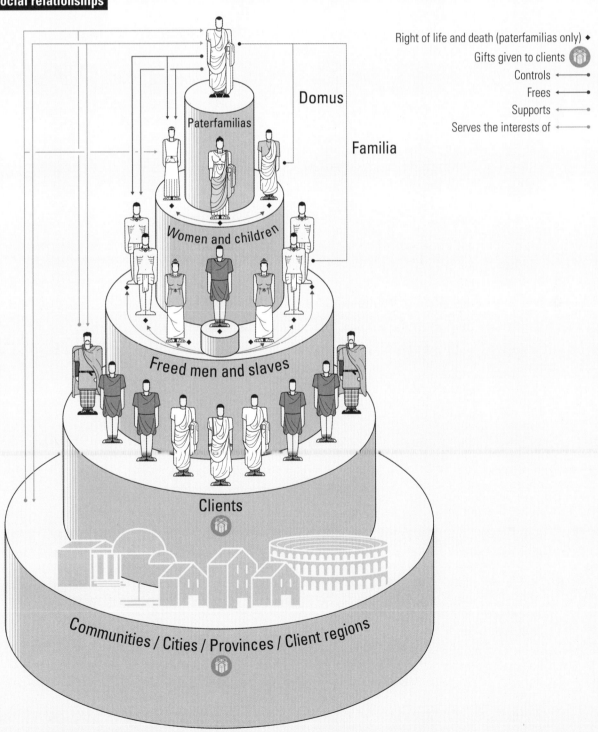

Right of life and death (paterfamilias only) ◆
Gifts given to clients
Controls
Frees
Supports
Serves the interests of

Domus

Familia

Paterfamilias

Women and children

Freed men and slaves

Clients

Communities / Cities / Provinces / Client regions

Stages in the life of a Roman woman

Under the tutelage/guardianship of:

Son | Husband | Father | Father-in-law | Priest

Takes part in religious ceremonies
Must remain a virgin
Can marry
Can divorce
May receive an inheritance (if she has three children)
Cannot touch her dowry or inherit
Does not have the right to vote
Cannot take part in legal process
Cannot take part in public or political life
Can be sold into slavery
Can be killed by her guardian

Baby

Child (–12 years)

Vestal (–12 years)

Woman (+12 years)

Empress

Divorcee

Matron / mother

Widow

Old woman

Once a girl child was accepted into the family by her paterfamilias after birth, she would play a role in family worship (as boys did) and, if she was high-born, could take part in some public activities such as festivals and even religious ceremonies. She was considered to be marriageable at the age of twelve. Depending on the type of marriage, she either fell under the tutelage of her husband or remained under that of her father; likewise, her dowry was controlled by her father or husband. A union with a non-Roman was considered a lesser type of marriage. Between the ages of six and ten, a girl could be chosen or 'taken' (capta) by the Grand Pontiff as a Vestal, to serve in the Temple of Vesta in the Forum, along with five other Vestals (six in later years). This practice

reputedly began in the royal era, and it was eventually banned by the Emperor Theodosius in 391 CE. Vestals served for thirty years and had to remain virgins for that period. They lived under the tutelage of the Grand Pontiff and enjoyed great privileges in their public life.

Under the Empire, the situation of married women, or 'matrons', improved slightly, although, in patrician families, husbands were chosen by the father, sometimes for girls as young as two or three. Divorce was relatively easy, but if a matron did not remarry or become a widow, she remained under the authority of her husband, father or father-in-law, depending on the circumstances.

These customs pertained to the upper classes – much less is known about the lives of women from other classes.

Slavery in the Roman world

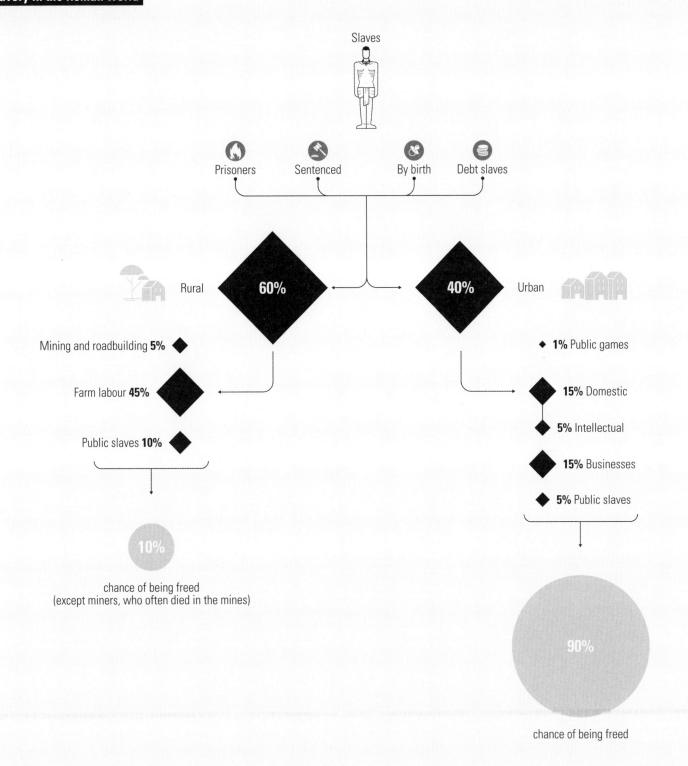

Slaves

Prisoners Sentenced By birth Debt slaves

Rural **60%**   **40%** Urban

Mining and roadbuilding **5%**

Farm labour **45%**

Public slaves **10%**

◆ **1%** Public games

15% Domestic

5% Intellectual

15% Businesses

5% Public slaves

10%

chance of being freed
(except miners, who often died in the mines)

90%

chance of being freed

A s in the rest of the ancient Mediterranean, slavery was commonplace in Rome. The majority of slaves originated as captives sold into slavery, but people could also be sentenced to slavery by law or fall into it because of debt – some individuals even sold themselves to their own creditor. The system was perpetuated by the birth of slaves' children. In fact, slavery was so pervasive that slaves outnumbered citizens up until the mid-2nd century CE, when large-scale wars of conquest became less common. Slaves did a variety of work. The least fortunate worked in mines – this was usually as a punishment, because they would not survive very long. The majority of slaves lived in rural areas; in fact, large estates and smaller farms were regularly run by slaves, often in the absence of their owners.

The conditions of these slaves would depend on whether they were farm labourers (often in chains) or overseers, but either way they had little hope of being freed. In contrast, the lot of urban slaves was often less arduous and their work more varied. Many performed domestic, manual or intellectual tasks, and some were placed in shops as traders. Slave labour was used by all business owners, including the organizers of spectacles. Slave owners could give permission for marriages between their charges, and often actively encouraged them to marry so that their *familia* could gain more members. The city of Rome, like other cities in Italy and the provinces, also possessed public slaves and, under the Empire, the emperor used personal slaves for administrative tasks and on his estates.

A MOSAIC OF CITY-STATES

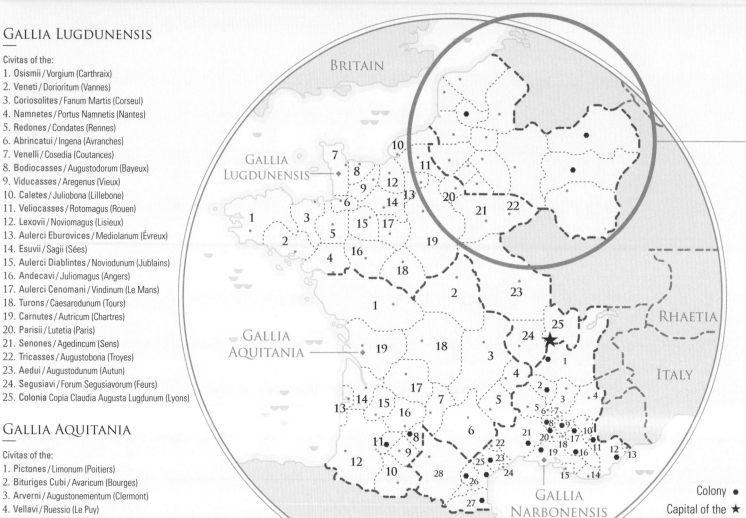

GALLIA LUGDUNENSIS

Civitas of the:

1. Osismii / Vorgium (Carthraix)
2. Veneti / Dorioritum (Vannes)
3. Coriosolites / Fanum Martis (Corseul)
4. Namnetes / Portus Namnetis (Nantes)
5. Redones / Condates (Rennes)
6. Abrincatui / Ingena (Avranches)
7. Venelli / Cosedia (Coutances)
8. Bodiocasses / Augustodorum (Bayeux)
9. Viducasses / Aregenus (Vieux)
10. Caletes / Juliobona (Lillebone)
11. Veliocasses / Rotomagus (Rouen)
12. Lexovii / Noviomagus (Lisieux)
13. Aulerci Eburovices / Mediolanum (Évreux)
14. Esuvii / Sagii (Sées)
15. Aulerci Diablintes / Noviodunum (Jublains)
16. Andecavi / Juliomagus (Angers)
17. Aulerci Cenomani / Vindinum (Le Mans)
18. Turons / Caesarodunum (Tours)
19. Carnutes / Autricum (Chartres)
20. Parisii / Lutetia (Paris)
21. Senones / Agedincum (Sens)
22. Tricasses / Augustobona (Troyes)
23. Aedui / Augustodunum (Autun)
24. Segusiavi / Forum Segusiavorum (Feurs)
25. Colonia Copia Claudia Augusta Lugdunum (Lyons)

GALLIA AQUITANIA

Civitas of the:

1. Pictones / Limonum (Poitiers)
2. Bituriges Cubi / Avaricum (Bourges)
3. Arverni / Augustonementum (Clermont)
4. Vellavi / Ruessio (Le Puy)
5. Gabali / Anderitum (Javols)
6. Ruteni / Segodunium (Rodez)
7. Cadurci / Divona (Cahors)
8. Lactorates / Lactora (Lectoure)
9. Ausci / Augusta Auscii (Auch)
10. Convenae / Lugdunum Convenarum (St-Bertrand de Comminges)
11. Elusates / Elusa (Eauze)
12. Tarbelli / Aquae Tarbellicae (Dax)
13. Boiates / Boios (Lamothe)
14. Bituriges Vivisci / Burdigala (Bordeaux)
15. Vasates / Cossium (Bazas)
16. Nitiobroges / Aginum (Agen)
17. Petrocorii / Vesunna (Périgueux)
18. Santoni / Mediolanum (Saintes)
19. Osismii / Vorgium (Carhaix)

GALLIA NARBONENSIS

1. Allobroges / Colonia Julia Vienna (Vienne)
2. Vocontii / Colonia Valentia (Valence)
3. Dea Augusta Vocontiorum (Die)
4. Vapincum (Gap)
5. Helvii / Alba Helvorum (Albe)
6. Tricastini / Augusta Tricastini (St-Paul-Trois-Chât.)
7. Vasio Julia Vocontiorum (Vaison-la-Romaine)
8. Colonia Firma Julia Sec. Arausio (Orange)
9. Meminii / Carpentoracte Meminorum (Carpentras)
10. Sogiontii / Sogiontiorum (Sisteron)
11. Reii / Col. Julia Aug. Apollinarium Reiorum (Riez)
12. Colonia Oct. Pacata Forum Julii (Fréjus)
13. Antipolis (Antibes)
14. Salyes / Tulia (Toulon)
15. Massilia (Marseilles)
16. Colonia Julia Augusta Aquae Sextiae (Aix)
17. Colonia Julia Apta (Apt)
18. Cabellio (Cavaillon)
19. Colonia Julia Paterna Arelatensium Sext. (Arles)
20. Glanum (St-Rémy)
21. Colonia Augusta Nemausus (Nîmes)
22. Volcae Arecomici / Claudia Luteva (Lodève)
23. Col. Julia Septimanorum Baeterrae (Béziers)
24. Agatha (Agde)
25. Col. Julia Paterna Narbo Martius (Narbonne)
26. Col. Julia Carcasso (Carcassonne)
27. Colonia Julia Ruscino (Château-Roussillon)
28. Volcae Tectosages / Tolosa (Toulouse)

Colony •
Capital of the ★
Three Gauls

0 km   100 km

I n the Roman world, a city (*polis, civitas*) was not merely an administrative unit, it was also a specific entity with its own constitution and legal status. 'Peregrine' or foreign cities (*civitates peregrinae*) implemented their own civic laws, while the institutions of Roman outposts, including *coloniae* (Roman colonies founded by veterans) and *municipia* (cities with Latin rights), reflected their Roman counterparts more closely. These variations in status were historically based, and often depended on whether the city had been conquered by Rome or assimilated more gradually. During the Empire, for instance, outposts sought to become Roman colonies, as this status was considered a badge of honour.

While colonies possessed fuller Roman rights, Latin rights were the keystone of the individual or collective status granted by Rome to allied cities in Italy from the 5th to 1st centuries BCE, and conferred some of the legal rights of a Roman city. In Italy, however, Latin rights came to be perceived as less desirable than full Roman citizenship and eventually sparked the Social War in 90 BCE. This was followed by a period in which cities or entire regions were integrated into the Empire, allowing the inhabitants of some provinces to be collectively awarded Latin rights. During the Empire, the full rights of Roman citizenship were granted to the magistrates of these cities and their families.

Furthermore, after the Social War, Romans of any status had two sets of rights: those of the city in which they were born and, if they were Roman citizens, those of the city of Rome itself. Cicero, for example, was a citizen of both Arpinum (in the Lazio region

The Three Gauls and Gallia Belgica in 170 CE

GERMANIA INFERIOR

GERMANIA SUPERIOR

GALLIA BELGICA

GALLIA LUGDUNENSIS

Forum Hadriani (Voorburg)

Ulpia-Noviomagus (Nijmegen)

Colonia Ulpia Traiana

Colonia Claudia Ara Agrippinensis (Cologne)

Civitas of the Menapii

Castellum Menapiorum (Cassel)

Civitas of the Morini

Tarvanna (Therouanne)

Civitas of the Atrebates

Civitas of the Nervii

Nemetacum (Arras)

Bagacum (Bavay)

Atuatuca (Tongeren)

Aquae Mattiacorum (Wiesbaden)

Civitas of the Ambiani

Samarobriva (Amiens)

Civitas of the Viromandui

Augusta Viromanduorum (St Quentin)

Civitas of the Treveri

Augusta Treverorum (Trier)

Borbetomagus (Worms)

Civitas of the Bellovaci

Caesaromagus (Beauvais)

Civitas of the Suessiones

Civitas of the Remi

Civitas of the Silvanectes

Augusta Suessionum (Soissons)

Durocortorum (Reims)

Civitas of the Mediomatrici

Divodurum (Metz)

Augustomagus (Senlis)

Civitas of the Meldi

Lantinum (Meaux)

Lutetia (Paris)

Brucomagus (Brumath)

Tullum (Toul)

Agedincum (Sens)

Civitas of the Leuci

Andemantunum (Langres)

— Roman roads
-·-· Province border
---- Civitas border
XXX Names of peoples
Provincial capital   Civitas
Vicus / settlement (known)
Temporary and permanent camps (known)

of Italy) and Rome. During the Empire, the civic status of Roman citizens depended on the city or province in which they were born. This dual citizenship came with doubled civic duties, especially for well-off citizens, who would take on commitments in their city of origin as magistrates and benefactors in parallel with attempts at an equestrian or senatorial career in Rome. Changing one's city of origin was virtually out of the question, although a settler in another city in Italy or the provinces could be granted the status of a resident, dependent on the acceptance of any inherent duties. The original populations of *civitates peregrinae* were also citizens of their own cities before – potentially – acquiring the right to Roman citizenship. After the Edict of Caracalla in 212 CE, however, all free men in the Empire automatically became Roman citizens.

Cities had their own institutions, which could either be indigenous or emulations of those in Rome itself. Overall, with the exception of peoples and tribes who did not belong to a city, most cities functioned in a similar way. They had a populace, who voted on laws and chose priests and magistrates. The latter were elected every year and governed the city. A local authority (a city senate, a council of decurions, or a *boule* in Greek territories) was made up of former magistrates and served in an advisory capacity. The magistrates dispensed justice: in the large cities, they judged almost all cases, but in more modest cities, the Roman governor presided over criminal cases on his regional rounds. The city magistrates were also responsible for collecting taxes.

II. GOVERNMENT, WORSHIP
AND SOCIAL NEEDS

THE ROMAN POLITICAL SYSTEM

Government during the Roman Kingdom
from the 8th to 6th centuries BCE

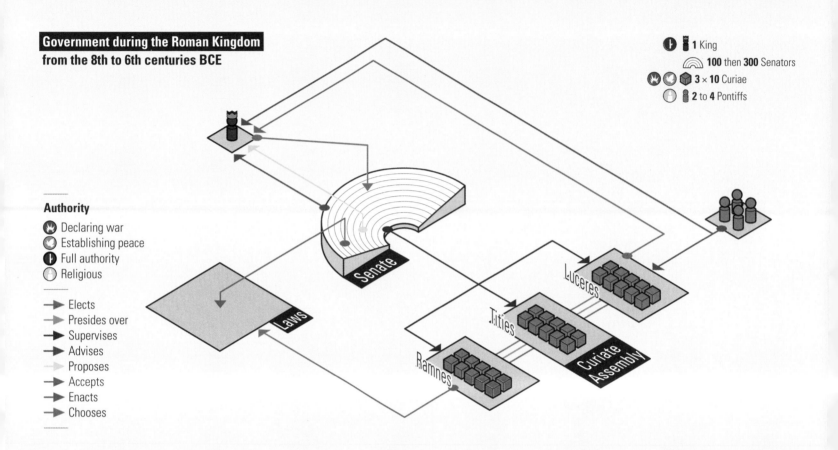

● ▮ **1** King
◠ **100** then **300** Senators
◉◉◈ **3 × 10** Curiae
● ▮ **2** to **4** Pontiffs

Authority

● Declaring war
◉ Establishing peace
● Full authority
○ Religious

→ Elects
→ Presides over
→ Supervises
→ Advises
→ Proposes
→ Accepts
→ Enacts
→ Chooses

I. BEFORE THE EMPIRE

Until the 4th century CE, the formal name of the Roman state was *res publica populi Romani Quiritium*: 'the republic of the Roman people of the Quirites'. *Res publica* meant 'the business or affairs of the people', while 'the Roman people' meant, for these purposes, Roman citizens as governed by magistrates and eligible to take part in military service and popular votes – in other words, it represented the state of Rome. The word 'Quirites' was an archaic word for those possessing citizenship. This official definition of the State therefore reflects the desire for extreme precision that was characteristic of much of Roman thinking.

The people of Rome were organized into groups or tribes known as *curiae*, which were also the groups from which soldiers were recruited. At the start of the royal era, the Curiate Assembly (*comitia curiata*) included three curiae – the Ramnes, the Tities and the Luceres – but later this figure would rise to 30, with each of the three original curiae being split into ten. This assembly remained in place until the end of the Republic, but by then its powers had been transferred to other institutions and it mainly served a symbolic and religious function. It also passed the *lex curiata*, a law that bestowed the power of command (*imperium*) on all upper-rank magistrates (consuls and praetors).

According to tradition, at the end of the royal era, a new Centuriate Assembly – the *comitia centuriata* – was created, based on divisions into classes. This structure was also used for the Roman army, which was billeted outside Rome, on the Campus Martius. During the Republican period, the populace was divided according to their wealth into 193 centuries (18 made up of those of equestrian or cavalry rank, 170 of infantry rank and 5 of miscellaneous or unarmed ranks). Citizens were classified into centuries every five years by the censors and divided into 35 tribes, identified by the place where they were registered as citizens (the city of Rome had four urban tribes). The Centuriate Assembly elected magistrates and priests, voted on laws and served as a tribunal for capital crimes and, after the 1st century BCE, for high treason. At first the Roman plebs had their own assembly, the Plebeian Council, which elected its own representatives (the plebeian tribunes) and passed resolutions (plebescites). Over time this council evolved into a second assembly (the *comitia tributa* or Tribal Assembly), which met in the Forum to vote on laws and elect lower-ranking magistrates (quaestors, aediles), as well as the plebeian tribunes and aediles. It could also serve as a court of justice for cases of public law.

The higher-rank magistrates (consuls and praetors) presided over the assemblies, the Senate (a council of 100, later 300 or 600, former magistrates) and the law courts. They controlled the army and governed both Rome and its provinces.

Government under the Roman Republic
3rd and 2nd centuries BCE

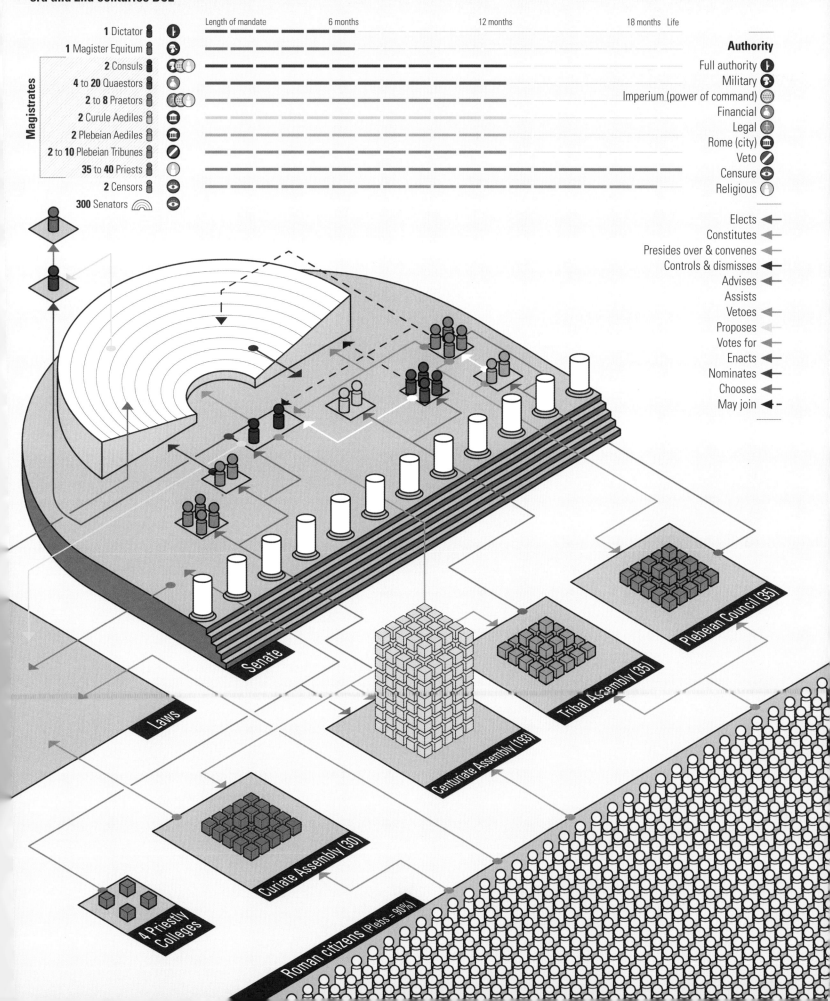

Magistrates

1 Dictator
1 Magister Equitum
2 Consuls
4 to 20 Quaestors
2 to 8 Praetors
2 Curule Aediles
2 Plebeian Aediles
2 to 10 Plebeian Tribunes
35 to 40 Priests
2 Censors
300 Senators

Length of mandate — 6 months — 12 months — 18 months — Life

Authority

Full authority
Military
Imperium (power of command)
Financial
Legal
Rome (city)
Veto
Censure
Religious

Elects
Constitutes
Presides over & convenes
Controls & dismisses
Advises
Assists
Vetoes
Proposes
Votes for
Enacts
Nominates
Chooses
May join

Senate

Laws

Centuriate Assembly (193)

Tribal Assembly (35)

Plebeian Council (35)

Curiate Assembly (30)

4 Priestly Colleges

Roman citizens (Plebs = 90%)

Government under the Roman Empire
1st century BCE to 3rd century CE

Emperor

Authority

- **!** Full authority
- **⊘** Right of veto

- ▶ Hails
- ▶ Constitutes
- ▶ Elects
- ▶ Oversees / Commands
- ▶ Advises
- Stationed in
- ▶ Vetoes
- ▶ Enacts
- ▶ Nominates

Office of Letters

Imperial Legate

Legion Legate

Military Tribunes

Imperial provinces

Laws

Legions / armies

II. THE IMPERIAL SYSTEM

The system of assemblies and magistrates remained unchanged throughout the first three centuries of the Empire, apart from the increase in the number of pairs of consuls elected every year, introduced by Augustus. This modification ensured a high enough number of top-level magistrates to govern the provinces and the army as promagistrates or legates and to take responsibility for overseeing infrastructure (food supplies, roads, the banks of the Tiber, aqueducts) and governing Rome and Italy. A major upheaval occurred, however, when the emperor took his place alongside the senators and magistrates.

The emperor took over responsibilities such as the governing of provinces in which troops were stationed, food distribution and public

order in both Rome and Italy. At the instigation of Claudius (r. 41–54 CE), an imperial administration gradually grew up. It was placed under the immediate authority of Roman equestrians, but the emperor was entitled to intervene in all matters. He was endowed with powers that had once belonged to the Roman magistrates, most notably the *imperium* of the upper magistrates (consuls and praetors) and the *potestas* of the plebeian tribunes. In the early years of the Empire, these powers were renewed every year, and then every five or ten years, but the renewal soon became a mere formality. Sometimes the emperor personally acted as a consul or conducted a census of the Roman people, but Domitian eventually placed the census permanently under the remit of the imperial administration. Jurisprudence was another

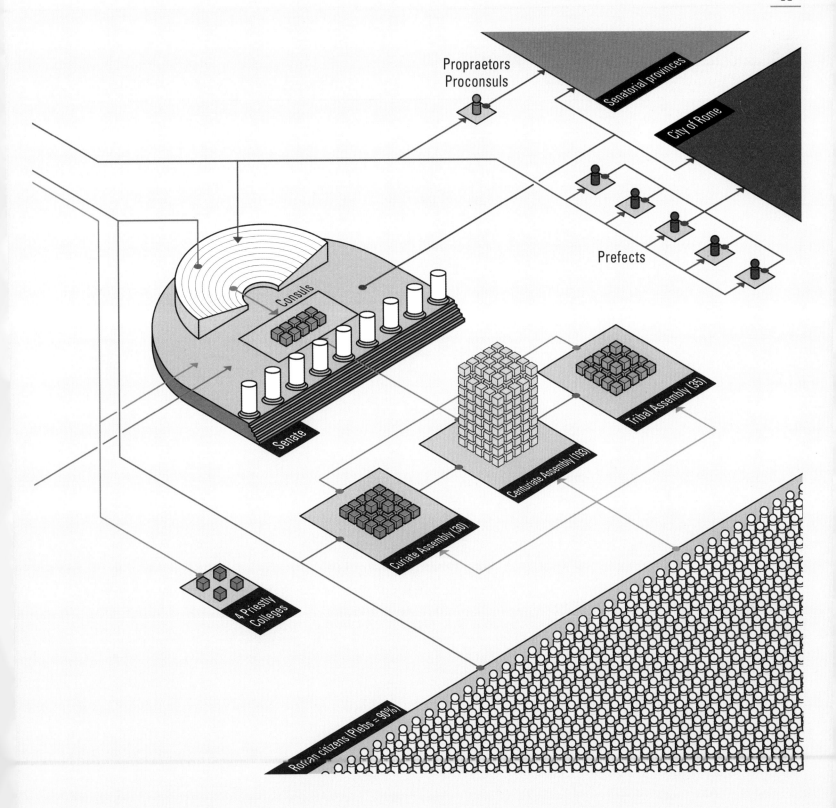

Propraetors
Proconsuls

Senatorial provinces

City of Rome

Prefects

Consuls

Senate

Centuriate Assembly (193)

Tribal Assembly (35)

Curiate Assembly (30)

4 Priestly Colleges

Roman citizens (Plebs = 90%)

area traditionally incumbent on the emperor, who dispensed justice on a daily basis. The election of magistrates quickly became an empty ceremony, as it was entirely dependent on the assent of the emperor. The political influence of posts such as consulship and praetorship waned as their administrative powers dwindled. The senators, meanwhile, focused their attention on the principal provincial governments and the posts responsible for major infrastructure.

After a gradual evolution, during which the imperial initiative became increasingly strong, a new system of government was introduced at the turn of the 4th century CE as a response to the chaos and invasions of the preceding three decades. In the 2nd century, the *juridici* had been appointed regional administrators

in Italy, but in the late 3rd century they were replaced by the post of *corrector* (at first one, and then two). The Roman provinces underwent similar changes. Diocletian combined them into larger dioceses and placed them under the control of Romans from the equestrian class, who represented the praetorian prefects but answered directly to the emperor. This reform put an end to the senators' influence over the provinces. Later, Diocletian decided to divide these dioceses into smaller units.

The creation of a law under the Republic and the Empire

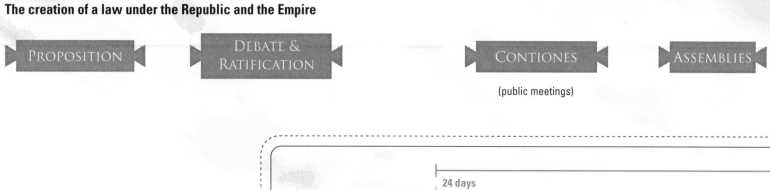

PROPOSITION

DEBATE & RATIFICATION

CONTIONES
(public meetings)

ASSEMBLIES

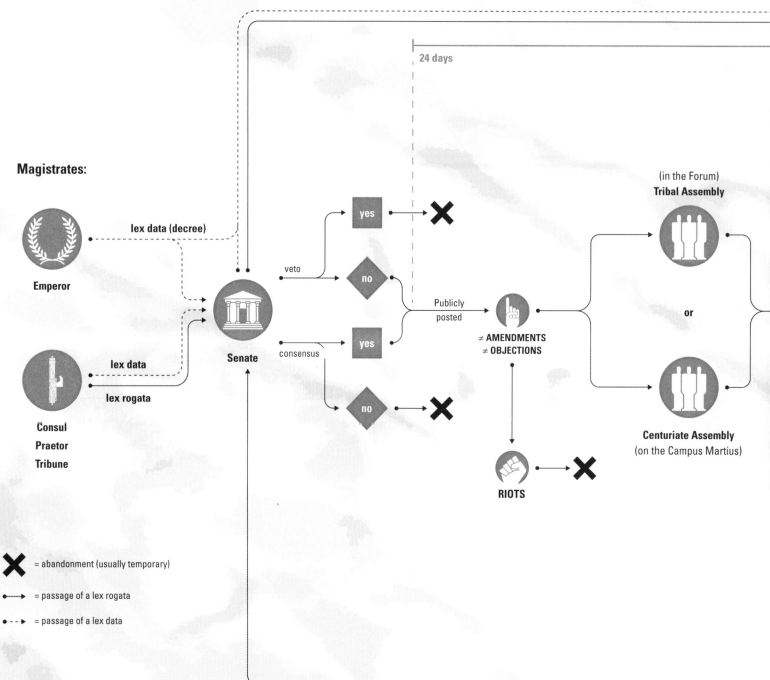

Magistrates:

lex data (decree)

Emperor

lex data

lex rogata

Consul
Praetor
Tribune

Senate

24 days

veto

consensus

yes

no

yes

no

Publicly posted

≠ **AMENDMENTS**
≠ **OBJECTIONS**

RIOTS

(in the Forum)
Tribal Assembly

or

Centuriate Assembly
(on the Campus Martius)

✖ = abandonment (usually temporary)

●—▶ = passage of a lex rogata

●--▶ = passage of a lex data

The shifting majority within the centuries

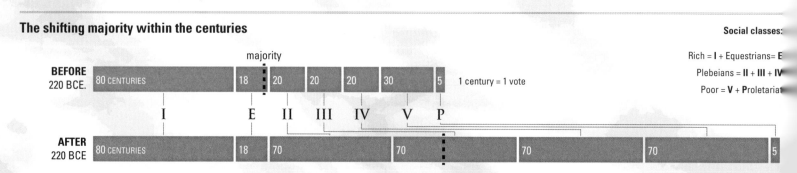

Social classes:

Rich = **I** + Equestrians= **E**

Plebeians = **II** + **III** + **IV**

Poor = **V** + Proletariat

majority

BEFORE
220 BCE.

| 80 CENTURIES | | 18 | 20 | 20 | 20 | 30 | 5 |

1 century = 1 vote

I   E   II   III   IV   V   P

AFTER
220 BCE.

| 80 CENTURIES | | 18 | 70 | 70 | 70 | 70 | 5 |

Roman law was one of the most remarkable achievements of the Roman people. As far back as the 5th century BCE, its underlying principles were publicly displayed in the Forum on the Twelve Tables. Over the course of centuries, these principles were honed into laws, voted either by the populace, via the Centuriate Assembly or by the plebeian tribunes. The laws proposed by the tribunes (known as plebiscites) only began to apply to all citizens in 287 BCE. By the end of the Republic, the Senate had to approve any proposals emanating from the plebeian tribunes, just as it did for those of other magistrates. The votes for any law were potentially subject to a veto from a consul or praetor, or a plebeian tribune. Generally speaking, laws were withdrawn if they proved unpopular in the public assemblies. The laws that were passed provided the basis for the body of law exercised both by jurists after the end of the Republic and subsequently by emperors. In 529 CE, the body of Roman law that had been accumulated up to that point was collected in the Code of Justinian, along with the laws of the imperial constitution.

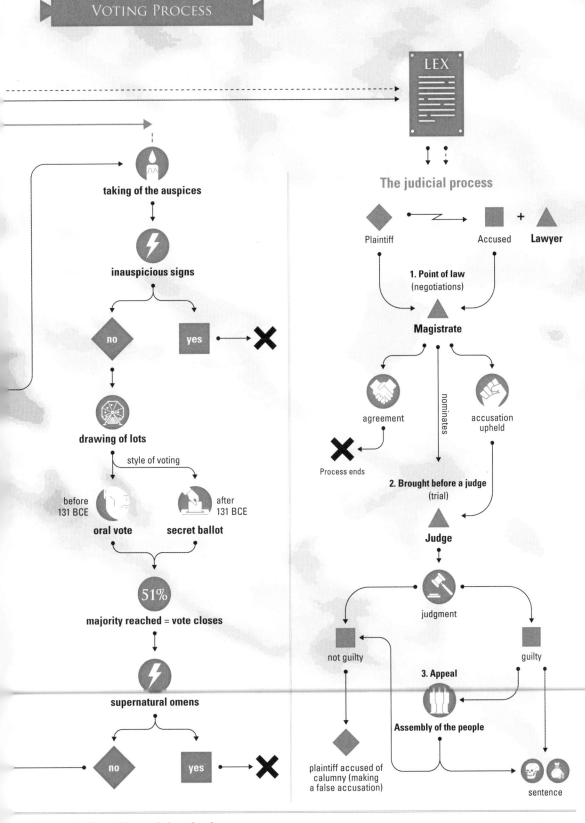

VOTING PROCESS

LEX

taking of the auspices

inauspicious signs

no / yes → ✗

drawing of lots

style of voting

before 131 BCE — oral vote

after 131 BCE — secret ballot

51% majority reached = vote closes

supernatural omens

no / yes → ✗

The judicial process

Plaintiff · Accused **+ Lawyer**

1. Point of law (negotiations)

Magistrate

agreement — Process ends ✗

nominates

accusation upheld

2. Brought before a judge (trial)

Judge

judgment

not guilty / guilty

3. Appeal

Assembly of the people

plaintiff accused of calumny (making a false accusation)

sentence

The evolution of Imperial authority

	Late Republic	Augustus	Tiberius	Hadrian
Emperor	—	▲ ● ⬡	▲ ● ⬡	▲ ● ⬡
Consilium Principis	—	—		▲ ● ⬡
Consuls	▲ ●			
Senate	▲ ⬡ ● ■ ★			
Assemblies	● ⬡ ■ ★	● ⬡ ■ ★	★	★

■ right to debate
▲ legislative rights
⬡ nominates magistrates
● manages finances
★ acclaims

The Cursus Honorum
2nd century BCE

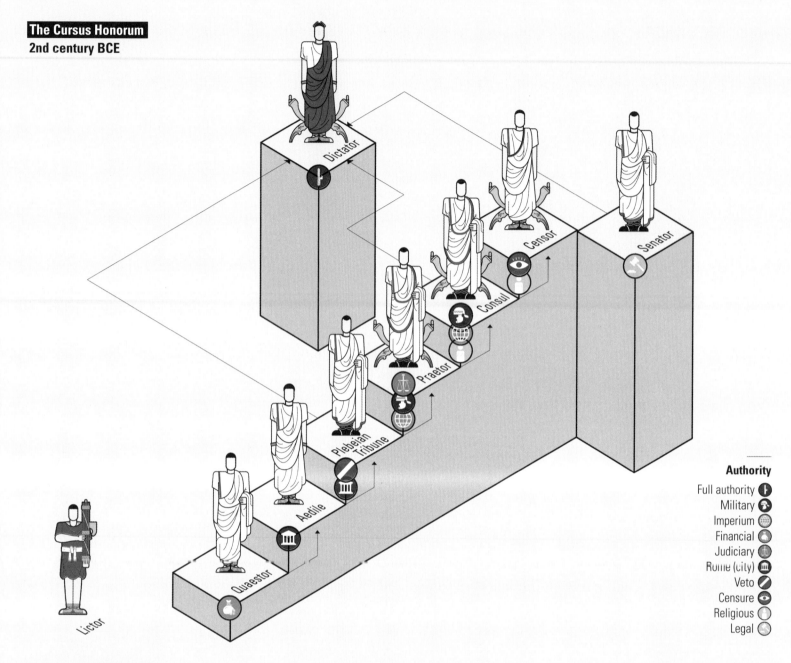

Authority

Full authority
Military
Imperium
Financial
Judiciary
Rome (city)
Veto
Censure
Religious
Legal

IV. THE MAGISTRATES

The executive power of the Roman State was always in the hands of elected magistrates. They grew in number after the emergence of the Republic in the 5th century BCE, but their power was constrained from the start of the Empire by the watchful presence of the emperor himself. The magistrates were all elected from the senatorial order or from the elite equestrian class. Very little is known about the processes used in the earliest centuries, but thereafter a young man could become a senator by being elected as a quaestor. The minimum age at which this became possible changed over time, but by the 2nd century BCE it was 28 years old. No matter how high he climbed (or failed to climb) on the career ladder, he would remain a senator, as long as he was not expelled by the censors. The position of aedile (accessible at the age of 37, then discretionary and, finally, at the age of 27 at the start of the modern era) would lead to praetorship (at around 40 years old) and, potentially, consulship. In the 5th century BCE, a time of fighting between the ancient patrician families of Rome and the newer arrivals, the plebs were granted the right to appoint tribunes to defend their interests. They were elected at the same time as the plebeian aediles by the Tribal Assembly of the Roman people, which included all citizens, unlike the Centuriate

Assembly, which was only open to the wealthy. The plebeian tribunes were sacrosanct and thus inviolate as far as the upper magistrates were concerned. They could appeal against sentences condemning a plebeian and they could apply a veto against all the actions of a particular magistrate, thereby annulling them. The ten tribunes gradually became part of the mechanism of government, although their powers were strictly confined to Rome. In the early days, back in the 4th century BCE, they could convoke the Senate and attack any decisions of magistrates that they considered excessive, but they had to use the Tribal Assembly system (*comitia tributa*) for legal proceedings. By 180 BCE at the latest, all the tribunes were senators.

The praetors (whose minimum age was 40 during the Republic, and 30 during the Empire) were endowed with *imperium*, the power to command and judge. This power was civil inside Rome's first mile and absolute beyond that. In contrast, the other magistrates possessed only *potestas*, the power to act in the name of the State. Like the consuls, the praetors wore the *toga praetexta*. The two consuls had to be at least 40 years old during the Republic and, at their youngest, 33 during the Empire. They possessed a higher level of *imperium*, subject to the same restrictions as that of the praetors.

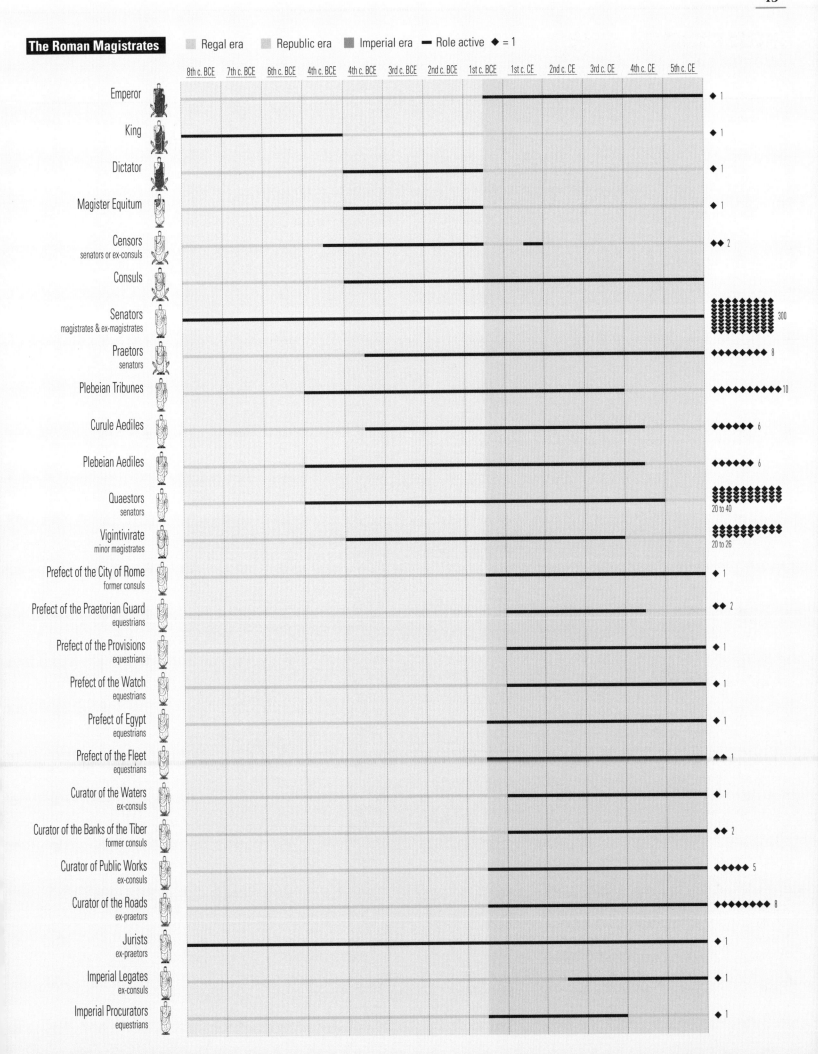

The Roman Magistrates

THE EMPEROR AND THE IMPERIAL DYNASTIES

I. THE EMPEROR'S POWERS AND TITLES

The role of emperor was based on three primary factors: dynastic links between emperors, civil authority, and military might. All three of these things were reflected in imperial titles. Apart from Tiberius, Caligula and Claudius, the emperors always followed the same formula of Imperator Caesar Augustus for their title. 'Imperator' defined their rank, 'Caesar' was a family name and 'Augustus' was an honorary title. These basic elements would then be complemented by their given names and, generally, the name of their adoptive father. All in all, therefore, emperorhood was kept within a single family whose power could last indefinitely.

The rest of the emperor's titles alluded to the powers bestowed on him by a law or by a vote in the assemblies. These usually included *pontifex maximus* ('grand pontiff') but could also include the title 'father of the country', as well as alluding to his tribunician power, acclamation as emperor, and holding a consulship or, potentially, the office of censor. Tribunician power meant that he possessed the authority and privileges of a plebeian tribune; it was granted for life but renewed every year (the number of years was therefore counted). Tribunician power enabled the emperor to attend sessions in the Senate and put forward motions, as well as opposing a veto against the decisions of the magistrates. Acclamation as emperor was a confirmation of his imperium, or power to command troops; it was agreed by the army and the Senate on his ascension to the throne and ratified every time the army achieved a victory.

These powers implied the capacity to run an imperial administration distinct from that of the annually elected magistrates. Emperors were surrounded by a civil service run by Roman equestrians, assisted by slaves and former slaves. The administrative system was headed by the equestrian *procuratores* working out of the Palatine. Some provinces or subsections of provinces were governed by equestrian prefects, while in Rome itself, the power of the Praetorian prefects was second only to that of the emperor.

How the authority of the emperor was reflected in his titles
The example of Trajan in 116 CE

personal name [praenomen]	family name [gentilice]	surname [cognomen]

MARCUS ULPIUS TRAIANUS

↓ *becomes*

IMPERATOR CAESAR, DIVI NERVAE FILIUS,

NERVA TRAIANUS OPTIMUS AUGUSTUS, GERMANICUS DACICUS PARTHICUS,

PONTIFEX MAXIMUS, TRIBUNICIA POTESTATE XX,

IMPERATOR XIII, PROCONSUL, CONSUL VI, PATER PATRIAE

The Emperor Caesar, son of the divine Nerva, Nerva Traianus, the most excellent and august, victorious in Germania, Dacia and Parthia, grand pontiff, holder of tribunician power for the 20th time, hailed emperor for the 13th time, proconsul, consul for the 6th time, father of the country

Military	**Administrative and legal**	**Religious**	**Victories**	**Family affiliation**	**Honorific**
Head of the armies	• Leader of Rome and the provinces of the Empire • First magistrate of the Empire • Because the emperor did not appoint consuls every year, the number of times is indicated	Grand pontiff: Head of the priestly colleges = a prestigious role in Roman public worship	• Victory titles were awarded by the Senate, during or after campaigns • These titles were publicly declared by the military in support of the emperor during military campaigns	• Caesar: belongs to the family of the Caesars • Divi Nervae filius: son of the divine emperor Nerva	Honorific title bestowed by the Senate a few months after the accession of each emperor

The imperial administration
under the High Roman Empire

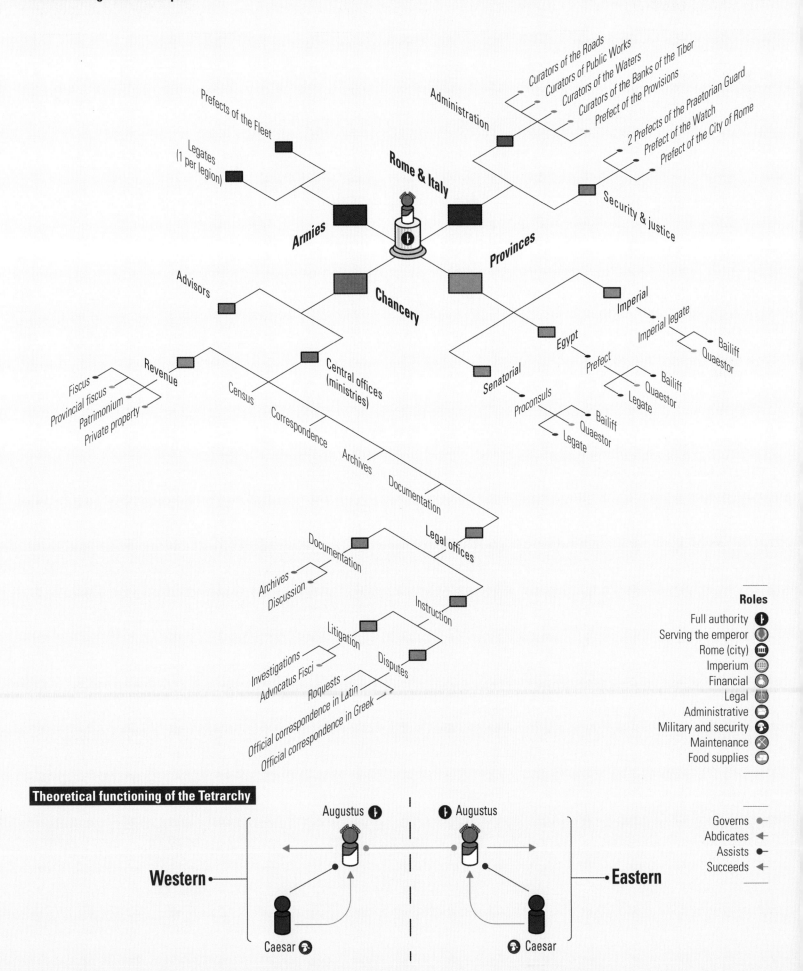

Prefects of the Fleet

Legates
(1 per legion)

Armies

Rome & Italy

Administration

Curators of the Roads
Curators of Public Works
Curators of the Waters
Curators of the Banks of the Tiber
Prefect of the Provisions

2 Prefects of the Praetorian Guard
Prefect of the Watch
Prefect of the City of Rome

Security & justice

Provinces

Chancery

Advisors

Revenue

Fiscus
Provincial fiscus
Patrimonium
Private property

Central offices
(ministries)

Census

Correspondence

Archives

Documentation

Imperial

Egypt

Senatorial

Imperial legate

Bailiff
Quaestor

Prefect

Bailiff
Quaestor
Legate

Proconsuls

Bailiff
Quaestor
Legate

Legal offices

Documentation

Archives
Discussion

Instruction

Litigation

Disputes

Investigations
Advocatus Fisci

Requests
Official correspondence in Latin
Official correspondence in Greek

Roles

Full authority
Serving the emperor
Rome (city)
Imperium
Financial
Legal
Administrative
Military and security
Maintenance
Food supplies

Theoretical functioning of the Tetrarchy

Augustus

Augustus

Western

Eastern

Caesar

Caesar

Governs
Abdicates
Assists
Succeeds

II. THE PRAETORIAN GUARD

The Praetorian Guard evolved from the bodyguards used by generals on the battlefield. In 23 BCE they were garrisoned outside the pomerium on the Viminal (near what is now Termini train station). In 2 BCE, Augustus plucked these elite troops from the legions and placed them under the command of two praetorian prefects of equestrian rank. He turned them into his private Praetorian Guard and stationed them in different areas of Rome. The unit initially consisted of nine cohorts of 500 men; this was later increased to ten cohorts, and then to double that number in the 2nd century. Septimius Severus distrusted the Praetorian Guard, however, and in 197 CE he replaced them with the Second Parthic Legion (garrisoned in Alba Longa), who served the same protective role. In the mid-3rd century, these troops were sent to the Eastern front, and after that point, there is little mention of the Praetorian Guard, although it continued to exist. Diocletian reduced the number of cohorts, and the unit was eventually dissolved altogether by Constantine the Great in 312.

The Praetorian cohorts were recruited in both Italy and the provinces, but their centurions were either young Roman equestrians or promoted soldiers from the Praetorian ranks. The Praetorian prefect served as the overall commander of the guard and the *speculatores* were commanded by a *trecenarius*. The Praetorian cohorts did not carry eagles but they had other insignia, and were not usually heavily armed. The cohorts were commanded by tribunes. The Julio-Claudian emperors maintained a mounted Germanic bodyguard, but these were replaced with 1,000 *equites singulares* ('personal horse guards') by Trajan. These were disbanded by Constantine after 312, and replaced by mounted *scholae*.

Armed forces permitted in Rome in 23 CE

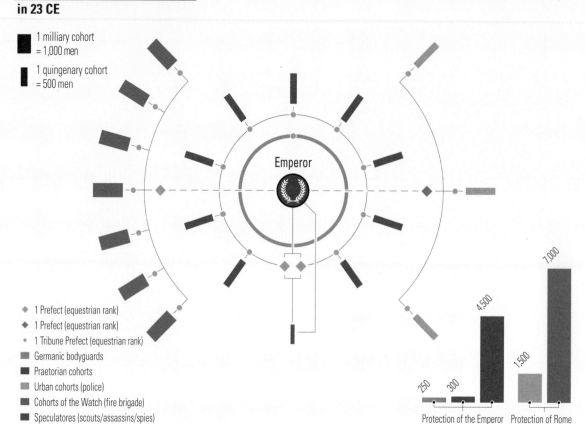

■ 1 milliary cohort = 1,000 men
▮ 1 quingenary cohort = 500 men

◆ 1 Prefect (equestrian rank)
◆ 1 Prefect (equestrian rank)
• 1 Tribune Prefect (equestrian rank)
■ Germanic bodyguards
■ Praetorian cohorts
■ Urban cohorts (police)
■ Cohorts of the Watch (fire brigade)
■ Speculatores (scouts/assassins/spies)

250 300 4,500 1,500 7,000
Protection of the Emperor   Protection of Rome

The changing number of Praetorian Guards

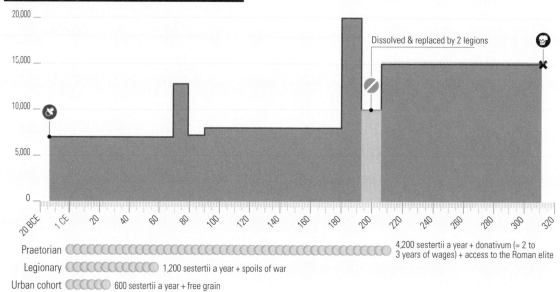

Dissolved & replaced by 2 legions

Praetorian   4,200 sestertii a year + donativum (= 2 to 3 years of wages) + access to the Roman elite
Legionary   1,200 sestertii a year + spoils of war
Urban cohort   600 sestertii a year + free grain

In battle
1st century CE

In battle
2nd century CE

Bodyguard
1st century CE

In battle
3rd century CE

Urban cohort
1st century CE

The changing number of provinces in the Empire

- ■ Conquered provinces
- ■ Division of one province into several
- ■ Merging of several provinces into one
- ▨ No change

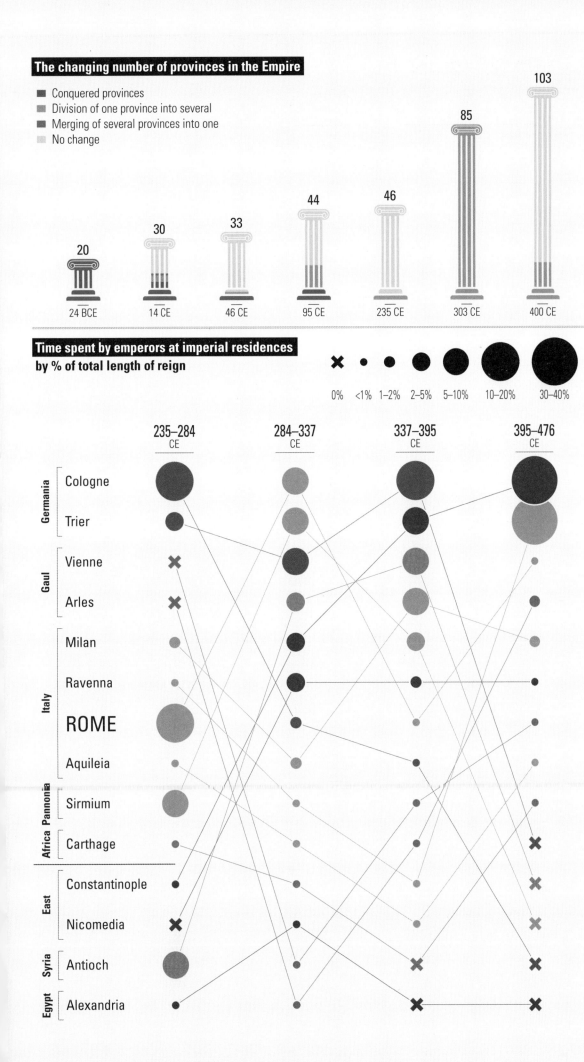

20 — 24 BCE
30 — 14 CE
33 — 46 CE
44 — 95 CE
46 — 235 CE
85 — 303 CE
103 — 400 CE

Time spent by emperors at imperial residences by % of total length of reign

✖ 0% • <1% • 1–2% ● 2–5% ● 5–10% ● 10–20% ● 30–40%

	235–284 CE	284–337 CE	337–395 CE	395–476 CE
Germania Cologne				
Trier				
Gaul Vienne				
Arles				
Italy Milan				
Ravenna				
ROME				
Aquileia				
Pannonia Sirmium				
Africa Carthage				
East Constantinople				
Nicomedia				
Syria Antioch				
Egypt Alexandria				

III. IMPERIAL RESIDENCES

Between Augustus and the Severan dynasty, the emperor's official base was on the Palatine in Rome, where an imposing palace with reception halls and administrative areas was built during the early Empire, under Domitian and the Severans. Then, in the late 3rd century CE, with the rise of the Tetrarchy, other fixed residences began to appear: in Nicomedia (Bithynia) and Antioch (Syria) for Diocletian, in Sirmium (Pannonia) for Galerius, in Milan for Maximian and in Trier for Constantius I.

This system changed under Constantine the Great. By 313 CE he was living in Arelate (now Arles), in Gaul, where he minted new coins and organized a synod in 314. He left Trier in 316 before going to Rome in 326 to celebrate his vicennalia (twenty years of rule). From 326 to 327, he spent the winter in Sirmium to remain on the alert against the Sarmatians. In late 327, he visited the Danube region and spent the winter in Nicomedia. In 329, he spent another winter in Sirmium, before establishing his capital, from 330 to 337, in Constantinople, which became another of his fixed residences.

Constantine's sons mostly used the same residences until 360, but later emperors moved around more, due to their military campaigns. Julian, for example, spent the winter of 356 in Vienne in southeastern Gaul. A year later, he was in Argentoratum (Strasbourg), but he spent the winters of 357–358 and 358–359 in Lutetia (Paris). The following winter found him back in Vienne; in 361 he went to Constantinople, then moved to Antioch in 362 to prepare an expedition into Persia.

In 395, Constantinople became the capital of the eastern part of the Empire, while in 402, under Honorius, Ravenna replaced Milan and Rome as capital of the Western Roman Empire, and remained so until 476.

1 The Julio-Claudians
27 BCE to 68 CE

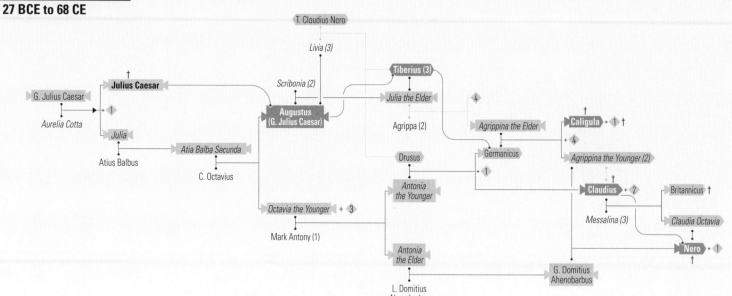

2 The Flavians
69 to 96 CE

3 The Antonines
96 to 192 CE

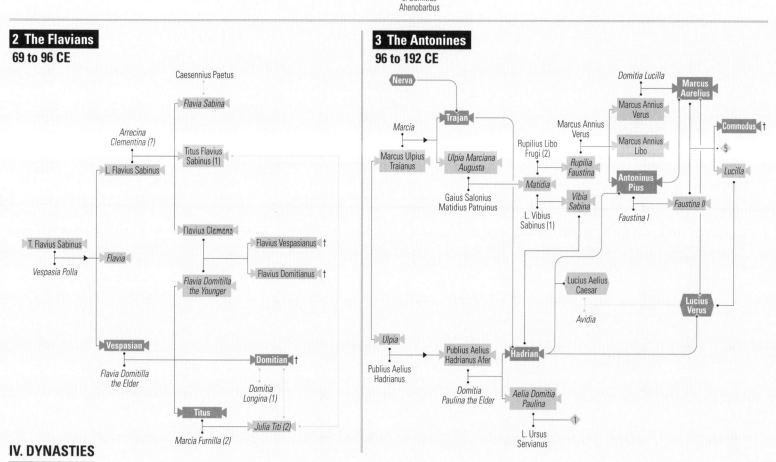

IV. DYNASTIES

Although imperial power was officially conferred via a series of ceremonies, laws and elections, it was heavily based on family ties. From the first years of the Second Triumvirate, Octavian took advantage of his family ties with Julius Caesar, by incorporating into his name, in 39 BCE, the title *divi filius*: 'son of the Divine (Julius)'. He also arranged for his wife to receive special honours and privileges, and he took on aides, such as his son-in-law Agrippa, who became members of his family. Adoption thus played a significant role in the creation of family links.

The term 'Julio-Claudian' is derived from the merging of the Julii, the descendants of Caesar, and the Claudii, through the mediation of Tiberius, the son-in-law of Augustus. Until 68 CE, emperors were chosen from this family bloc, but by that year the Julio-Claudian

dynasty had reached its limits. After two years of civil wars sparked by a struggle for power, a new dynasty took over: the Flavians, led by Vespasian. He was succeeded by his two sons, Titus and Domitian.

The system instituted by Augustus had made it possible to move from one dynasty to another, even if the cost was a civil war. With the Flavians, for the first time Roman power had fallen into the hands of a family originally from Italy (more specifically Rieti), and not from Rome itself. Later on, under Trajan and his successors, imperial power would be held by a dynasty whose ancestors were Roman colonists from Spain, while a Roman family, the Septimii, originally from Libya and Asia Minor, founded the Severan dynasty after settling in Rome. With the arrival of the Tetrarchy (joint rule by four leaders), emperors were recruited from military families with modest backgrounds from

4 The Severans
193 to 235 CE

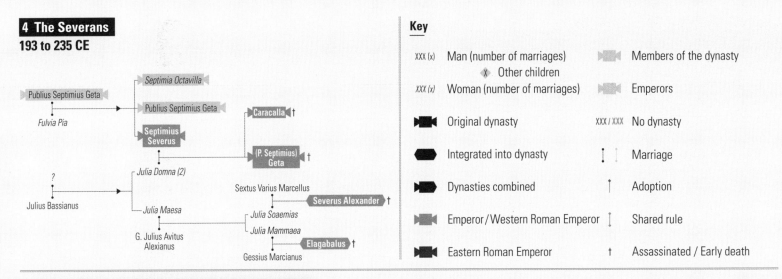

Key

XXX (x)	Man (number of marriages)
✕	Other children
XXX (x)	Woman (number of marriages)
	Original dynasty
	Integrated into dynasty
	Dynasties combined
	Emperor / Western Roman Emperor
	Eastern Roman Emperor

	Members of the dynasty
	Emperors
XXX / XXX	No dynasty
↕ ↕	Marriage
↑	Adoption
↕	Shared rule
†	Assassinated / Early death

5 The Constantinians, Valentinians and Theodosians
284 to 457 CE

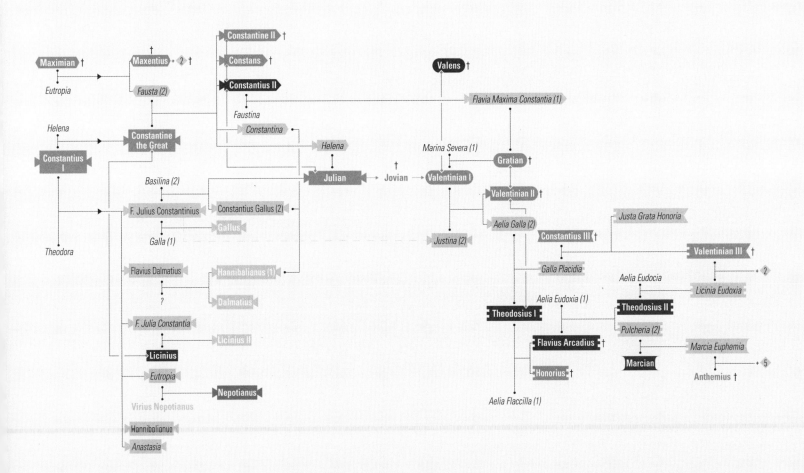

the Danube region, who constituted, from Constantine onwards, a dynasty primarily founded on marriage. The final dynasty, which descended from Valentinian I, was founded on the same principles.

Within this process of dynastic succession, violence always remained a risk. If senatorial opposition became too strong in the face of malfeasance by an emperor considered to be tyrannical, as Caligula was in 41 CE, the incumbent would generally be overthrown and the position entrusted to another member of the family. The most serious crises, however, involved confrontations between multiple claimants, all without any dynastic legitimacy. These conflicts were only resolved when one of the pretenders gained the upper hand by military and political means, enabling him to found a new dynasty. This was the case in 96 CE, with the Antonines, who were themselves

replaced in 193 by the Severans, although the accompanying civil war lasted until 197. The Severans retained power until 235, after which there followed a half-century of conflicts of all kinds.

The system of the Tetrarchy, which re-established a relative peace, was originally constructed around an artificial family structure: two *augusti* appointed two *caesarae*, whom they adopted or gave in marriage to their daughters, and the four of them ruled together over the Roman world. This configuration of dynasties through adoption or marriage would prevail until practically the end of the Western Empire.

V. A CHRONOLOGY OF THE EMPERORS

Seven major dynasties succeeded each other between the victory of Octavian over Mark Antony in 30 BCE and the fall of the Western Empire in 476 CE. Up until 235, the Julio-Claudians, the Flavians, the Nerva-Antonines and the Severans pacified and expanded Rome's provincial Empire. At the same time, they developed a central administration that made it possible to govern this enormous array of cities, as well as codifying a body of civil law that played a key role in the gradual unification of the Roman world.

Under the Julio-Claudians (30 BCE–68 CE), the Roman Empire was pacified and conquests were consolidated, for the time being, as far as the Rhine, the Danube and Syria, while Rome's political

system was reformed and an imperial administration put into place. Under the Flavians (70–96), the imperial administration continued to grow and there was further pacification of the Rhine and Danube frontier. The Nerva-Antonines (96–193) then achieved new conquests on the Danube and in Arabia.

After a civil war, the Severans (193–235) tried to pacify the borders with the Euphrates, the Danube and the Rhine. The period embracing the Antonines and the Severans, considered the Golden Age of the Roman Empire, came to a grim end in 235, sparking 35 years of civil wars and invasions. This chaos set the stage for the creation of the new imperial regime of the Tetrarchy. The Empire

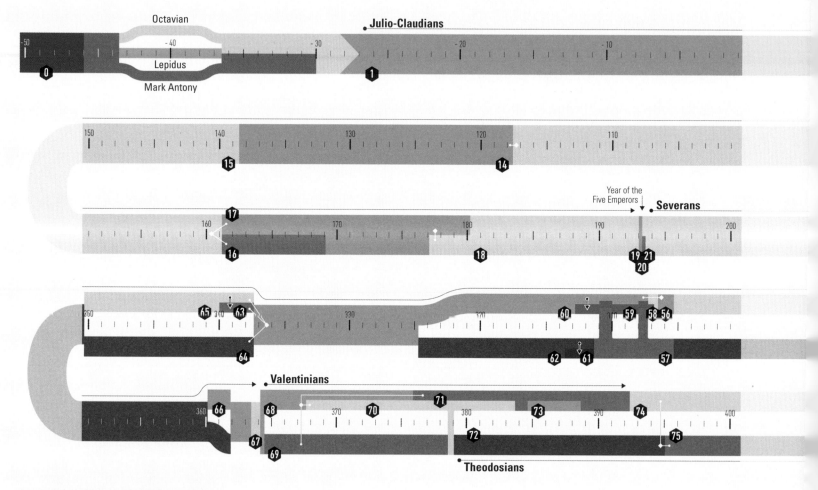

Details from the lives of the emperors

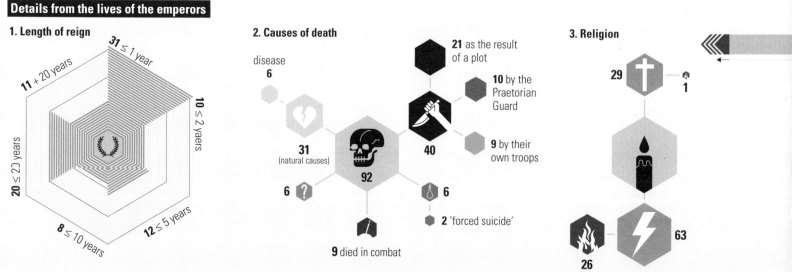

1. Length of reign

31 ≤ 1 year
11 + 20 years
10 ≤ 2 yaers
20 ≤ 2) years
8 ≤ 10 years
12 ≤ 5 years

2. Causes of death

disease
6

21 as the result of a plot

10 by the Praetorian Guard

31 (natural causes)

92

40

9 by their own troops

6 ?

6

2 'forced suicide'

9 died in combat

3. Religion

29

1

26

63

was then pacified, and the system of government was transformed by the partition of the Empire into two zones. In 312, however, Constantine's victory over Maxentius led to the reunification of the Empire, under the rule of the Constantinians (312–363).

The dynasty of Valentinian I (364–455) saw an increasing 'barbarization' of the army. The Empire was invaded yet again and imperial power gradually crumbled in the Western region but was strengthened in the East. After Valentinian III, the emperors were little more than puppets subject to the whims of barbarian kings until, eventually, the last emperor of the Western Roman Empire, Romulus Augustulus, was deposed in 476.

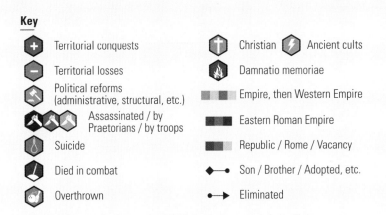

Key

- ✚ Territorial conquests
- ➖ Territorial losses
- ⚒ Political reforms (administrative, structural, etc.)
- Assassinated / by Praetorians / by troops
- Suicide
- Died in combat
- Overthrown
- ✝ Christian
- ⬡ Ancient cults
- Damnatio memoriae
- Empire, then Western Empire
- Eastern Roman Empire
- Republic / Rome / Vacancy
- ◆→ Son / Brother / Adopted, etc.
- ●→ Eliminated

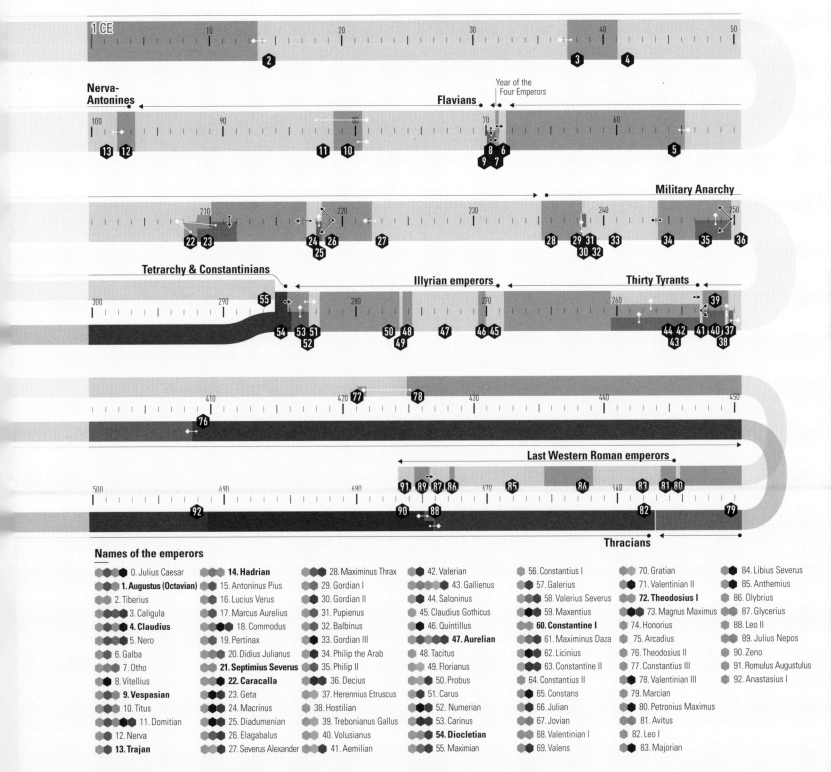

Year of the Four Emperors

Nerva-Antonines

Flavians

Military Anarchy

Tetrarchy & Constantinians

Illyrian emperors

Thirty Tyrants

Last Western Roman emperors

Thracians

Names of the emperors

- 0. Julius Caesar
- **1. Augustus (Octavian)**
- 2. Tiberius
- 3. Caligula
- **4. Claudius**
- 5. Nero
- 6. Galba
- 7. Otho
- 8. Vitellius
- **9. Vespasian**
- 10. Titus
- 11. Domitian
- 12. Nerva
- **13. Trajan**
- **14. Hadrian**
- 15. Antoninus Pius
- 16. Lucius Verus
- 17. Marcus Aurelius
- 18. Commodus
- 19. Pertinax
- 20. Didius Julianus
- **21. Septimius Severus**
- **22. Caracalla**
- 23. Geta
- 24. Macrinus
- 25. Diadumenian
- 26. Elagabalus
- 27. Severus Alexander
- 28. Maximinus Thrax
- 29. Gordian I
- 30. Gordian II
- 31. Pupienus
- 32. Balbinus
- 33. Gordian III
- 34. Philip the Arab
- 35. Philip II
- 36. Decius
- 37. Herennius Etruscus
- 38. Hostilian
- 39. Trebonianus Gallus
- 40. Volusianus
- 41. Aemilian
- 42. Valerian
- 43. Gallienus
- 44. Saloninus
- 45. Claudius Gothicus
- 46. Quintillus
- **47. Aurelian**
- 48. Tacitus
- 49. Florianus
- 50. Probus
- 51. Carus
- 52. Numerian
- 53. Carinus
- **54. Diocletian**
- 55. Maximian
- 56. Constantius I
- 57. Galerius
- 58. Valerius Severus
- 59. Maxentius
- **60. Constantine I**
- 61. Maximinus Daza
- 62. Licinius
- 63. Constantine II
- 64. Constantius II
- 65. Constans
- 66. Julian
- 67. Jovian
- 68. Valentinian I
- 69. Valens
- 70. Gratian
- 71. Valentinian II
- **72. Theodosius I**
- 73. Magnus Maximus
- 74. Honorius
- 75. Arcadius
- 76. Theodosius II
- 77. Constantius III
- 78. Valentinian III
- 79. Marcian
- 80. Petronius Maximus
- 81. Avitus
- 82. Leo I
- 83. Majorian
- 84. Libius Severus
- 85. Anthemius
- 86. Olybrius
- 87. Glycerius
- 88. Leo II
- 89. Julius Nepos
- 90. Zeno
- 91. Romulus Augustulus
- 92. Anastasius I

RELIGION

Like all the cities in the Roman world, Rome itself was home to a wide range of religions and religious communities, and a unifying religion only emerged with the advent of Christianity. Like the 2,000 to 3,000 cities in the Roman world, Rome had its own public cult, as did every family and private group (guilds, professional associations, etc.). People did not become a member of a religious community by choice but rather, in the case of a public cult, through birth, the acquisition of citizenship (after serving as an auxiliary in the army, for example) or manumission. In the private sphere, membership of a religious cult was determined by birth into a particular family, or entrance into it through marriage, adoption or sale in the case of slaves. Only membership of a college or association involved a personal choice.

These religions were not structured around revelations, holy scriptures or dogma but instead followed ancestral traditions and decisions taken by the leaders of the public or private cults. The primary concern was ritual obligations that linked specific divinities to particular groups of Romans, enlisting them as partners in their worldly undertakings. The soul and its wellbeing in the great beyond were irrelevant to this type of cult. In public cults, priests were responsible for maintaining holy law, monitoring rituals and preserving the patrimony of the gods. The main participants in ceremonies were the consuls, the praetors and the emperor, as well as selected groups of priests.

All foreign cities and communities had their own religion, and *peregrini* who lived in another city would be admitted into its religion. Ancient cities such as those in Greece and Asia Minor maintained their own traditions, while cities in Northern Europe quickly created religions similar to those of Rome, although there was no question of 'conversion'. On the whole, foreign cities kept their own religion and gods, and even if they became *municipia* they could still choose their own gods and rituals. They also remained free to select their own pantheon and rites if they acquired the status of a colony, but a nod to Roman traditions would now be expected. The Roman gods were widely known in the provinces, thanks to the presence of colonies or garrisoned troops, and, by the same token, foreign divinities were brought to Rome by travellers and merchants, or even as a result of battles (some gods would then be 'evoked' – called to Rome – or associated with a particular victory).

Rome's official public cult was a matter for all Roman citizens. Ceremonies were performed to benefit the health of the Roman people (or rather, the Roman State) and, later on, for that of the emperor; they involved officially recognized divinities and followed a calendar of rituals and festivals. Public cults drew on ritual offerings and divinatory consultations. Offerings ranged from small quantities of incense and statuettes to large statues, altars and temples, although the most common form was a banquet, which took the form of a sacrifice. An animal or plant would be given up to a divinity before being killed or destroyed, with one part burnt in the fire of the altar and the other part eaten by the celebrants. In rituals involving gods of the underworld, the offerings would be completely burnt, as no living human could share a banquet with them. Rituals were conducted at both regular and one-off festivals, and they were often associated with games (chariot races, spectacles, staged hunts).

Divinatory rites involved the consultation of auspices and oracles. Auspices were often linked with observations of the flight and behaviour of birds. Magistrates would even take an augur or haruspex with them on journeys outside Rome, to take auspices before sunrise that would favour or prohibit any action that the magistrate was planning to take. The Sibylline Books, three scrolls mostly containing verses written in Greek, were an oracle specific to Rome. A college of priests – the *decimviri* and later the *quindecimviri* – consulted the books in times of crisis in search of advice and recommended rituals to ward off disastrous events. They would report their findings to the Senate, where they would be debated and then acted on by the consuls.

The gods of the public cult originated from Latium, central Italy and – in some cases, as the Roman State extended its field of influence – Africa, Greece and Greater Greece (Magna Graecia). As emperors succeeded one another, new divinities were admitted into the official pantheon, often as the fulfilment of a *votum*, a vow to build a temple or make sacrifices to a particular god in the event of a military victory. Augustus, for example, erected the temples of Apollo Palatinus and Mars Ultor, Vespasian favoured Isis and Serapis, and Aurelian invoked Sol Invictus in 274 in a vow before a war against Palmyra. Sometimes a whole new cult was assimilated from elsewhere, as in the case of Sol Invictus Elagabal. The latter was the sun god of the temple-city of Emesa, in Syria, and was imported to Rome by Emperor Elagabalus, who had formerly served as the god's high priest. Once such divinities were officially accepted, they became 'Roman'.

After the death of Julius Caesar in 44 BCE, official religious practices were complemented by imperial cults that elevated rulers to the status of a deified mortal or *divus*. Philosophers had long debated the idea that exceptional people could attain immortality, and this speculation was eventually solidified into a custom that combined heroic Greek-style funeral rites and the myths of Hercules and Aesculapius, the only two human beings who had been elevated to dwell among the gods without being dead. The myth of the apotheosis of Hercules provided a particularly influential model, and one participant at the cremation of a dead emperor was specifically charged with observing whether the spirit or lifeforce of the emperor had flown up to the heavens. An apparition of this kind would testify to his status as a *divus* deserving of worship and dedicated priests. In the Eastern Empire, emperors received honours equivalent to those of gods while they were still alive (although they did not actually become gods); in the Western Empire, it was their genius, or divine double, that was worshipped, along with their virtues.

Private cults were no different from public cults in terms of either the rituals that were performed or the gods that were venerated. Alongside family-specific divinities like the genius of the paterfamilias, the Lares (tutelary deities) and the Manes (spirits of dead ancestors), families would also worship one or more of Rome's traditional gods, depending on their background. Private individuals were expected to participate in public ceremonies, and they were also permitted to make sacrifices in public temples outside of official rituals. Foreigners living in Rome, or any other city, had the right to worship as they pleased in private. As for professional guilds and associations, these had their own religious calendar and rites. All these private cults gave rise to autonomous congregations in which the celebrants were heads of families or annually appointed heads of associations.

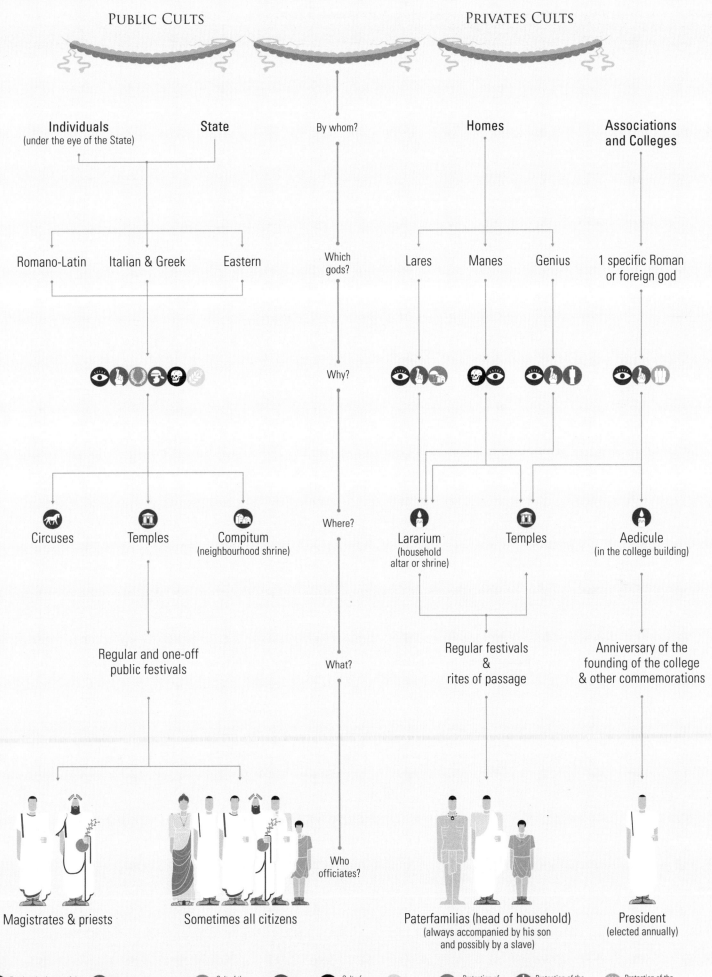

PUBLIC CULTS

PRIVATES CULTS

Individuals
(under the eye of the State)

State

By whom?

Homes

Associations and Colleges

Which gods?

Romano-Latin   Italian & Greek   Eastern

Lares   Manes   Genius

1 specific Roman or foreign god

Why?

Where?

Circuses   Temples   Compitum
(neighbourhood shrine)

Lararium
(household altar or shrine)

Temples

Aedicule
(in the college building)

What?

Regular and one-off
public festivals

Regular festivals
&
rites of passage

Anniversary of the
founding of the college
& other commemorations

Who officiates?

Magistrates & priests

Sometimes all citizens

Paterfamilias (head of household)
(always accompanied by his son
and possibly by a slave)

President
(elected annually)

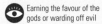 Earning the favour of the gods or warding off evil  Worldly business matters   Cult of the Emperor   War   Cult of the dead   Harvests   Protection of the household 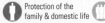 Protection of the family & domestic life   Protection of the college or association

The major Roman gods, with their patronages, origins and dates of first appearance

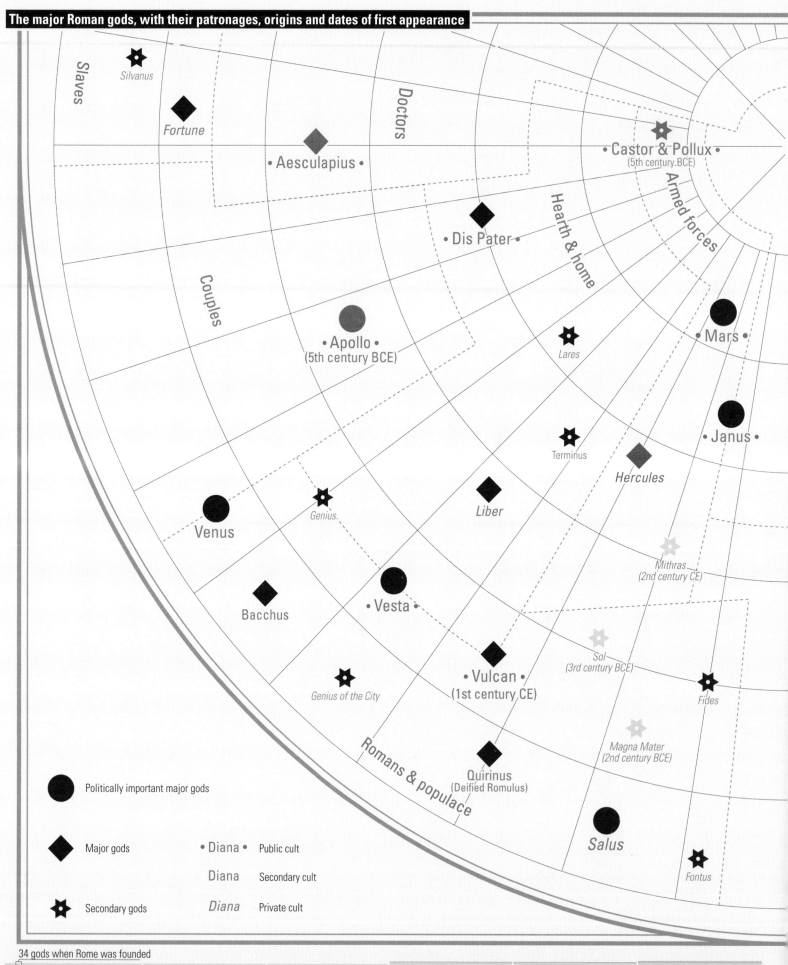

Slaves

Silvanus

Fortune

Doctors

Aesculapius

Castor & Pollux
(5th century BCE)

Armed forces

Dis Pater

Hearth & home

Couples

Apollo
(5th century BCE)

Lares

Mars

Terminus

Janus

Hercules

Venus

Genius

Liber

Mithras
(2nd century CE)

Bacchus

Vesta

Sol
(3rd century BCE)

Genius of the City

Vulcan
(1st century CE)

Fides

Magna Mater
(2nd century BCE)

Romans & populace

Quirinus
(Deified Romulus)

Salus

Fontus

⬤ Politically important major gods

◆ Major gods

✹ Secondary gods

• Diana • Public cult

Diana Secondary cult

Diana Private cult

34 gods when Rome was founded

8th century BCE   7th century BCE   6th century BCE   5th century BCE   4th century BCE   3rd century BCE

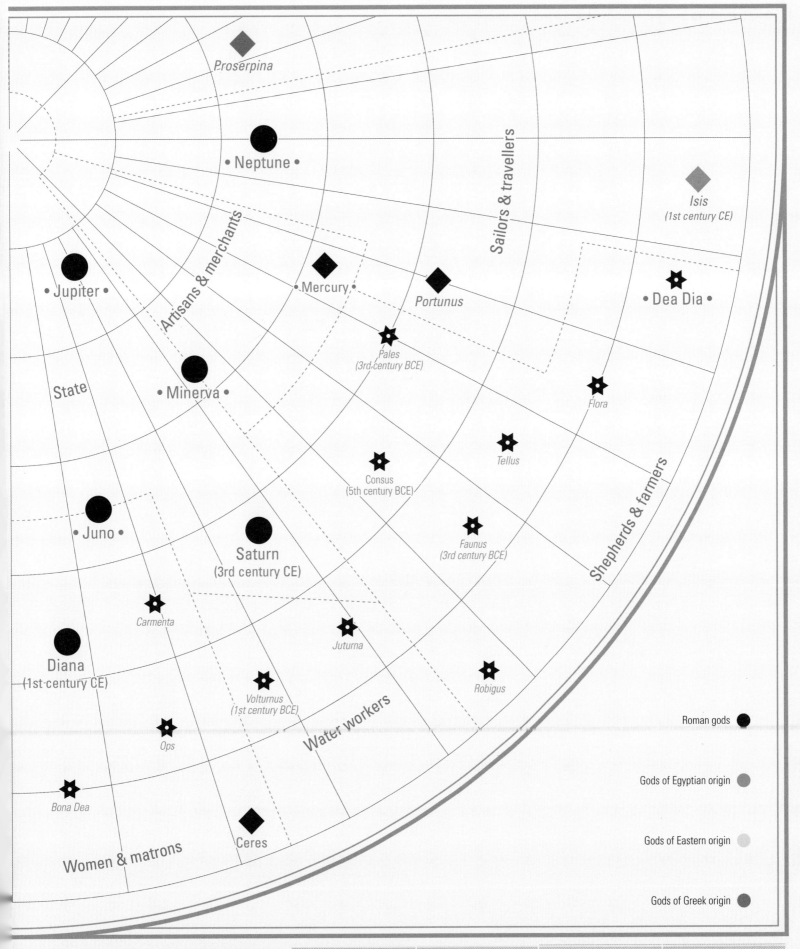

Proserpina

Neptune

Isis
(1st century CE)

Sailors & travellers

Artisans & merchants

Jupiter

Mercury

Portunus

Dea Dia

Pales
(3rd century BCE)

Flora

State

Minerva

Tellus

Consus
(5th century BCE)

Shepherds & farmers

Juno

Saturn
(3rd century CE)

Faunus
(3rd century BCE)

Carmenta

Juturna

Robigus

Diana
(1st century CE)

Volturnus
(1st century BCE)

Water workers

Ops

Bona Dea

Ceres

Women & matrons

Roman gods

Gods of Egyptian origin

Gods of Eastern origin

Gods of Greek origin

2nd century BCE   1st century BCE   1st century CE   2nd century CE   3rd century CE   4th century CE

The two principal types of Roman temple

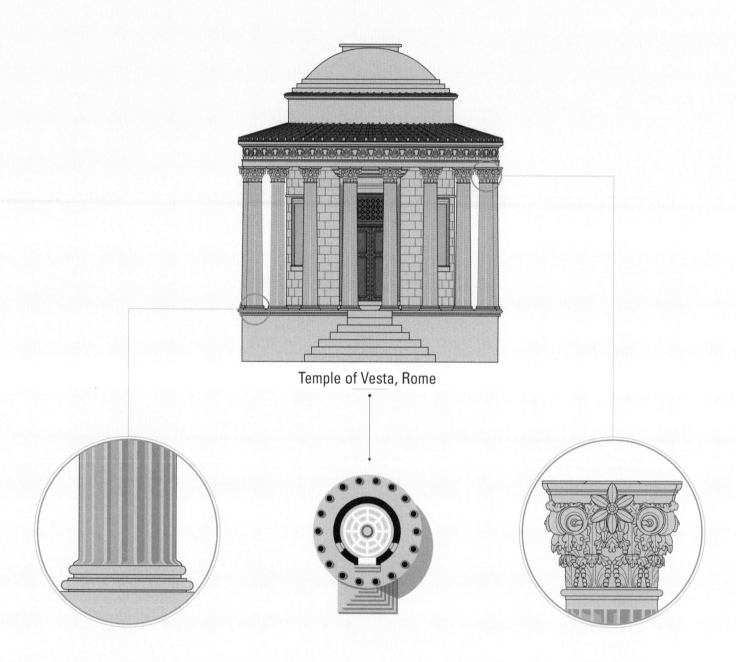

Temple of Vesta, Rome

II. PLACES OF WORSHIP

Gods that were welcomed into the Roman public cult were given an earthly residence. This would be a consecrated space with an altar, a shrine or a temple, which could possibly be surrounded by a sacred wood and have its own well. The most important temples were situated in or near the fora, while others could be found in the city regions of Rome or elsewhere in the city's territory. Temples were generally quadrangular and were based around a *templum* (hence their name), a sacred space that was established by means of augury. Temples comprised an enclosed, raised area (*cella*) surrounded by columns and fronted by a portico (*pronaos*), which

was reached by steps. The cella contained a devotional statue; some temples, such as the Capitol, had three cellae, each with a separate divinity. The devotional altar would be set in front of the temple, while the courtyard surrounding it could be filled by a sacred grove. Sacred spaces were forbidden to mortals, except for the purposes of worship or maintenance. The square around the temple was often endowed with porticoes, used to shelter worshippers and to hold banquets. (Porticoes were profane and thus open to mortals.) Temples for deities of foreign origin, like the double temple of Isis and Serapis, could have special features, such as, in this case, wells with 'Nile' water.

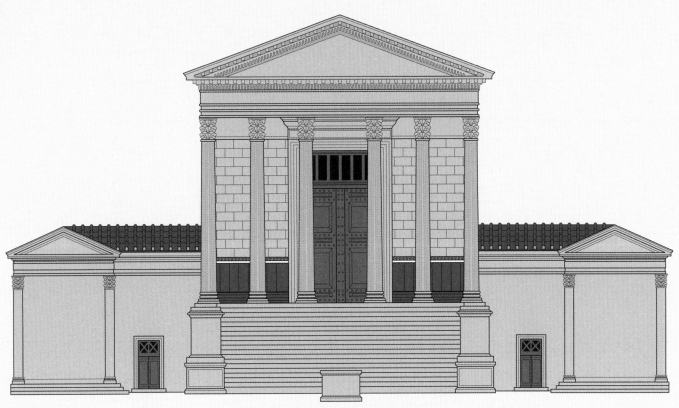

Temple of Jupiter, Ostia Antica

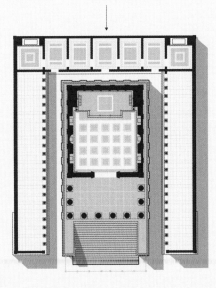

The Roman Forum held the circular Temple of Vesta, which contained a fire that was never extinguished and probably served to validate all Rome's public sacrifices, as it seems that their sacrificial fires were all lit from its flames. There were other round temples in Rome, such as the Temple of Hercules Invictus in the Forum Boarium, which was Greek in style (with no podium), but the best-known today is the Pantheon, which was devoted to twelve major gods. Military camps also had a small sanctuary in their 'chapel' of insignias.

Private places of worship tended to be simpler affairs. Houses had a shrine for their Lares and the genius (divine tutelary spirit) of the father and mother of the family. The shrine took the form of a niche with small statues or a painted wall with an altar in front of it, either in the kitchen or in the communal living area or garden. Altars to the Manes (the souls of the deceased) were set up outside cities.

Religious ceremonies conducted by an organization or guild generally took place in front of an aedicule on its premises. The places of worship used by *peregrini* took their own particular forms, as did the synagogues of the Jewish communities.

Important religious roles in Rome

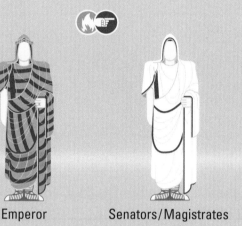

Priestly college
Role — Gods
Name
Method of recruitment — Rank
Name and historical era
• Royal • Republic • Empire

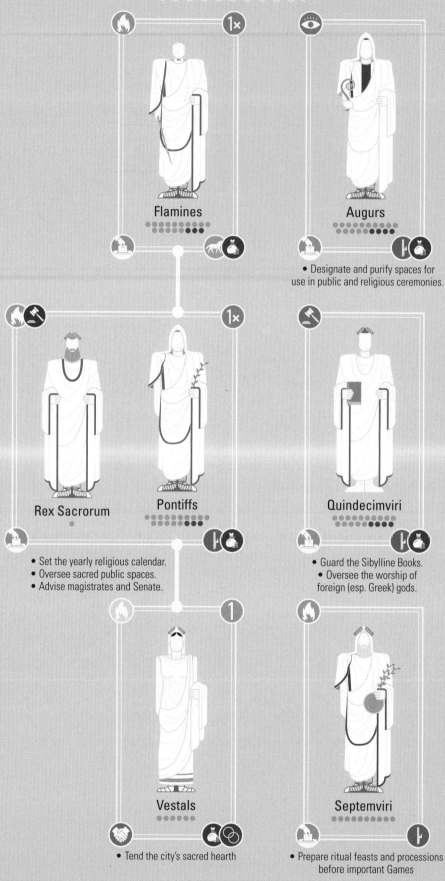

Flamines

Augurs
• Designate and purify spaces for use in public and religious ceremonies.

Rex Sacrorum   **Pontiffs**
• Set the yearly religious calendar.
• Oversee sacred public spaces.
• Advise magistrates and Senate.

Quindecimviri
• Guard the Sibylline Books.
• Oversee the worship of foreign (esp. Greek) gods.

Vestals
• Tend the city's sacred hearth

Septemviri
• Prepare ritual feasts and processions before important Games

Emperor   **Senators/Magistrates**
• May address priests and the senate on religious questions.
• Are consulted regarding correct behaviour in religious matters.

Nomination of priests (Imperial period)

Diplomacy

Augury and interpretation of divine signs

Overseeing sacred rites / Overseeing foreign cults

Veneration of a god / gods by members of a college

Elected / Chosen

Cult celebration (pre-Roman / Roman / Imperial period)

Equestrian / senatorial / patrician / aristocratic rank

Calendar of fixed Roman festivals

Agricultural rites   Rites to ward off evil   War rites   Civic rites

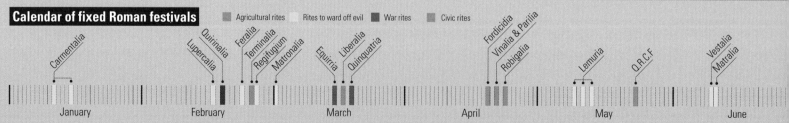

Carmentalia
Lupercalia   Quirinalia   Feralia   Terminalia   Regifugium   Matronalia
Equirria   Liberalia   Quinquatria
Fordicidia   Vinalia & Parilia   Robigalia
Lemuria
Q.R.C.F
Vestalia   Matralia

January   February   March   April   May   June

Sodales Augustales

1

●●●●●●●●●●●●
●●●●●●●

Sodales Titii

1

●●●●●●●●●●
●●●

Arval Brethren

1

●●●●●●●●●
●●

Fetiales

●●●●●●●●●●●●
●●●●

• Safeguard the relationship between Rome
and its gods and foreign lands
• Make proclamations of peace and war

Luperci

1

●●●●●●●●●●● (x2)

Haruspex

Religious leaders of
foreign communities
(e.g. rabbi)

Salii

1

●●●●●●●●●● (x2)
●●

• Guard the shield of Mars
• Celebrate some warrior rites

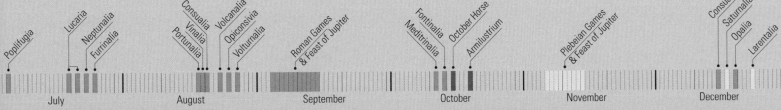

Poplifugia · Lucaria · Neptunalia · Furrinalia · Consualia · Vinalia · Portunalia · Volcanalia · Opiconsivia · Volturnalia · Roman Games & Feast of Jupiter · Fontinalia · Meditrinalia · October Horse · Armilustrium · Plebeian Games & Feast of Jupiter · Consualia · Saturnalia · Opalia · Larentalia

July   August   September   October   November   December

III. A MAJOR FESTIVAL: THE SAECULAR GAMES

Following a series of portents in the year 1 BCE, the Sibylline Books were consulted and interpreted as recommending a revival of the ancient Saecular Games, which marked the end of one generation (*saeculum*) and solicited good health for the coming one. In total, these games were held three times – in 17 BCE and 88 and 204 CE – before Constantine put an end to the tradition in 213.

The festival was celebrated by the quindecimviri (members of the priestly colleges) and Roman matrons, and was watched by the people of Rome. After various preparatory ceremonies, the Games started on the night of 31 May–1 June, in an ancient place of worship, the Tarentum, close to the Temples of Dis Pater and Proserpina, gods

of the underworld. The three days of the Games always included a night-time ceremony – to celebrate the passing of the preceding generation – and a daytime ceremony – to greet the arrival of the new generation. Over the course of three nights, the quindecimviri made sacrifices to, respectively, the Parcae (the three Fates), the Lucinae (goddesses of childbirth), and Terra Mater (the Earth Mother). All of these sacrifices were burnt offerings. On completing them, the priests went, every night, to a specially erected wooden theatre near the Tarentum, to watch the games and performances. Meanwhile, on the Capitoline, in front of the Temple of Juno, the empress and 109 matrons selected by the priests spent three nights in vigil and

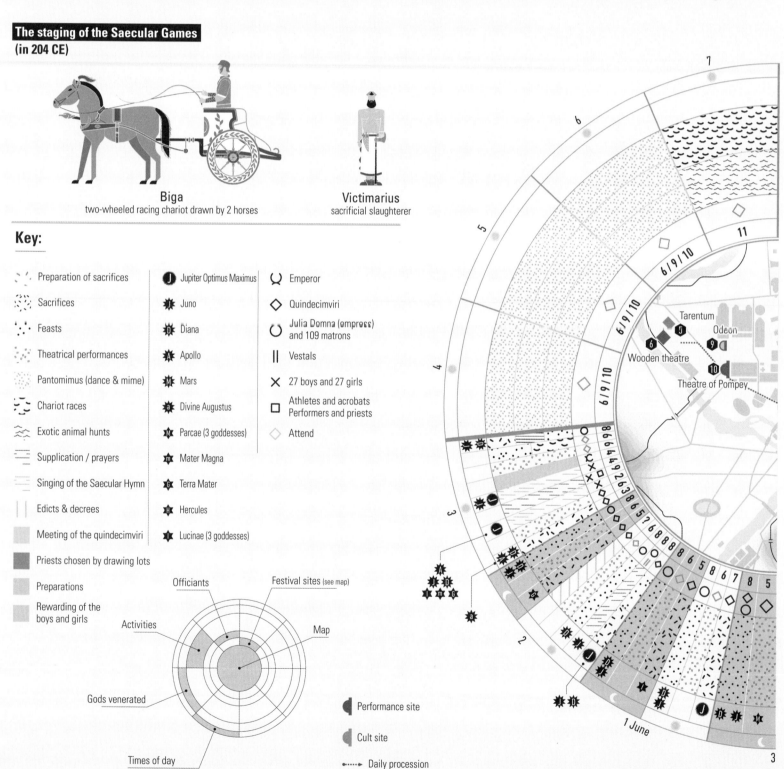

The staging of the Saecular Games
(in 204 CE)

Biga
two-wheeled racing chariot drawn by 2 horses

Victimarius
sacrificial slaughterer

Key:

- Preparation of sacrifices
- Sacrifices
- Feasts
- Theatrical performances
- Pantomimus (dance & mime)
- Chariot races
- Exotic animal hunts
- Supplication / prayers
- Singing of the Saecular Hymn
- Edicts & decrees
- Meeting of the quindecimviri
- Priests chosen by drawing lots
- Preparations
- Rewarding of the boys and girls

- Jupiter Optimus Maximus
- Juno
- Diana
- Apollo
- Mars
- Divine Augustus
- Parcae (3 goddesses)
- Mater Magna
- Terra Mater
- Hercules
- Lucinae (3 goddesses)

- Emperor
- Quindecimviri
- Julia Domna (empress) and 109 matrons
- Vestals
- 27 boys and 27 girls
- Athletes and acrobats Performers and priests
- Attend

Officiants — Festival sites (see map)

Activities

Map

Gods venerated

Times of day

- Performance site
- Cult site
- Daily procession

at a *sellisternium* (feast), at which places were set for Juno and Diana. In the morning, the quindecimviri made sacrifices on the Capitoline on 1 June (to Jupiter) and 2 June (to Juno and Diana) and on the Palatine on 3 June (to Apollo and Diana). After these sacrifices, they would attend performances at the wooden theatre, while the 109 matrons celebrated another feast dedicated to the same two goddesses. On the second day, the matrons made supplications to Juno, assisted by two Vestals under orders from the emperor. On the morning of 3 June, the priests, having made their sacrifices and attended the performances, returned to the Temple of Apollo and Diana, where 27 boys and 27 girls sang the Saecular Hymn, composed by the poet

Horace. They then accompanied the children, along with the athletes and performers from the final spectacles, to the Capitoline, where the children repeated the Saecular Hymn in front of the Temples of Juno and Jupiter. After offering rewards to the participating children, the priests watched the performances for the last time and then presided over chariot races in a temporary circus built near the wooden theatre. At the same time, the 109 matrons made sacrifices to Juno and Diana, and during their banquet they listened to the children performing the hymn and rewarded them appropriately. There were more spectacles on 4–6 June, before the festival finally came to an end with chariot races and staged hunts on 7 June.

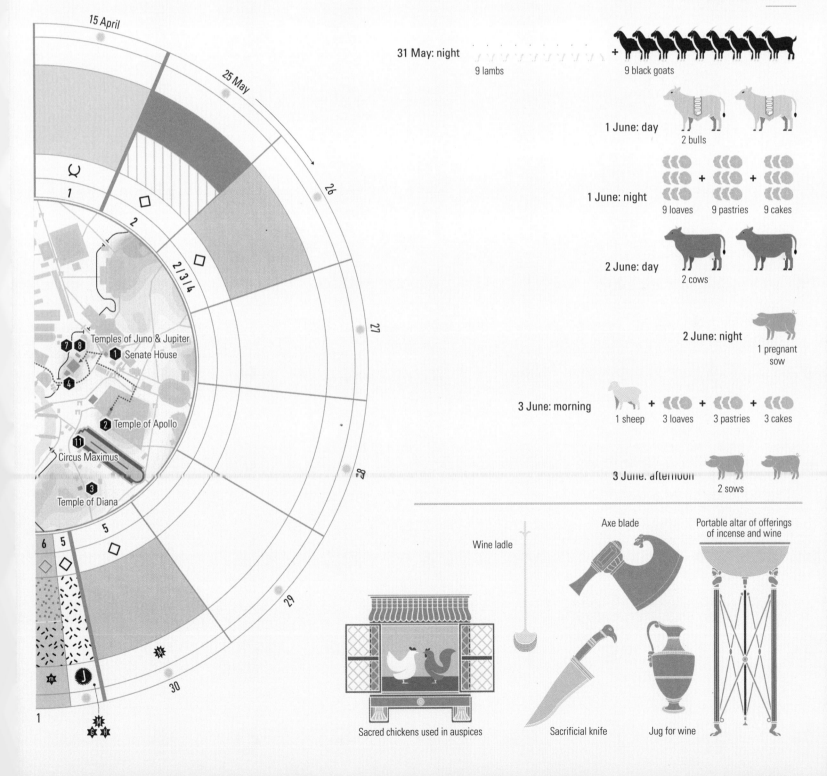

IV. JEWISH COMMUNITIES AND THE SPREAD OF CHRISTIANITY

There were Jewish communities in Rome, and in many other cities, from the 1st century BCE onwards. They had the right to practise their religion and follow Jewish law. In 65 CE, however, the Jewish revolt against the Romans in Judea led to a catastrophe: the destruction of the temple in Jerusalem in 70 CE. After being the public religion of a kingdom, with its own clergy and temple, Judaism now became one religion among many in the Roman world. Nevertheless, Judaism thrived after 71 CE, both in synagogues, where the community met for prayers, rituals and festivals, and in private homes.

In the early 1st century, in the time of Tiberius, a Jewish movement led by Jesus of Nazareth began to gain followers in Judea. Under pressure from the priests in the Temple, Jesus of Nazareth was arrested and executed by the Roman prefect of Judea. Then, thanks to the efforts of missionaries such as Paul, a Jewish Roman citizen from Tarsus, Christian communities began to emerge, particularly in big cities. Christianity separated from Judaism in 90 CE, but it was not until the 2nd century that explicit Roman references to Christians were first recorded – by Tacitus, in his account of the Jewish War of 70. A letter to the Emperor Trajan from Pliny the Younger, the governor of Bithynia-Pontus, describes the spread of the Christian faith and the Roman attitude towards it. Until that point, anyone accused of being a Christian was sentenced to death, but Trajan discouraged this practice by decreeing the same punishment for accusers if their denunciation was not proven. Despite occasional unrest, such as the persecutions in Lugdunum (Lyons) in 177, the persecution of Christians was neither widespread nor constant. In reality, the only people executed for publicly refusing to renounce their religion were provocateurs accused of treason.

It is true that the Roman State did fiercely repress Christianity in the second half of the 3rd century, but it ultimately failed in its attempts and Christianity continued to grow. When Constantine the Great defeated the last (pagan) pretender to imperial power, he went on to legalize Christianity in 312. The Church finally came out of hiding and established its own places of worship. Furthermore, within a century, Christianity was declared the only authorized religion in the Empire and had the support of the emperors, although it did split into various sects and regional churches.

Menorah
(Jewish)

Fish and cross
(Christian)

◉ Patriarchate ◉ Archdiocese ◉ Diocese
✝✝✝ Christian community in the 1st / 2nd century / 325 CE
■ Spread of Christianity in the 3rd century
■ Spread of Christianity in the 4th century
■ Spread of Christianity in the 5th century
★ Settlements from Jewish diaspora of the 3rd century
→ Movement of Jewish diaspora
- - - Borders of the Roman Empire in the late 3rd century
🔥 Anti-Christian persecution before the 3rd century

The spread of Christianity (by % of the total population of the Empire)

1. 177 CE: Persecution of Christians in the Empire (martyrs of Lyon)
2. 202 CE: Ban on any Jewish or Christian proselytism
3. 250 CE: Persecution of Christians (death of St Cyprian)
4. 260 CE: Edict of toleration of Christianity
5. 301 CE: Armenia becomes the first state to adopt Christianity as its official religion, when Gregory the Illuminator converts King Tiridates III
6. 303 CE: Persecution of Christians
7. 311 CE: Edict of Serdica (toleration of Christianity)

8. 312 CE: Edict of Maximinus (persecuting Christians)
9. 313 CE: Edict of Milan (toleration)
10. 331 CE: Inventory of temple property, confiscations
11. 341 CE: First ban on pagan sacrifices
12. 356 CE: Ban on sacrifices and closing of temples in the East
13. 361 CE: Reestablishment of paganism and anti-Christian measures
14. 381 CE: Second Council of Constantinople. Reinstated ban on pagan sacrifices

15. 382 CE: Polytheism is rejected as the state religion and the Altar of Victory is removed from the Senate House
16. 385 CE: Ban on sacrifices and examining the entrails of victims
17. 386 CE: Destruction of temples in Syria, Egypt, Africa
18. 391 CE: Ban on traditional private cult worship in Rome
19. 392 CE: Ban on traditional (polytheistic) cults in the Empire
20. 399 CE: Destruction of rural pagan temples & Temple of Caelestis
21. 435 CE: Reinstated ban on pagan sacrifices

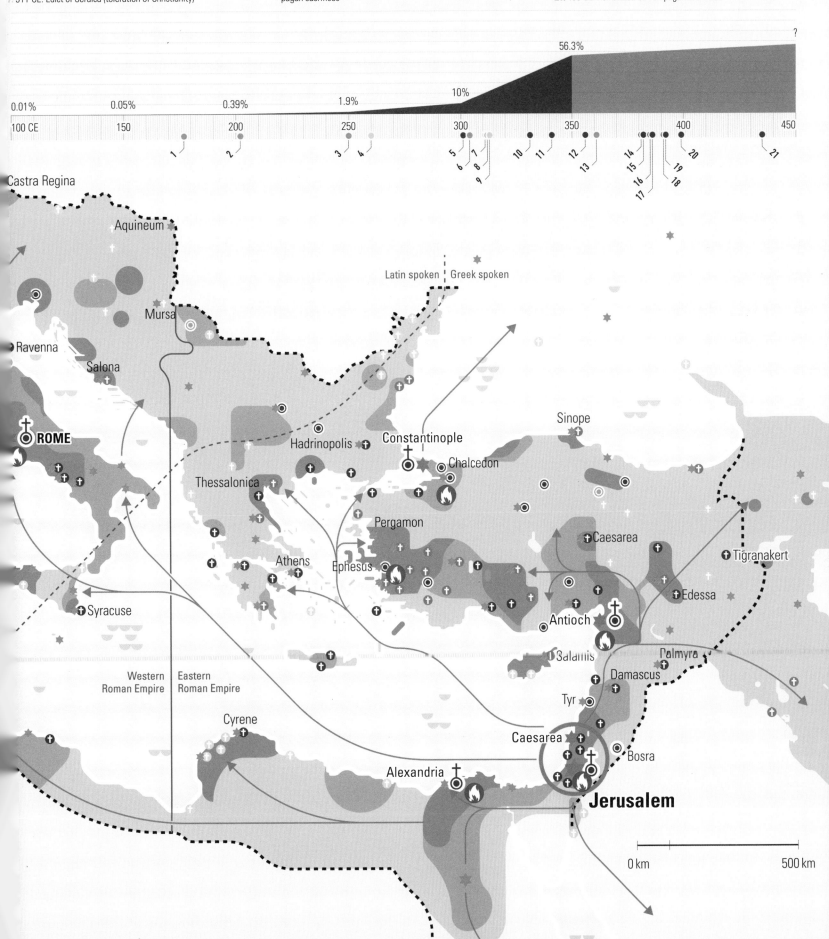

56.3%

10%

0.01%   0.05%   0.39%   1.9%

100 CE   150   200   250   300   350   400   450

Castra Regina

Aquineum

Latin spoken | Greek spoken

Mursa

Ravenna

Salona

ROME

Hadrinopolis

Constantinople

Sinope

Chalcedon

Thessalonica

Pergamon

Caesarea

Athens

Tigranakert

Ephesus

Syracuse

Edessa

Antioch

Western Roman Empire   Eastern Roman Empire

Salamis   Palmyra

Damascus

Tyr

Cyrene

Caesarea   Bosra

Alexandria

Jerusalem

0 km   500 km

THE ROMAN ECONOMY

The wars of the republican period allowed Rome to pacify first Italy and the Western Mediterranean and then, during the 2nd and 1st centuries BCE, the Eastern Mediterranean and the surrounding lands. By the beginning of the modern era, it was possible to travel in safety all over the Roman Empire, from Gibraltar to the Black Sea, from Scotland to the Rhine and from the Danube to the Sahara. This situation gave rise to what could be cautiously described as a 'global economy' that developed for two hundred years, before suffering the effects of political turmoil and invasions in the middle of the 3rd century. There was an upswing with the relative stability of the early 4th century but the economy never recovered the buoyancy of the preceding centuries, due to pressure on the Rhine and Danube from nomadic peoples and the consolidation of a new capital, Constantinople, in the richest half of the Empire. In the 5th century CE, the Western Empire fell into disarray and its economy quickly fell apart.

What exactly was the nature of the Roman economy? The economics of the ancient world have long been the subject of theoretical debate, largely on account of the daunting state of the primary sources. Written sources are usually patchy, and although archaeology is providing an increasing quantity of raw data, it remains difficult to interpret. Who owned the industrial sites that have been discovered? How were the estates and workshops organized, and how much profit did they make? The best-preserved evidence – ceramics, for example – give rise to some more tricky questions: were these objects valued items or merely utilitarian? Amphorae have been found in their thousands in shipwrecks and archaeological digs, but do they constitute a reliable record of wine and oil production?

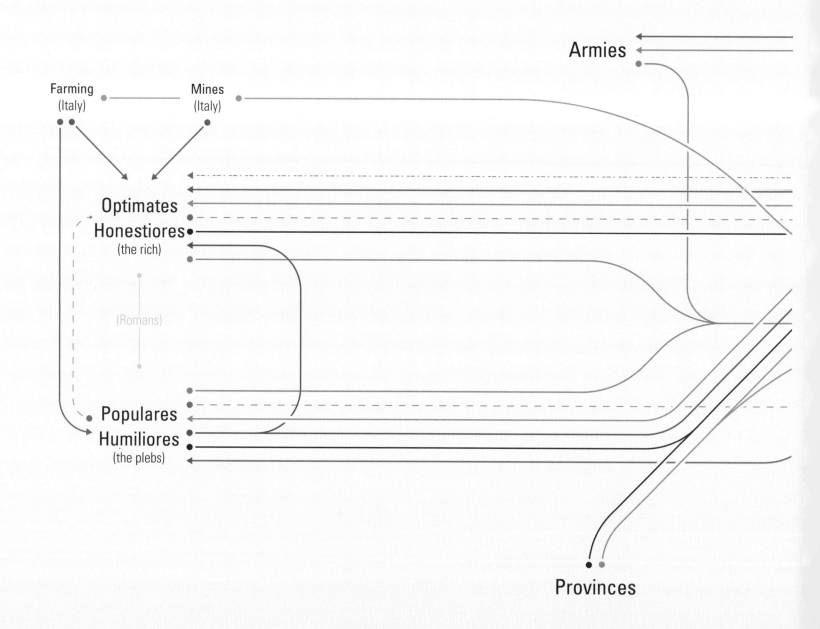

They were once thought to have been used for wine alone, but archaeologists were subsequently able to demonstrate – to widespread surprise – that the Romans also used barrels for this purpose.

Land was the best investment in ancient times, with a yield of around 6%, but contemporary writings suggest that financial affairs were not driven by cold-headed calculations. Agriculture was not seen as part of a market economy but instead focused on subsistence. As far as we can tell, trade and industry were always marginal and only the production and sale of luxury items (gemstones, pearls, perfumes, spices) seem to have been greatly profitable. Data on more basic commodities (oil, wine, ceramics) is only available for a few periods, such as the end of the Republic, although there is evidence of an awareness at the start of the Empire of the agricultural potential of whole swathes of North Africa and the West. Plenty

of questions are still unanswered, however – not to mention the constraints on research imposed by gaps in the chronology and shortfalls in the information available on certain topics, as well as the theoretical arguments that have been propounded in relation to the economics of the ancient world. These veer between a 'primitivist' outlook (mirroring ideas discussed by Moses Finley and Peter Garnsey) that views economics within the context of culture and politics, and a 'modernist' approach that views the Roman economy as the benchmark for the economies of the modern world. A middle course has been steered by Claude Nicolet and Paul Veyne, who acknowledge the specificities of the economic philosophy of the period but nevertheless attempt to quantify its supplies and demands.

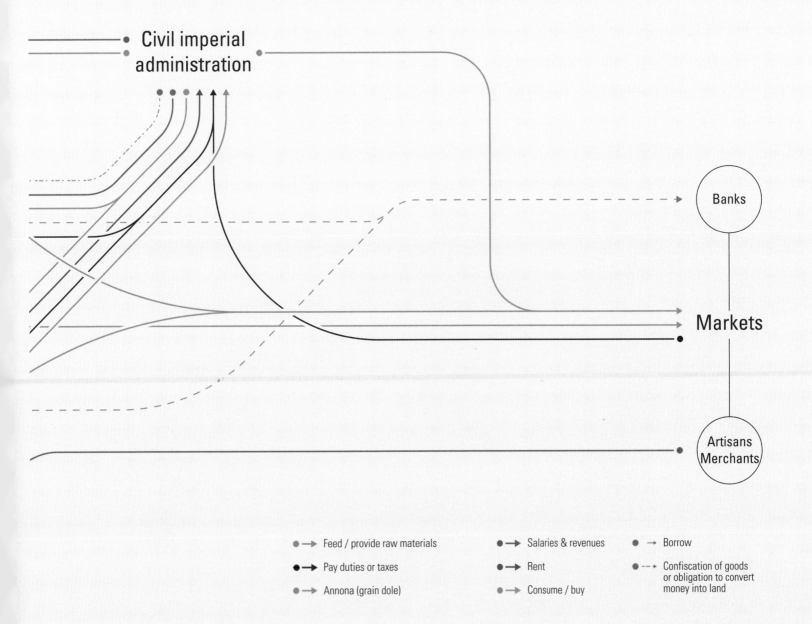

Civil imperial administration

Banks

Markets

Artisans Merchants

● → Feed / provide raw materials

● → Pay duties or taxes

● → Annona (grain dole)

● → Salaries & revenues

● → Rent

● → Consume / buy

● → Borrow

● --→ Confiscation of goods or obligation to convert money into land

II. THE NEEDS OF ROME, ITALY AND THE EMPIRE

The Roman economy in the republican period was focused on satisfying basic needs, particularly food. Feeding Rome was a political problem in itself, as shortages could spark unrest. Part of the economy was therefore based on maintaining supplies of wheat and, later, oil, but these products were not subject to the vagaries of commercial transactions: the *Annona*, or grain dole, was guaranteed by the State and the aristocracy. The importance of the Annona to Rome is reflected in the rapid population drop in the 4th century, after the founding of Constantinople. Other major cities relied on the patronage of local aristocrats, who supplemented food supplies from their private estates and handed out provisions to their 'clients'.

The Roman economy was not a free-for-all, and times of crisis could trigger interventions by the Senate (during the Republic), or later by the emperor. The emperors granted legal and fiscal privileges to merchants and transporters of wheat to Rome (from Alexandria in the reigns of Claudius to Commodus, and later from other parts of Africa). Many needs were covered by local and regional suppliers but some goods – ceramics, tiles, bricks, metal, marble – were imported. There is evidence of trading networks but their dynamics are still unclear. Tiles and bricks, for example, could be used as ballast during sea journeys, which may explain how bricks manufactured during a slow period on a farming estate in Latium could end up in a building in Africa. Moreover, the stamps found on bricks and tiles show that the army was a major producer of these items, both for itself and for public buildings in the cities near its camps. From the late 1st century CE onwards, bricks were needed for imperial construction projects in Rome (public baths, temples, forums, porticoes), and demand was such that all brickworks were soon requisitioned. Marble, granite and metal were probably the building materials that travelled furthest; stone was widely used for public works, and quarries and mines were often imperial property.

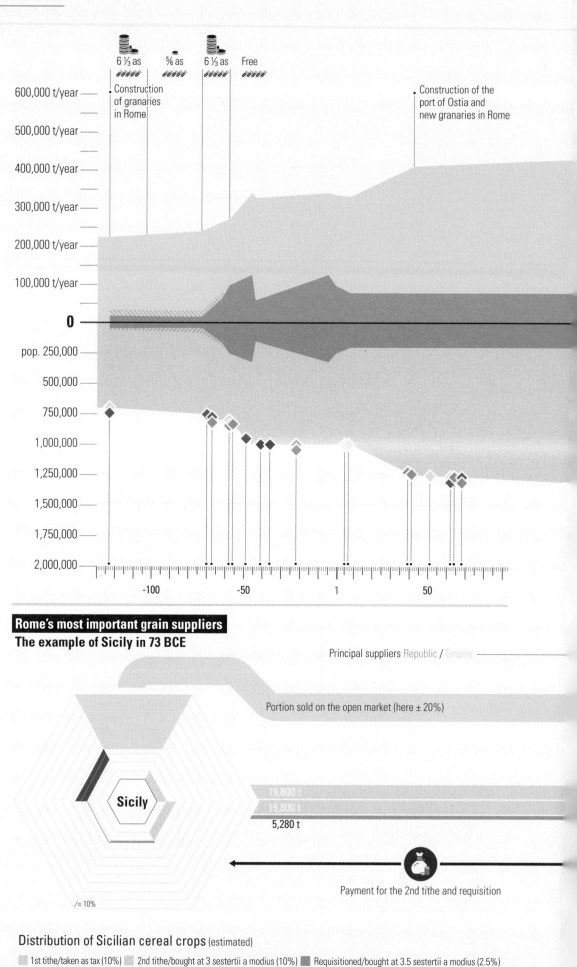

Rome's most important grain suppliers
The example of Sicily in 73 BCE

Principal suppliers Republic / Empire

Portion sold on the open market (here ± 20%)

Sicily

19,800 t
19,800 t
5,280 t

Payment for the 2nd tithe and requisition

/ = 10%

Distribution of Sicilian cereal crops (estimated)

- 1st tithe/taken as tax (10%)
- 2nd tithe/bought at 3 sestertii a modius (10%)
- Requisitioned/bought at 3.5 sestertii a modius (2.5%)
- Cut taken by the prefect (± 0.7%)
- Kept as seed for sowing (± 12.5%)
- Consumed locally/kept in reserve/sold abroad (± 64.3%)

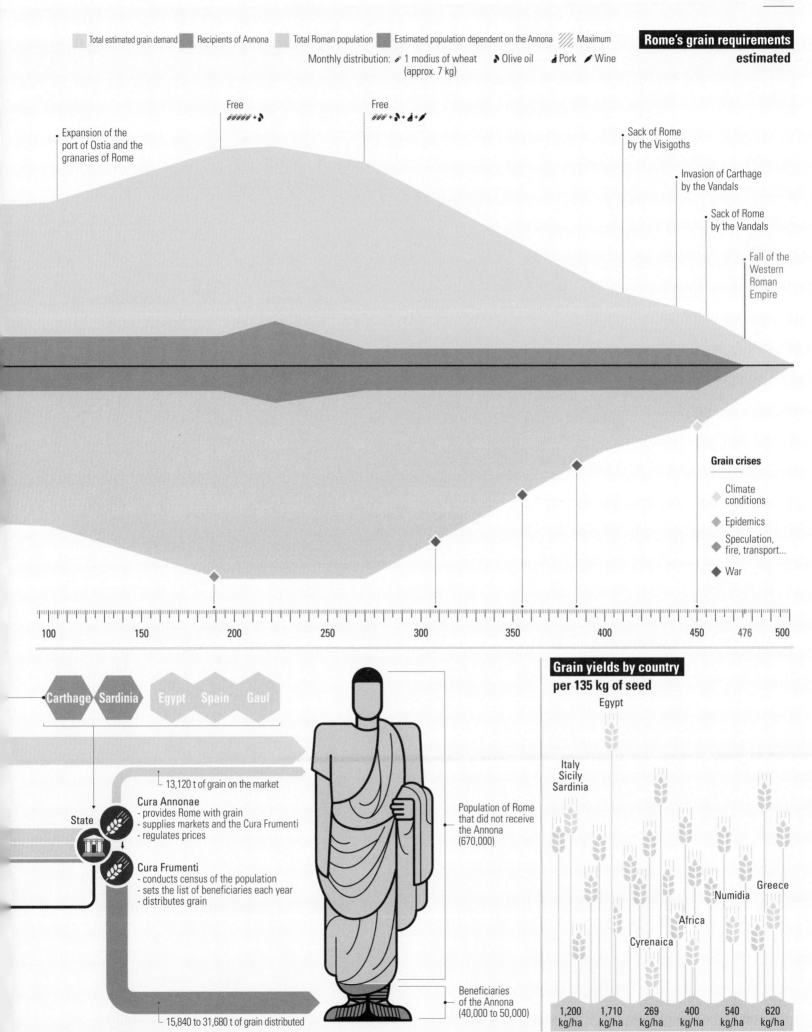

Rome's grain requirements
estimated

Total estimated grain demand | Recipients of Annona | Total Roman population | Estimated population dependent on the Annona | Maximum

Monthly distribution: 🌾 1 modius of wheat (approx. 7 kg) 🍶 Olive oil 🍖 Pork 🍷 Wine

Free
🌾🌾🌾🌾🌾 + 🍶

Free
🌾🌾🌾 + 🍶 + 🍖 + 🍷

Expansion of the port of Ostia and the granaries of Rome

Sack of Rome by the Visigoths

Invasion of Carthage by the Vandals

Sack of Rome by the Vandals

Fall of the Western Roman Empire

Grain crises

◇ Climate conditions
◆ Epidemics
◆ Speculation, fire, transport...
◆ War

100 150 200 250 300 350 400 450 476 500

Carthage Sardinia Egypt Spain Gaul

13,120 t of grain on the market

Cura Annonae
- provides Rome with grain
- supplies markets and the Cura Frumenti
- regulates prices

State

Cura Frumenti
- conducts census of the population
- sets the list of beneficiaries each year
- distributes grain

Population of Rome that did not receive the Annona (670,000)

Beneficiaries of the Annona (40,000 to 50,000)

15,840 to 31,680 t of grain distributed

Grain yields by country
per 135 kg of seed

Egypt

Italy Sicily Sardinia

Greece

Numidia

Africa

Cyrenaica

| 1,200 kg/ha | 1,710 kg/ha | 269 kg/ha | 400 kg/ha | 540 kg/ha | 620 kg/ha |

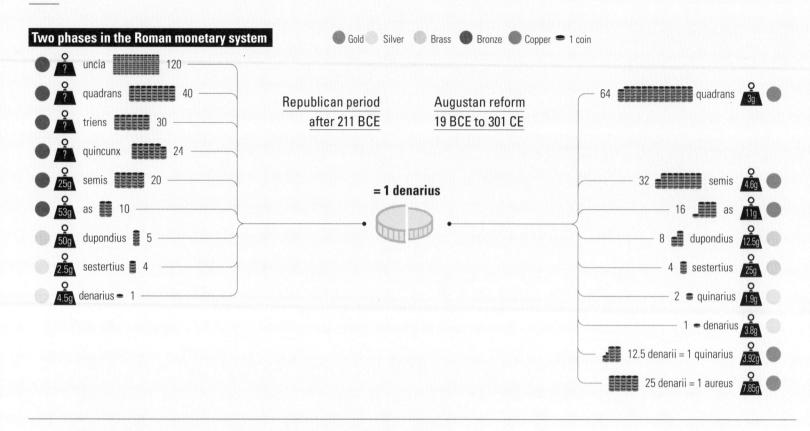

Two phases in the Roman monetary system

Legend: Gold · Silver · Brass · Bronze · Copper · 1 coin

Republican period after 211 BCE | Augustan reform 19 BCE to 301 CE

= 1 denarius

Republican period (left):
- uncia — 120
- quadrans — 40
- triens — 30
- quincunx — 24
- semis (25g) — 20
- as (53g) — 10
- dupondius (50g) — 5
- sestertius (2.5g) — 4
- denarius (4.5g) — 1

Augustan reform (right):
- 64 quadrans (3g)
- 32 semis (4.6g)
- 16 as (11g)
- 8 dupondius (12.5g)
- 4 sestertius (25g)
- 2 quinarius (1.9g)
- 1 denarius (3.8g)
- 12.5 denarii = 1 quinarius (3.92g)
- 25 denarii = 1 aureus (7.85g)

Depreciation and devaluation, as seen in the example of the silver denarius
(weight of coin and % of silver)

Legend: Alloy · Silver

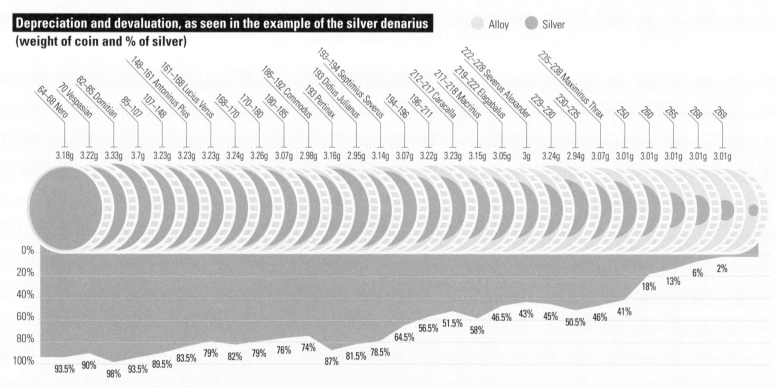

Period / Ruler	Weight	% silver
64–68 Nero	3.18g	93.5%
70 Vespasian	3.22g	90%
82–85 Domitian	3.33g	98%
85–107	3.7g	93.5%
107–148	3.23g	89.5%
148–161 Antoninus Pius	3.23g	83.5%
161–168 Lucius Verus	3.23g	79%
168–170	3.24g	82%
170–180	3.26g	79%
180–185	3.07g	76%
186–192 Commodus	2.98g	74%
193 Pertinax	3.16g	87%
193 Didius Julianus	2.95g	81.5%
193–194 Septimius Severus	3.14g	78.5%
194–196	3.07g	64.5%
196–211	3.22g	56.5%
212–217 Caracalla	3.23g	51.5%
217–218 Macrinus	3.15g	58%
219–222 Elagabalus	3.05g	46.5%
222–228 Severus Alexander	3g	43%
229–230	3.24g	45%
230–235	2.94g	50.5%
235–238 Maximinus Thrax	3.07g	46%
250	3.01g	41%
260	3.01g	18%
265	3.01g	13%
268	3.01g	6%
269	3.01g	2%

Roman coinage went through four principal phases. Until the 4th century BCE, coins consisted first of nuggets of untreated bronze and then of marked bronze ingots that were valued according to their weight. In the late 3rd century BCE, at the time of the Second Punic War (when soldiers needed to be paid), Rome introduced a monetary system with silver and bronze coins, based on the Greek model. The system was reformed in 19 BCE and remained stable for the first three centuries of the Empire. Coinage in silver and gold (introduced by Julius Caesar) was complemented by a series of submultiples in less precious metals; bronze was abandoned. The sestertius, which had been a tiny piece of silver

during the Republic, became a coin made with an alloy of copper and zinc, similar to tin, while the as was made from pure copper. The sestertius became the monetary unit for the Roman economy, while the denarius was primarily used for wages and census calculations.

Over time, devaluation began to occur more frequently. Under Septimius Severus, the concentration of silver in a denarius was reduced from 70% to 50%. In around 215, Caracalla, having increased his soldiers' wages, created a new coin that enabled him to pay them: an antoninius, which had the same weight as one and a half denarii and contained a 50% concentration of silver. The antoninius gradually lost its intrinsic value, to such

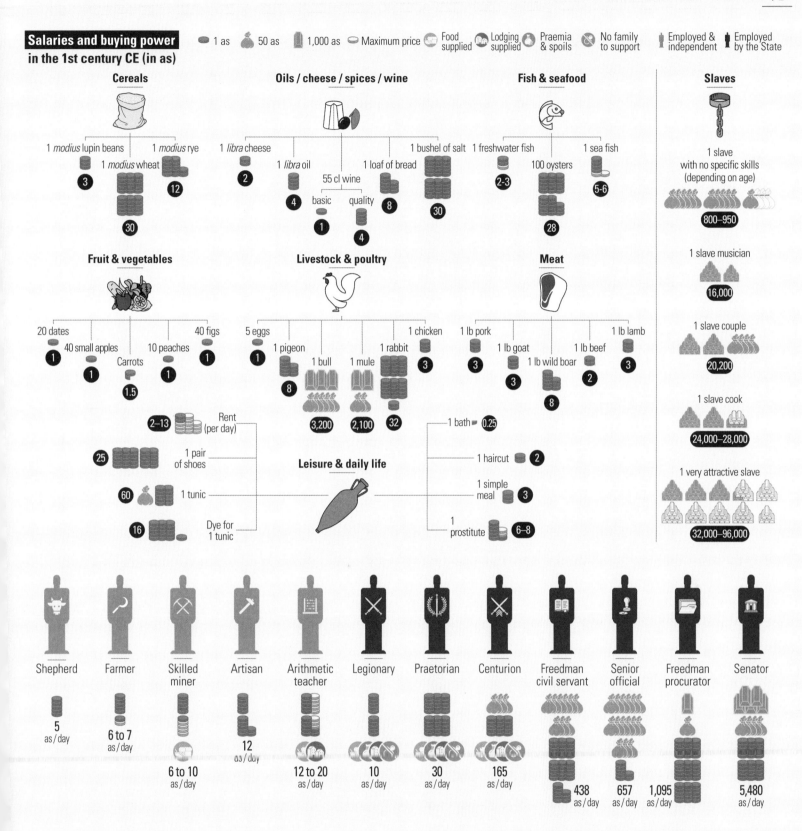

an extent that under Claudius Gothicus (r. 268–270), silver accounted for no more than 3 or 4% of its content, and it looked more like a bronze coin. By this time, the sestertius, which was worth one eighth of an antoninius, was barely being minted.

In late 294, Diocletian introduced a new reform of the monetary system and created new coins: the argenteus or silver denarius, which had the same value as Nero's old denarius, and three bronze coins, including the large follis or nummus, which contained a low percentage of silver. The monetary unit was still the denarius, despite its depreciated value. In around 311, Constantine devalued the gold standard by creating the solidus (around 4.5 g of pure gold). This new currency was issued in considerable quantities, but its stability could only be maintained through the confiscation of significant stocks of gold hoarded in pagan temples. Nevertheless, it remained a safe investment until the 11th century, even under the Byzantine Empire.

Roman currency was not at the mercy of market forces, for it was controlled and managed by the Senate during the Republic and then by the emperors, who controlled the economy by introducing measures against usury and debt and, on occasion, loans. One of the benefits of Rome's conquest of the known world was undoubtedly the establishment of the denarius as a standard monetary unit for trade and taxation.

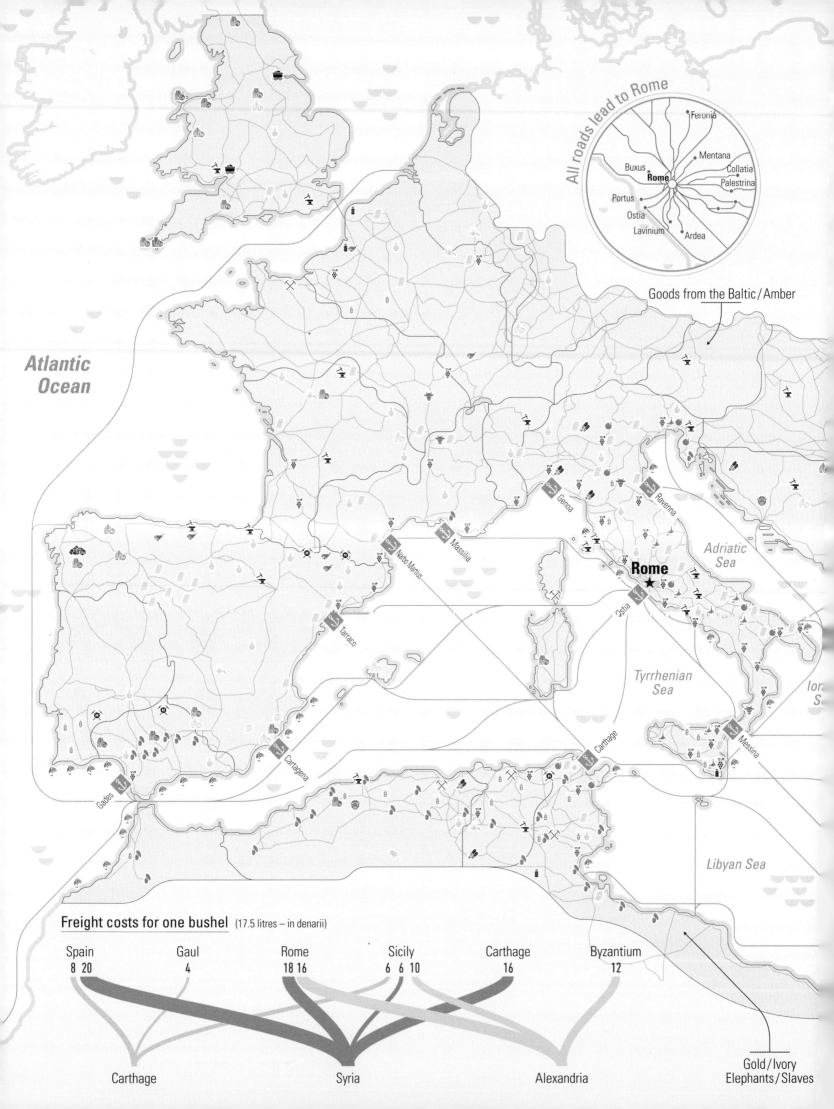

Atlantic Ocean

All roads lead to Rome

Feronia

Mentana

Buxus · Collatia

Rome · Palestrina

Portus

Ostia

Lavinium · Ardea

Goods from the Baltic / Amber

Genoa

Ravenna

Massilia

Adriatic Sea

Nabo Martius

Tarraco

Rome

Ostia

Cartagena

Tyrrhenian Sea

Ion S

Carthage

Messina

Gades

Libyan Sea

Freight costs for one bushel (17.5 litres – in denarii)

Spain	Gaul	Rome	Sicily	Carthage	Byzantium
8 20	4	18 16	6 6 10	16	12

Carthage

Syria

Alexandria

Gold / Ivory
Elephants / Slaves

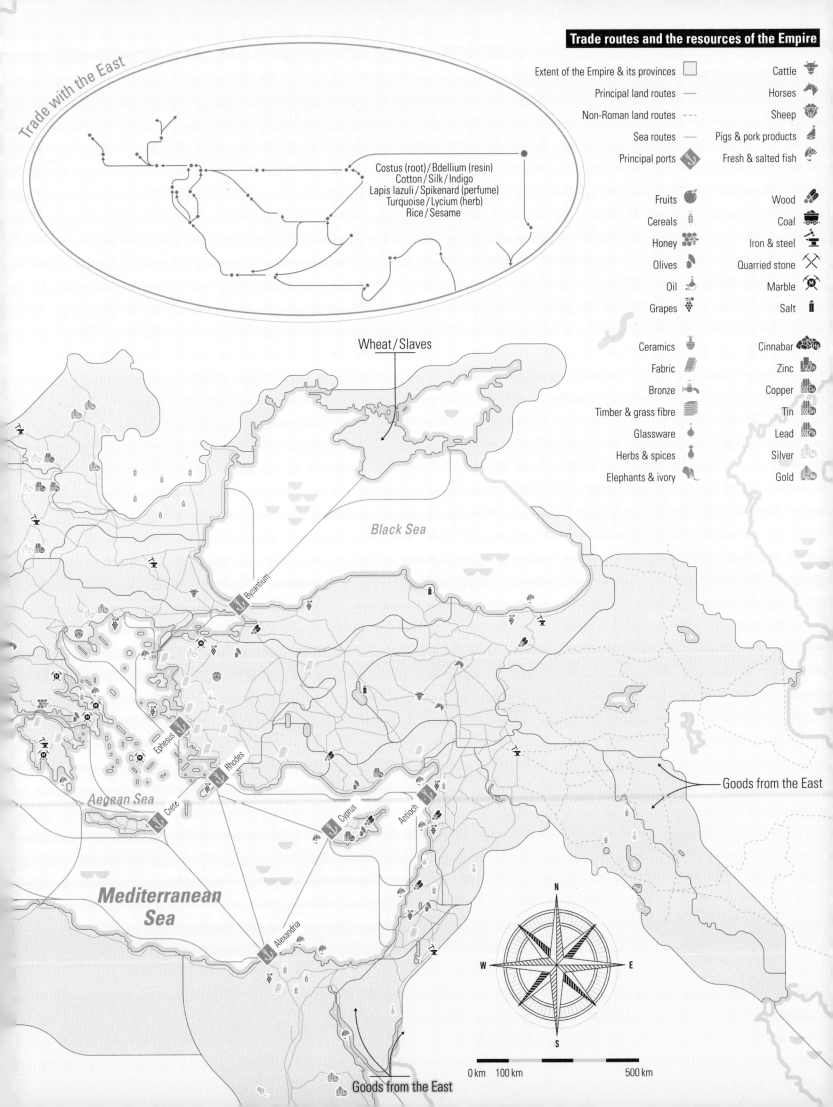

Trade routes and the resources of the Empire

Trade with the East

Extent of the Empire & its provinces
Principal land routes
Non-Roman land routes
Sea routes
Principal ports

Cattle
Horses
Sheep
Pigs & pork products
Fresh & salted fish

Fruits
Cereals
Honey
Olives
Oil
Grapes

Wood
Coal
Iron & steel
Quarried stone
Marble
Salt

Ceramics
Fabric
Bronze
Timber & grass fibre
Glassware
Herbs & spices
Elephants & ivory

Cinnabar
Zinc
Copper
Tin
Lead
Silver
Gold

Costus (root) / Bdellium (resin)
Cotton / Silk / Indigo
Lapis lazuli / Spikenard (perfume)
Turquoise / Lycium (herb)
Rice / Sesame

Wheat / Slaves

Black Sea

Byzantium

Ephesus
Rhodes
Crete
Cyprus
Antioch

Aegean Sea

Goods from the East

Mediterranean
Sea

Alexandria

Goods from the East

0 km   100 km   500 km

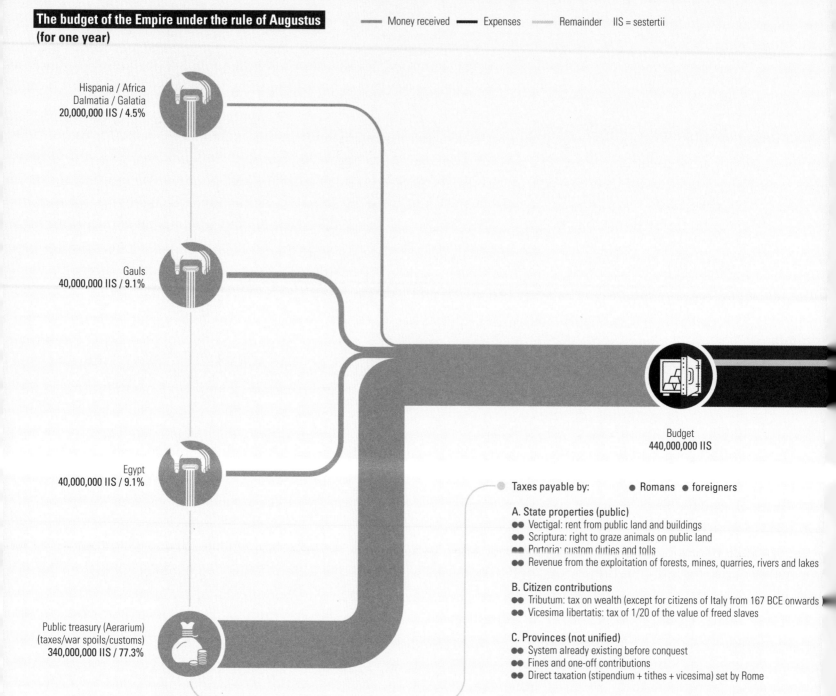

The budget of the Empire under the rule of Augustus (for one year)

—— Money received   ▬▬ Expenses   ⋯⋯ Remainder   IIS = sestertii

Hispania / Africa
Dalmatia / Galatia
20,000,000 IIS / 4.5%

Gauls
40,000,000 IIS / 9.1%

Egypt
40,000,000 IIS / 9.1%

Public treasury (Aerarium)
(taxes/war spoils/customs)
340,000,000 IIS / 77.3%

Budget
440,000,000 IIS

Taxes payable by: ● Romans ● foreigners

A. State properties (public)
●● Vectigal: rent from public land and buildings
●● Scriptura: right to graze animals on public land
●● Portoria: custom duties and tolls
●● Revenue from the exploitation of forests, mines, quarries, rivers and lakes

B. Citizen contributions
●● Tributum: tax on wealth (except for citizens of Italy from 167 BCE onwards)
●● Vicesima libertatis: tax of 1/20 of the value of freed slaves

C. Provinces (not unified)
●● System already existing before conquest
●● Fines and one-off contributions
●● Direct taxation (stipendium + tithes + vicesima) set by Rome

III. STATE REVENUE AND EXPENDITURE

Alongside the expenses incurred by annual military campaigns, and later by the upkeep of a permanent army, Rome also needed wheat to feed its people. During the Empire, Rome needed 150,000–200,000 tons of grain annually, rising to 270,000–400,000 tons under the Severans, while the army alone consumed 100,000 tons of wheat per year (around 1 kg per person/day) and 150,000 tons under the Severans. These necessities were covered by taxes and the imperial estates. Under Diocletian, the army also began to buy provisions on the free market, although little is known about the role of private commerce in food supplies. It seems that the official Annona covered around 60% of the total requirements for wheat (and later oil), while wealthy families provided the remaining 40% to their 'clients' and dependents via their private estates.

In addition to the revenue received from Egypt from the reign of Augustus onwards, the Roman State imposed numerous taxes,

both direct and indirect. The long and complex history of these taxes reflects the history of Rome's conquests. After 167 BCE, Roman citizens in Italy no longer had to pay the tributum (direct tax) but they were still subject to a series of indirect taxes (under Augustus, for example, 5% on manumissions, 4% on the sale of slaves, 5% on collateral inheritances) and possibly rental payment for public places and land. The tributum was imposed in the provinces (apart from in those few fortunate cities subject to Italic law), along with a panoply of other taxes, land rents and customs duties (such as the 2.5% charged the Gauls for crossing frontiers such as the Alps). These taxes were levied by local authorities in the cities, by Roman functionaries at toll gates and, under the Republic, by the publicans, Romans of the equestrian class who collected provincial taxes for the State. During the Empire, governors' finances and the imperial assets were managed by equestrian procurators.

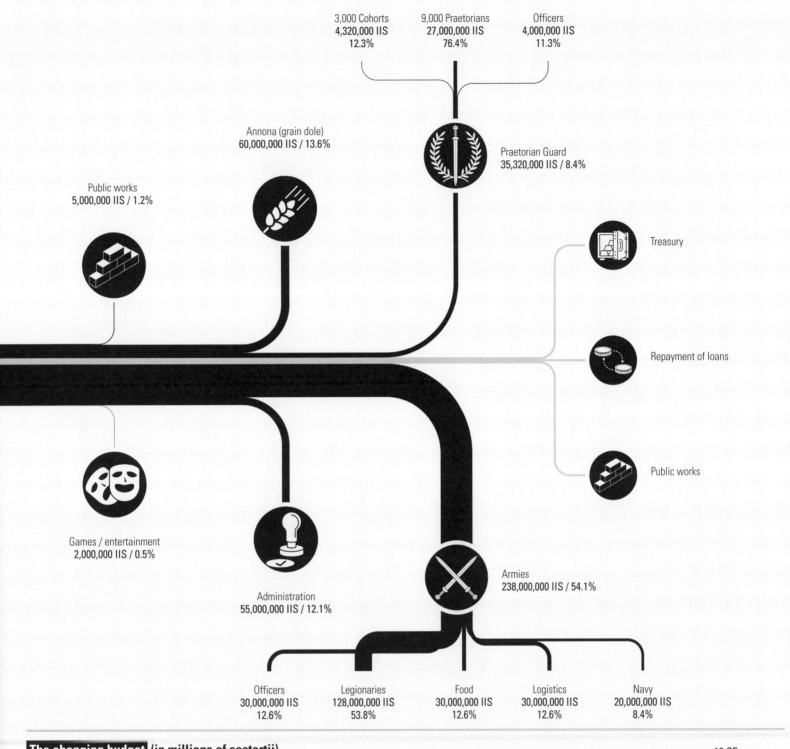

3,000 Cohorts
4,320,000 IIS
12.3%

9,000 Praetorians
27,000,000 IIS
76.4%

Officers
4,000,000 IIS
11.3%

Annona (grain dole)
60,000,000 IIS / 13.6%

Praetorian Guard
35,320,000 IIS / 8.4%

Public works
5,000,000 IIS / 1.2%

Treasury

Repayment of loans

Public works

Games / entertainment
2,000,000 IIS / 0.5%

Administration
55,000,000 IIS / 12.1%

Armies
238,000,000 IIS / 54.1%

Officers
30,000,000 IIS
12.6%

Legionaries
128,000,000 IIS
53.8%

Food
30,000,000 IIS
12.6%

Logistics
30,000,000 IIS
12.6%

Navy
20,000,000 IIS
8.4%

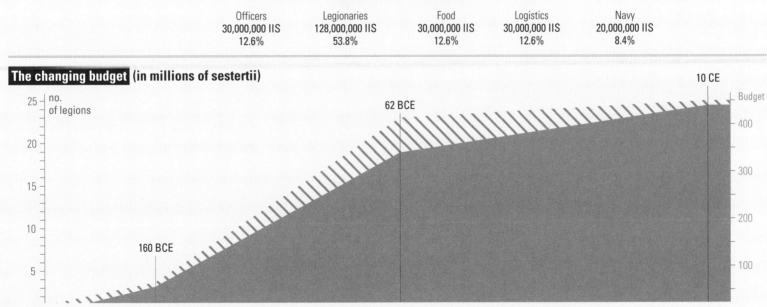

The changing budget (in millions of sestertii)

10 CE

25 — no.
of legions

62 BCE

Budget

20

400

15

300

160 BCE

10

200

5

100

III. ROME'S MILITARY MIGHT

THE ROMAN LEGIONS

I. FROM THE ROYAL PERIOD TO THE IMPERIAL ARMY

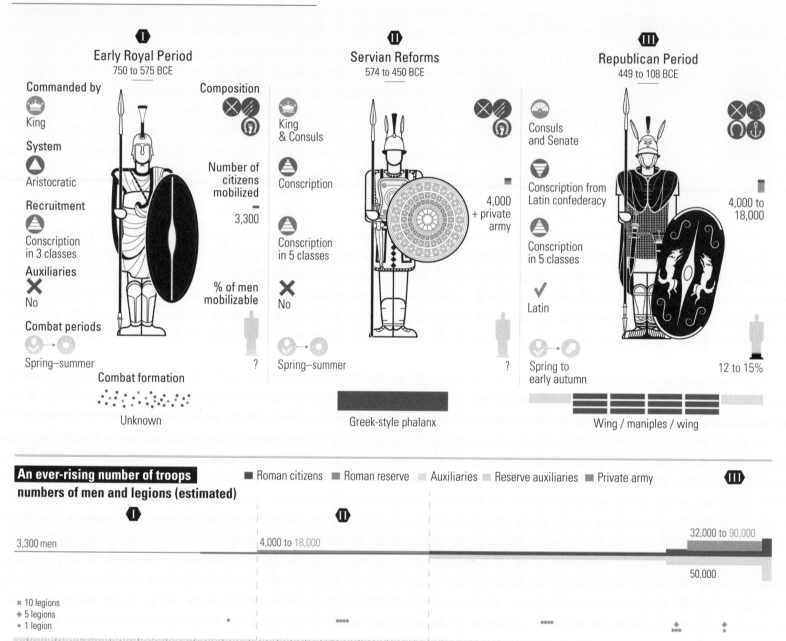

I

Early Royal Period
750 to 575 BCE

Commanded by
King

System
Aristocratic

Recruitment
Conscription
in 3 classes

Auxiliaries
✗ No

Combat periods
Spring–summer

Composition
King
& Consuls

Conscription

Conscription
in 5 classes

**Number of
citizens
mobilized**
3,300

**% of men
mobilizable**
?

Combat formation
Unknown

II

Servian Reforms
574 to 450 BCE

King
& Consuls

Conscription

Conscription
in 5 classes

✗ No

Spring–summer

?

4,000
+ private
army

Greek-style phalanx

III

Republican Period
449 to 108 BCE

**Consuls
and Senate**

Conscription from
Latin confederacy

Conscription
in 5 classes

✓ Latin

Spring to
early autumn

4,000 to
18,000

12 to 15%

Wing / maniples / wing

An ever-rising number of troops
numbers of men and legions (estimated)

■ Roman citizens ■ Roman reserve ■ Auxiliaries ■ Reserve auxiliaries ■ Private army   **III**

I   **II**

3,300 men

4,000 to 18,000

32,000 to 90,000

50,000

✗ 10 legions
◆ 5 legions
• 1 legion

740 BCE | 720 | 700 | 680 | 660 | 640 | 620 | 600 | 580 | 560 | 540 | 520 | 500 | 480 | 460 | 440 | 420 | 400 | 380 | 360 | 340 | 320 | 300 | 280 | 260 | 240 | 220

The Roman army changed and grew considerably over the course of the eleven centuries during which it succeeded in conquering, and then retaining, the lands that became the Roman Empire. Nevertheless, it was markedly less powerful than is commonly thought. It was substantially less skilled on the battlefield than most of its contemporaries, such as the professional armies of the Carthaginians and the Hellenistic kingdoms, or the barbarian peoples who essentially lived to make war. Despite these deficiencies, however, Rome succeeded in dominating all its enemies between the 6th century BCE and the 1st century BCE, and its army subsequently went on to protect the Roman world for another four centuries. There are two basic reasons for this accomplishment. Firstly, Rome

encouraged the integration of new citizens. Consequently, it had enormous reserves of mobilizable manpower from the Punic Wars onwards, and during the Empire this enabled it to react to rebellions and to early incursions by barbarians. Secondly, the Romans were always aware of the technical shortcomings of their army and its equipment, and their troops would be supplemented by auxiliaries – more effective combat units generally made up of allies of Rome (until 78 BCE, when all free men in Italy became Roman citizens).

The system of conscripted recruitment from the five most wealthy classes of citizens prevailed until the end of the 2nd century BCE. By that point, the war zones had become increasingly distant and the army had turned professional, although it still

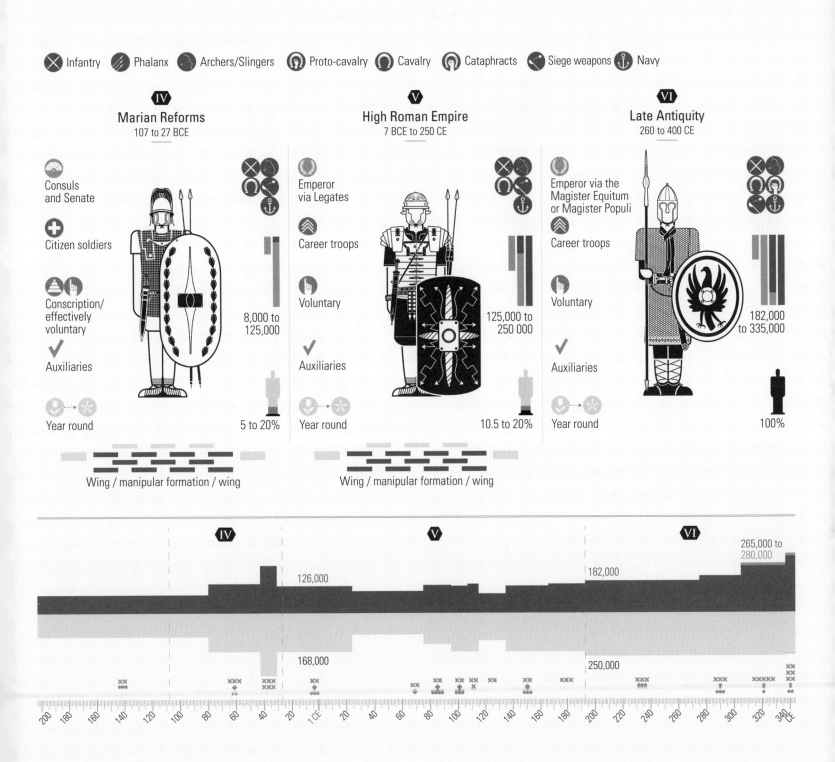

Infantry Phalanx Archers/Slingers Proto-cavalry Cavalry Cataphracts Siege weapons Navy

IV
Marian Reforms
107 to 27 BCE

Consuls and Senate

Citizen soldiers

Conscription/ effectively voluntary

Auxiliaries

Year round

8,000 to 125,000

5 to 20%

Wing / manipular formation / wing

V
High Roman Empire
7 BCE to 250 CE

Emperor via Legates

Career troops

Voluntary

Auxiliaries

Year round

125,000 to 250 000

10.5 to 20%

Wing / manipular formation / wing

VI
Late Antiquity
260 to 400 CE

Emperor via the Magister Equitum or Magister Populi

Career troops

Voluntary

Auxiliaries

Year round

182,000 to 335,000

100%

IV   V   VI

265,000 to 280,000

126,000

182,000

168,000

250,000

200 180 160 140 120 100 80 60 40 20 1 CE 20 40 60 80 100 120 140 160 180 200 220 240 260 280 300 320 340 CE

comprised a combination of citizens backed up by auxiliaries. By the birth of the Empire, recruitment came primarily from the most Romanized provinces in Italy. By 70 CE, recruitment in Italy started to peter out and the focus switched to recruiting Roman citizens from the most Romanized provinces elsewhere: Gallia Narbonensis (southern France), Spain and Africa Proconsularis. Trajan, however, encouraged continued recruitment in Italy, offering subsidies for the education of poor boys who might one day grow up to be legionaries. Although this strategy did not prove entirely successful, Trajan nevertheless managed to recruit four whole legions in Italy, and Marcus Aurelius assembled two for new conquests or, if required, the defence of Italy against barbarians.

From the 2nd century CE onwards, however, legions were primarily recruited in the provinces in which they were stationed, although there was a constantly changing mix. Under the Julio-Claudians, between a third and a half of all legionaries came from the provinces, but this rose to three-quarters under the Flavians and Trajan. Under Hadrian, 93% of the Legio III Augusta, stationed in Africa, came from North Africa. For a long time, the armies of northeastern Europe were recruited in Gallia Narbonensis, Spain and Macedonia, but in the 3rd century they soon began to be recruited in situ, often from the sons of veterans. In that period, the majority of legionaries originated from the Danubian and Balkan provinces.

II. THE COMPOSITION OF A LEGION

A Roman legion, in the form that it is best known (particularly from the 1st century BCE to the 3rd century CE), comprised ten cohorts of around 500 foot soldiers, each commanded by a military tribune, under the orders of the legion's legate (*legatus Augusti*). The military tribunes were chosen by the emperor from the sons of senators and equestrians, as well as from candidates proposed by city leaders. The length of their service depended on their origin. Nine out of the ten cohorts consisted of three maniples, each comprising two centuries of around 80 men, while the tenth – actually numbered as the first – had double the number of troops. The military tribunes and centurions were granted a hierarchical position that reflected the rank of their cohort or century. Thus, a centurion in the first century of the 1st cohort (the *primipile*) formed part of his legion's military command and was usually its most experienced soldier.

These foot soldiers were complemented by four *turmae* (squadrons of about 30 horsemen), each commanded by a decurion (equivalent in rank to a centurion). A legion also had around 1,400 servants and grooms (*calones*) who took care of menial tasks such as transport and maintenance, and helped the legionaries with everyday operations such as distributing water and pitching tents.

In late antiquity, the number of legions increased but they contained fewer men; in practice, the field army was largely made up of mobile military units.

Composition of a sample legion
in 50 CE

Legionary
4,480 (64.1%)

Decanus
640 (9.16%)

640 contubernia
5,120 (73.26%)

Cornicen
59

Signifer
59

Optio
59

Centurion
59

59 century command units
236 (3.4%)

Cavalrymen
120 (1.7%)

Aeneator
6

Aquilifer
1

Tribune/Prefect
7

Legate
1

1 legion command unit
15 (0.2%)

Scout
10

Mounted scout
65

Intelligence/reconnaissance
75 (1.1%)

Combatants:
6,602 combatants

Auxiliary cavalry
1,036 (14.8%)

Support:
385 men

Total:
8,982 men
4,623 animals
145 chariots
69 siege engines

Logistics:
1,995 men
4,623 animals
145 chariots

Ballistas
10

Catapults
59

Artillery
± 215 (3.1%)

Servants/grooms
1,995 (29.5%)

Mules
1,910 (28.25%)

Horses
2,648 (39.1%)

Oxen
64 (1%)

2 or 4-wheel chariots
145 (2.1%)

Logistics

Engineers
± 85 (1.2%)

Support
± 85 (1.2%)

Support
± 170 (2.4%)

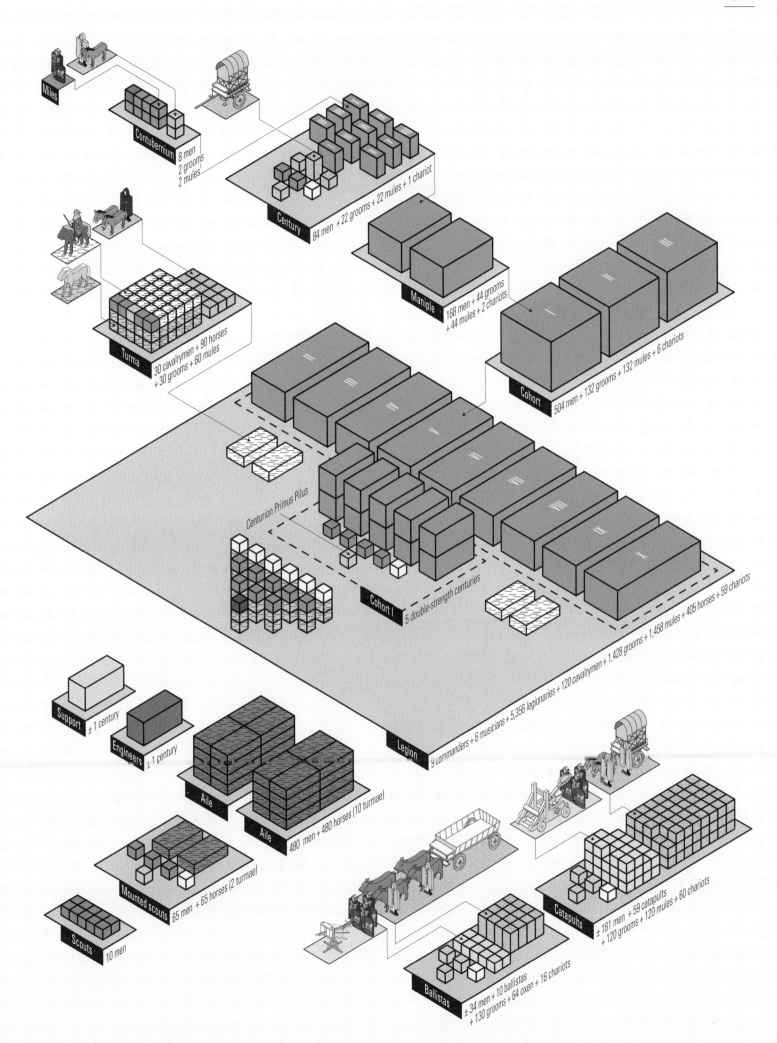

Miles

Contubernium 8 men
2 grooms
2 mules

Century 84 men + 22 grooms + 22 mules + 1 chariot

Maniple 168 men + 44 grooms
+ 44 mules + 2 chariots

Cohort 504 men + 132 grooms + 132 mules + 6 chariots

Turma 30 cavalrymen + 90 horses
+ 30 grooms + 60 mules

Centurion Primus Pilus

Cohort I 5 double-strength centuries

Legion 9 commanders + 6 musicians + 5,356 legionaries + 120 cavalrymen + 1,428 grooms + 1,458 mules + 405 horses + 59 chariots

Support ± 1 century

Engineers ± 1 century

Aile

Aile 480 men + 480 horses (10 turmae)

Mounted scouts 65 men + 65 horses (2 turmae)

Scouts 10 men

Ballistas ± 34 men + 10 ballistas
+ 130 grooms + 64 oxen + 16 chariots

Catapults ± 181 men + 59 catapults
+ 120 grooms + 120 mules + 60 chariots

III. THE CAMPS

There were two types of camp that provided legions with shelter: marching camps and permanent encampments. The former were designed to last the length of an annual campaign, at most, and they changed very little after the 3rd century BCE. They could vary in size, from around 20 hectares to more than 50, depending on the number of legions involved in a campaign, not to mention auxiliaries and logistical support. According the writings of Pseudo-Hyginus, one legion required a camp measuring about 470 by 700 m. Its rampart would be 1.8 m high. Smaller variants were also constructed, generally keeping the same proportions, although one camp near Hanover, from the late 1st century BCE, was square and covered around 20 hectares. It would sleep around 20,000 soldiers (three legions plus logistical support).

These camps, complete with a palisade, rampart, ditch and four gates, would be built extraordinarily quickly at the end of a day by a squad of soldiers, while another squad kept guard. This speed of construction would amaze enemy troops, and provides a good example of the efficiency, discipline and training of the Roman army.

Although camps could vary in their design, the underlying principles remained constant: at the heart of the camp was the *principia* (camp headquarters), along with the *praetorium* (commanders' quarters) and the *sacellum* (a shrine where the legion's standard was kept), surrounded by bodyguards and the first cohort. This layout enabled the commanders to observe the entire camp and issue orders with ease. A camp was divided into three main sections, arranged lengthwise on either side of the central praetorium and crossed by three main paths or streets: the *via principalis*, which ran lengthwise, and two transverse streets, the *via praetoria*, in front of the praetorium, and the *via decumana*, behind the praetorium and in front of the *quaestorium*, where the camp treasurer (quaestor) was based. These streets were connected to the camp gates. The soldiers were equipped with tents for eight men (a *contubernium*) measuring around 3 × 3 m, with a space in front for weapons and beasts of burden, plus the calones or grooms who looked after them.

The spaces in front of and behind the praetorium (the *praetendura* and the *retendura*, respectively) were occupied by auxiliary units.

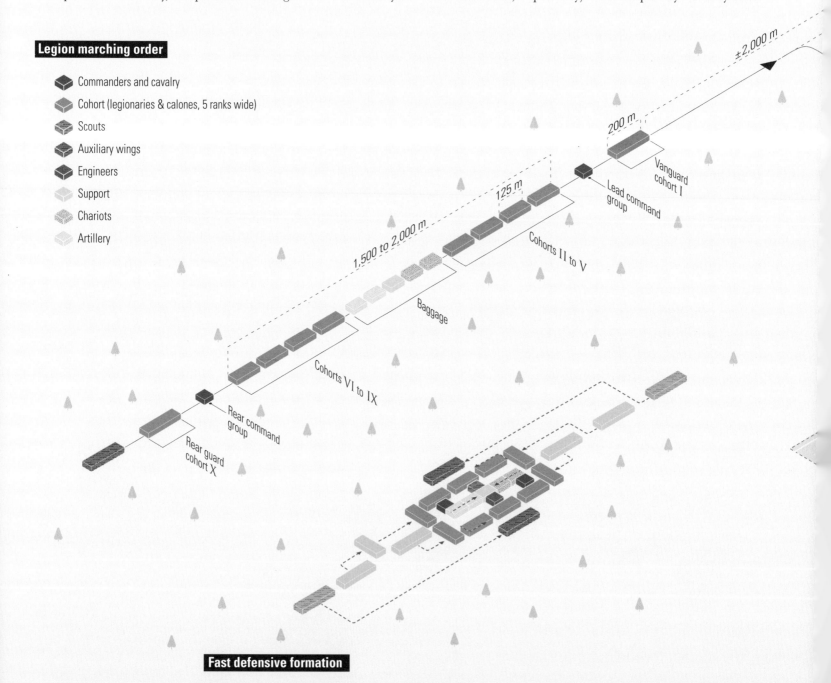

Legion marching order

- Commanders and cavalry
- Cohort (legionaries & calones, 5 ranks wide)
- Scouts
- Auxiliary wings
- Engineers
- Support
- Chariots
- Artillery

±2,000 m

200 m

Vanguard cohort I

Lead command group

125 m

Cohorts II to V

1,500 to 2,000 m

Baggage

Cohorts VI to IX

Rear command group

Rear guard cohort X

Fast defensive formation

Construction stages of a marching camp

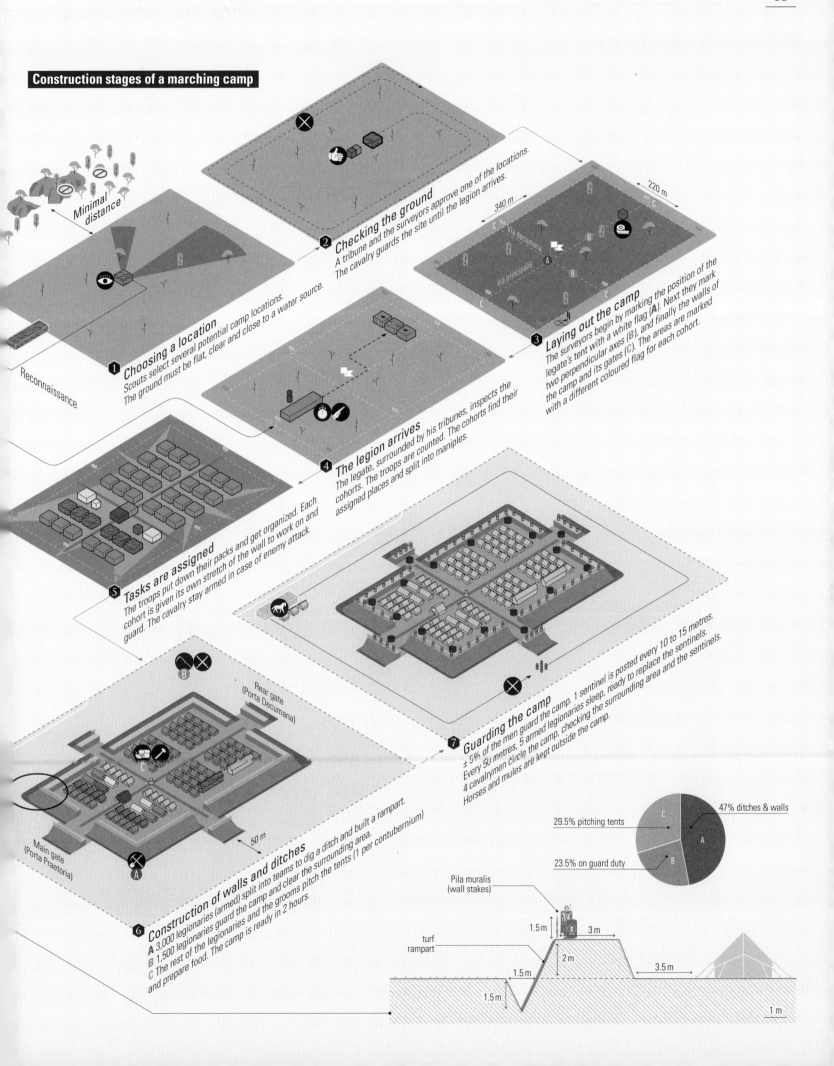

Minimal distance

Reconnaissance

1 **Choosing a location**
Scouts select several potential camp locations.
The ground must be flat, clear and close to a water source.

2 **Checking the ground**
A tribune and the surveyors approve one of the locations.
The cavalry guards the site until the legion arrives.

3 **Laying out the camp**
The surveyors begin by marking the position of the legate's tent with a white flag (**A**). Next they mark two perpendicular axes (**B**), and finally the walls of the camp and its gates (**C**). The areas are marked with a different coloured flag for each cohort.

220 m
340 m

Via decumana
Via principalis
C B A B C
N

4 **The legion arrives**
The legate, surrounded by his tribunes, inspects the cohorts. The troops are counted. The cohorts find their assigned places and split into maniples.

5 **Tasks are assigned**
The troops put down their packs and get organized. Each cohort is given its own stretch of the wall to work on and guard. The cavalry stay armed in case of enemy attack.

6 **Construction of walls and ditches**
A 3,000 legionaries (armed) split into teams to dig a ditch and built a rampart.
B 1,500 legionaries guard the camp and clear the surrounding area.
C The rest of the legionaries and the grooms pitch the tents (1 per contubernium) and prepare food. The camp is ready in 2 hours.

Rear gate
(Porta Decumana)

Main gate
(Porta Praetoria)

50 m

7 **Guarding the camp**
± 5% of the men guard the camp. 1 sentinel is posted every 10 to 15 metres. Every 50 metres, 5 armed legionaries sleep, ready to replace the sentinels. 4 cavalrymen circle the camp, checking the surrounding area and the sentinels. Horses and mules are kept outside the camp.

47% ditches & walls
29.5% pitching tents
23.5% on guard duty
A B C

Pila muralis
(wall stakes)

turf rampart

1.5 m
3 m
1.5 m
2 m
1.5 m
3.5 m
1.5 m
1 m

The different types of Roman camp

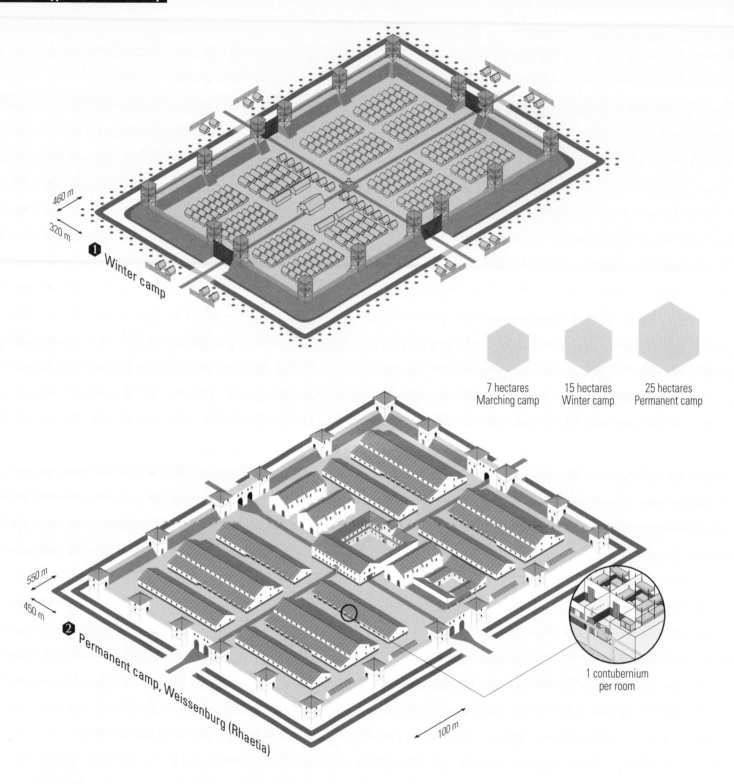

460 m
320 m
❶ Winter camp

7 hectares
Marching camp

15 hectares
Winter camp

25 hectares
Permanent camp

550 m
450 m
❷ Permanent camp, Weissenburg (Rhaetia)

1 contubernium
per room

100 m

As military campaigns became longer, the Roman army would spend the winter in more comfortable camps equipped with more substantial structures, such as towers. Archaeological evidence has revealed, however, that these later camps were still laid out according to the same model described by Polybius and, in more detail, by Pseudo-Hyginus, although the *via principalis* now tended to mark the centre of the camp's longest side. Nevertheless, some excavated camps have revealed configurations different from those described by Pseudo-Hyginus. Moreover, as the Roman army increasingly focused its attention on protecting its borders and consolidating its presence in the provinces, so its camps became more permanent. They still followed the same template as the marching

camps, but the tents were replaced by buildings with a dormitory and an armoury. The camps were now surrounded by a wall with stone towers rather than a palisade, and this perimeter could itself be surrounded by two or even three ditches. The overall surface area remained similar, however. For example, the large camp in Lambaesis, in present-day Algeria, which was built between 115 and 120 CE, measured 420 × 500 m (21 hectares) and accommodated 12,000 men.

Once the Empire's frontiers had been established, their defences were boosted by a system of fortifications – although some of these, in Germania and on the Danube, originally served to initiate conquests and only took on a defensive role in response to relentless attacks from barbarians. In the 3rd century, these border fortifications

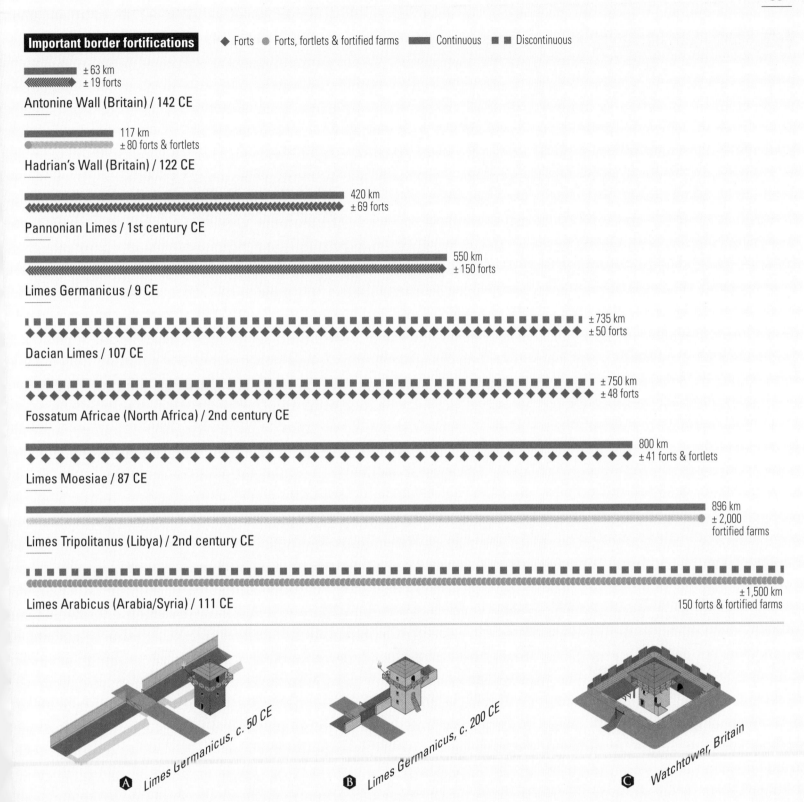

Important border fortifications ◆ Forts ● Forts, fortlets & fortified farms ▬▬ Continuous ■ ■ Discontinuous

±63 km
±19 forts

Antonine Wall (Britain) / 142 CE

117 km
±80 forts & fortlets

Hadrian's Wall (Britain) / 122 CE

420 km
±69 forts

Pannonian Limes / 1st century CE

550 km
±150 forts

Limes Germanicus / 9 CE

±735 km
±50 forts

Dacian Limes / 107 CE

±750 km
±48 forts

Fossatum Africae (North Africa) / 2nd century CE

800 km
±41 forts & fortlets

Limes Moesiae / 87 CE

896 km
±2,000 fortified farms

Limes Tripolitanus (Libya) / 2nd century CE

±1,500 km
150 forts & fortified farms

Limes Arabicus (Arabia/Syria) / 111 CE

Ⓐ *Limes Germanicus, c. 50 CE*   Ⓑ *Limes Germanicus, c. 200 CE*   Ⓒ *Watchtower, Britain*

came to be known as limes. Although some of these were border walls complemented by camps and forts, as in Britain and along the Rhine and Danube, this was not always the case. The frontier of Roman Africa, the Fossatum Africae ('ditch of Africa'), did not at all resemble the continuous defensive barriers with ramparts used in the North, as this model was not viable there. Instead, a large area was monitored by the army, which kept watch of the movements of nomads and their relationships with the local tribal peoples, peasant villages and semi-nomadic herders. The priority was to protect sources of water and position troops to the rear of the fortresses of the Legio III Augusta, in order to block the way at key points. In contrast, in the 2nd–3rd centuries, Northern territories

began to acquire continuous walls and ditches, along with a chain of watchtowers and forts, defended by smaller fortlets and auxiliary units (*numeri*), reinforced by a significant number of legionary camps.

The urgent need for defence in the late 3rd century CE and throughout the following century led to a reorganization of the army into *comitatenses* and *ripenses* (from *ripa*, or 'river bank'), later known as *limitanei* (from 'limes'). The comitatenses were stationed in cities and resembled the old legions in their political commitment and loyalty to the emperor, while the limitanei, who comprised two thirds of the total forces, were still billeted in camps and could be called upon to defend border areas and bear the brunt of any attempted invasions.

The 'triple line' formation in action

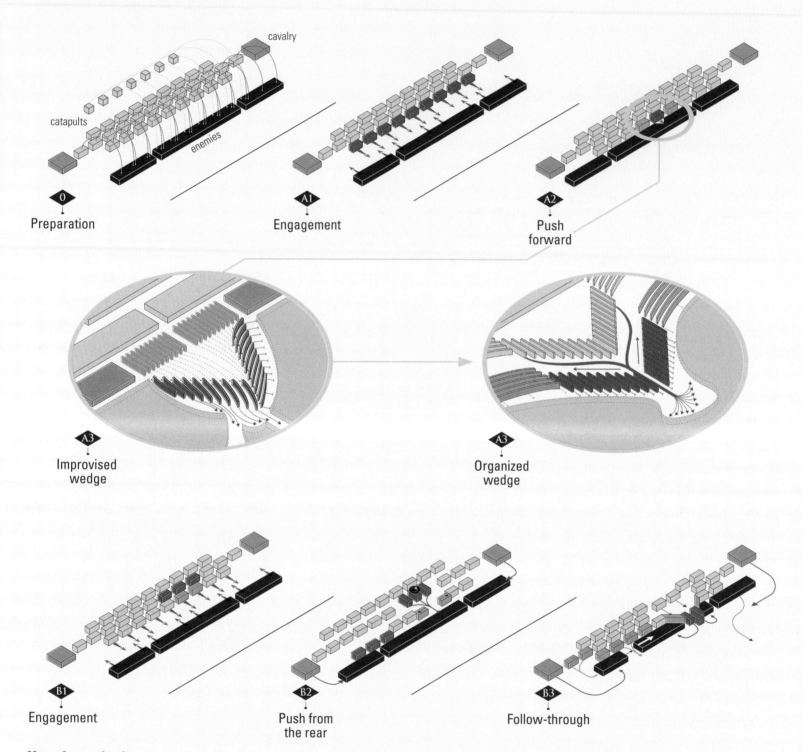

0 Preparation

catapults

enemies

cavalry

A1 Engagement

A2 Push forward

A3 Improvised wedge

A3 Organized wedge

B1 Engagement

B2 Push from the rear

B3 Follow-through

How it worked:

0. The legions are deployed in a checkered formation called a quincunx, in three staggered lines, allowing the second line to move forward easily through the first line to relieve them, while maintaining cohesion and avoiding breaks in the line. The legionaries begin the attack with projectile weapons, using javelins, arrows, slings and catapults to weaken the enemy.

A1. Frontal engagement begins. With the cohesion provided by the century and the flexibility offered by the maniples, the legion can withstand shock tactics or break through the lines.

A2. When ordered to push forward, each century in the first line tries to break through the enemy ranks.

A3. When one century manages to break through the ranks, its sister century pushes forward, entering the breach while protecting the flanks of the centuries in front, while nearby maniples push to disrupt a possible counterattack. If the combatants, exhausted by the fight, cannot continue the push, the two centuries create a space to let a maniple from the second line pass through to continue the push. Several points in the line can therefore be attacked at the same time.

B1. The legion can also take the lead in order to create a deep break. Three maniples from the second line, supported by two from the first line, must break through the opposing line.

B2. The two maniples on the front line move aside to let the assault group pass. The whole legion then pushes, maintaining its cohesion and breaking the enemy line.

B3. When the enemy line breaks, the other maniples rush into the breaches to smash the enemy ranks. The cavalry wings are then deployed, either to pursue fugitives, or to block the enemy rear. All of these tactics require units that can manoeuvre quickly and efficiently on the battlefield. Orders are given by trumpet or horn. Much more mobile than the older heavy phalanxes, this army can beat a larger enemy force. However, the cavalry is essential to protect the wings and rear of the legion.

IV. A LEGION IN COMBAT

By the 2nd century BCE, the Roman army, apart from its frequent wars of attrition, would generally make the initial attacking move on the battlefield, first by hurling *pila* (javelins) when the front line was within 25 to 30 m of the enemy and then by charging, accompanied by battle cries. The previous military model, inspired by Greek phalanxes, had proved too cumbersome, especially on uneven terrain. Roman legions had not formerly been trained to manoeuvre, fight in smaller units or beat a retreat. They subsequently acquired greater flexibility, which allowed them, for example, to defeat the Macedonian army at the Battle of Pydna in 168 BCE, when the manipular legion, with its cohorts (a line measuring 145 m × 6.5 m, with the 1st cohort stretching to 245 m × 6.5 m), proved its ability to adapt to all different types of terrain. Furthermore, when the army was on the march, still structured into cohorts, maniples and

centuries, it could adopt a three-lined battle formation (*acies triplex*) relatively quickly if it came under attack. The first line comprised the youngest soldiers of all, the *hastati*, carrying javelins; the second was made up of the more mature *principes*, while the third were *triarii*, the most experienced soldiers, each armed with a long spear (*hasta*). The first two lines contained 120 to 160 men, while the third had 60.

A legion's commander was usually positioned behind the second line of principes, where he had an excellent view of the field of battle and was visible to all his troops. The standard-bearers, trumpeters (*tubicines*) and horn-blowers (*cornicines*), not to mention the *tesserarii* (messengers), enabled him to communicate with his different units. If the emperor went to the front, he would take up the same position, protected by horsemen (*equites singulares*) and Praetorian guards.

Alternative formations

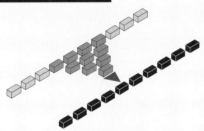

Wedge formation

The lines are concentrated in the centre in order to break through enemy lines.

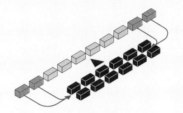

Single line defence

Maniples are deployed in a single line to overlap the enemy flanks and protect their own.

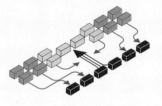

Cannae tactic (weak centre)

The centre is deliberately left weak to encourage an enemy attack, which can then be surrounded.

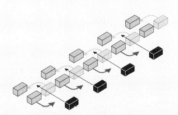

Zama tactic

Channels are created between maniples to encourage the enemy to push forward, where they will be trapped and eliminated.

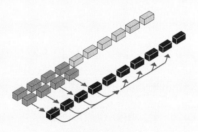

Strong flank

One side of the flank has a double row of troops, designed to break through the enemy line and attack them from the rear.

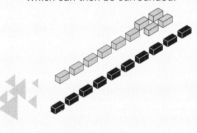

Protected flank

One flank is protected by a natural obstacle (mountains, river, etc.), so cavalry and auxiliaries are placed on the opposite flank.

Standard legion manoeuvres

Triple line

The standard deployment.

Relief

To relieve the first line, the second line pushes through between the first line troops and continues the push forward.

Testudo (tortoise)

A defensive formation used to form a barrier and protect against enemy arrows and other projectile weapons.

Wedge formation

Designed to break through enemy defences.

The career of one Roman legionary: Titus Valerius Marcianus

Boyhood/Adolescence — Serving legionary — Combat — Retirement/*Honesta missio*

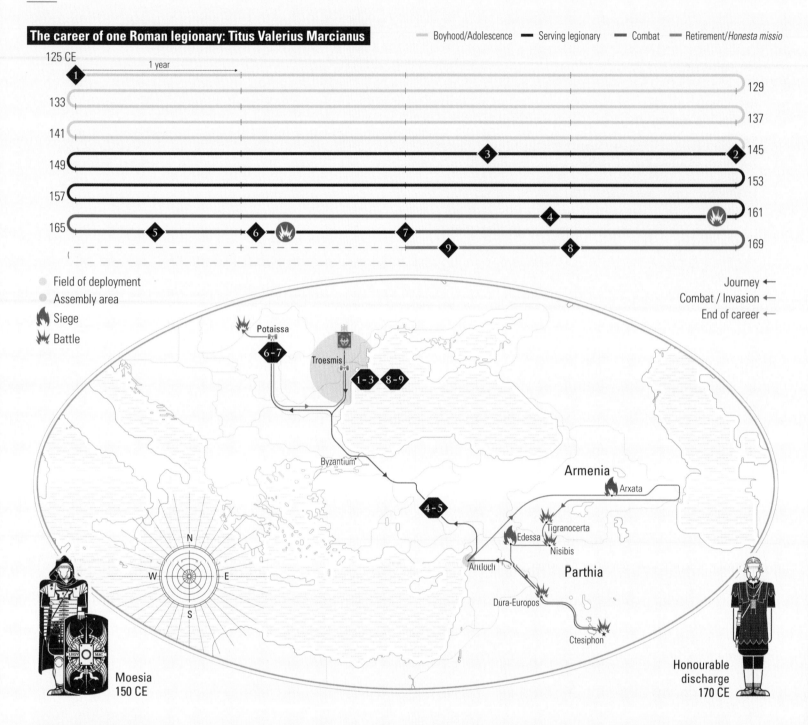

Field of deployment

Assembly area

Siege

Battle

Journey ←
Combat / Invasion ←
End of career ←

Moesia
150 CE

Honourable
discharge
170 CE

V. THE LEGIONARIES

Roman legionaries were extremely mobile. They usually moved around in columns, four to six men in width and 2.5–4.2 km long (excluding their logistical support). In order to ensure that it remained sufficiently fit for combat, every legion conducted a marching exercise of around 15 km three times a month on a *campus*, an exercise ground near the encampment. Here, the soldiers also engaged in combat training with wooden gladiator swords and bucklers woven from willow, which were heavier than the weapons normally used. They also probably practised various manoeuvres, such as crossing enemy lines and pincer movements, as well as wedge and tortoise (*testudo*) formations.

Aside from training, the soldiers' main task in a legion camp was to keep watch over the surrounding area. They also participated in public works projects – primarily for the army itself, such as building strategic roads using materials mined from quarries or bricks, which were duly stamped with the legion's seal. For non-military building

projects, a legion would provide specialists such as surveyors, architects and engineers. The ultimate task of the legions, of course, was to intervene in military crises, whether they occurred close to their garrison or far away in another province. An entire legion might be mobilized for a war and stay several years in one area, or they might return to their base camp as soon as the fighting was over (particularly in cases of an uprising or civil war). From the mid-2nd century onwards, however, it became unusual for entire legions to travel, as they generally preferred to dispatch vexillations (detachments the size of a cohort) to form a battle unit on a particular site. After a minimum of 25 years of service, a legionary could obtain an honourable discharge (*honesta missio*), provided that he had not committed any serious infraction. On discharge, he would receive the portion of his salary that had been retained by the legion treasury and received a farewell bonus or a plot of land in a colony. He would already have received regular substantial bonuses (*donativi*) while serving.

1. Birth of Titus Valerius Marcianus in 125 CE, 30 km from Troesmis, Moesia. His father is an army veteran.

2. He volunteers at the age of 20 and is recruited in 145 CE by the Legio V Macedonica, based in Troesmis, Moesia.

3. Principal postings for 16 years: police duties and border patrol.

4. In 161, the Parthian War of Lucius Verus begins, with a Roman defeat. In 162, the Legio V Macedonica is sent to Antioch, with five other legions and five *vexillationes* (temporary detachments). The forces are assembled and trained before reconquering Armenia and crushing the Parthians by taking their capital. Titus Valerius is 37 years old.

5. In 165, after 20 years of service, he is classed as a veteran, and is promoted to the rank of *beneficiarius consularis*. He no longer has to do daily chores and is attached to the prefect of a wing, the commander of a legion or the governor of a province. His job still involves administrative, logistical or police duties.

6. In 166, the Marcomannic Wars begin. The legion is posted to its new camp in Potaissa, Dacia.

7. From 167 to 170, he takes part in the Marcomannic Wars, probably behind the lines.

8. In 170, at the age of 45 and after 25 years of service, he leaves the legion. He turns down the option of a plot of land in an Italian colony of former soldiers and chooses instead to take the *honesta missio* (honourable discharge) payment of 3,000 denarii (equivalent to 10 years of salary) plus the 250 denarii left in his army account. He returns to Troesmis where his family live.

9. In 170, he marries Marcia Basilissa, sister-in-law of a legionary. His offspring and date of death are unknown.

Recruitment and training

Volunteer citizen aged 18 to 21

Arrival at camp — Physical examination — Criminal record checked — Enrolment approved — Military oath

Training (1+2 = practised daily from *calone* to centurion)

1 physical: Marching*, Obstacle course, Swimming, Riding
2 weapons: Sword & shield, Pilum, Bow and arrow, Sling, Siege weapons
3 manoeuvres: Battle line, Doubling ranks, Square
4 construction: Encampments, Bridges & roads, Earthworks & quarries, Brickmaking, Towns

* The 2 types of march (done 3 times a month)

5 hr — ± 40 kg — All weathers

quick march / *plenus gradus*: ± 7.6 km/h
standard march / *gradus militaris*: ± 6.4 km/h

32 km — 38 km

0 km — 5 — 10 — 15 — 20 — 25 — 30 — 35 — 40 km

The principal duties of a legionary

● Primary ● Secondary ● Other

Combat — Guarding borders — Earthworks & construction — Police duties — Guarding & working in mines — Colonization — Administration

Punishments

Manual chores — Reduction of rations — Reduction in pay — Reduction of rank — Beating — Whipping — Stoning — Crucifixion — Decimation (1 in 10 killed)

Minor infractions — Insubordination, theft, lying, immoral behaviour; 3rd conviction for the same offence — Desertion — Serious defeat, mutiny

The weapons and equipment of the legions were regularly improved. During the early centuries of the Republic, mobilized men were responsible for providing their own heavy hoplite weaponry. In the 3rd century BCE, the long sword was replaced by the short *gladius*, better suited to hand-to-hand fighting. Legionaries wore their swords on the right, while centurions wore theirs on the left. During the 1st century CE, the coat of mail (9–12 kg) was superseded by articulated body armour (*lorica segmentata*, 6–8 kg).

There were further changes to weapons and equipment during the Empire. The *pilum* was replaced by the longer *hasta* when legionaries began to be aligned in eight ranks, while cavalry soldiers forsook the *gladius* in favour of the longer *spatha*. By the 3rd century, the front-line troops (*phalangarii*) were using hastae, the next

line (the *lancearii*) had lances, and behind them were the archers (*sagittarii*). As for shields, the bulky rectangular *scutum* gave way to the round buckler (*parma*, *clipeus*), while chainmail (in the West) and scale armour (in the East) replaced the articulated armour. All equipment was supplied by the army, but it was purchased out of soldiers' wages and then requisitioned when they demobilized.

Legionaries carried some of their equipment – arms, tools, food – when they were marching or involved in operations, although every contubernium had a cart or mule to transport the heaviest items. Apart from the food carried by each legionary, a legion had to provide 18.4 tons of daily food rations and animal feed. A military command usually calculated food rations in 17-day stretches, which meant that riverboats took on a vital role in the replenishment of supplies.

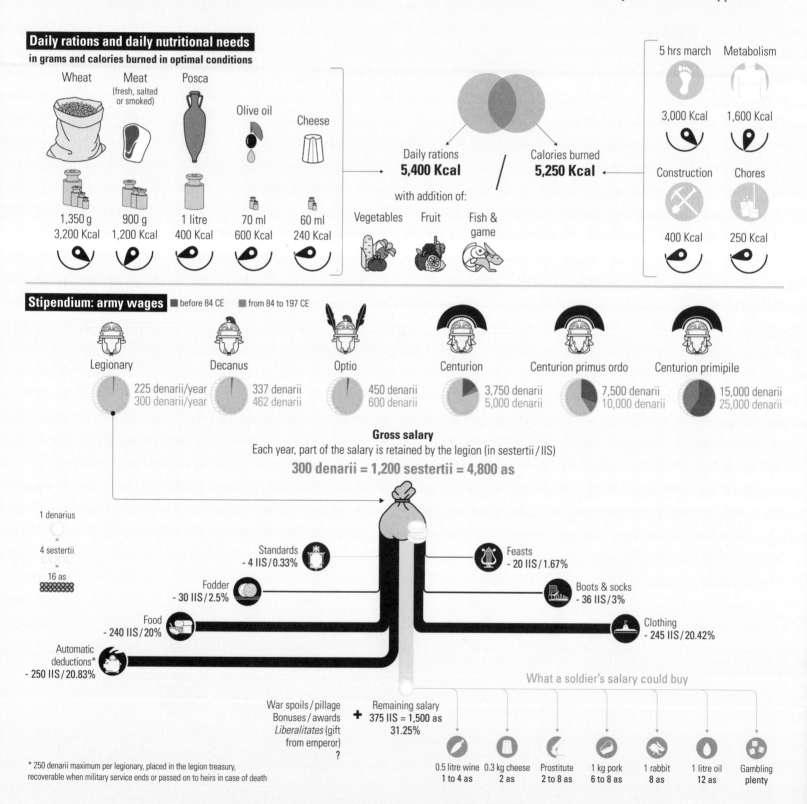

Daily rations and daily nutritional needs
in grams and calories burned in optimal conditions

Wheat	Meat (fresh, salted or smoked)	Posca	Olive oil	Cheese
1,350 g	900 g	1 litre	70 ml	60 ml
3,200 Kcal	1,200 Kcal	400 Kcal	600 Kcal	240 Kcal

Daily rations
5,400 Kcal

Calories burned
5,250 Kcal

with addition of:
Vegetables   Fruit   Fish & game

5 hrs march — 3,000 Kcal
Metabolism — 1,600 Kcal
Construction — 400 Kcal
Chores — 250 Kcal

Stipendium: army wages   ■ before 84 CE   ■ from 84 to 197 CE

Legionary	Decanus	Optio	Centurion	Centurion primus ordo	Centurion primipile
225 denarii/year	337 denarii	450 denarii	3,750 denarii	7,500 denarii	15,000 denarii
300 denarii/year	462 denarii	600 denarii	5,000 denarii	10,000 denarii	25,000 denarii

Gross salary
Each year, part of the salary is retained by the legion (in sestertii / IIS)

300 denarii = 1,200 sestertii = 4,800 as

1 denarius
=
4 sestertii
=
16 as

Standards
- 4 IIS / 0.33%

Fodder
- 30 IIS / 2.5%

Food
- 240 IIS / 20%

Automatic deductions*
- 250 IIS / 20.83%

Feasts
- 20 IIS / 1.67%

Boots & socks
- 36 IIS / 3%

Clothing
- 245 IIS / 20.42%

What a soldier's salary could buy

War spoils / pillage
Bonuses / awards
Liberalitates (gift from emperor)
?

+ Remaining salary
375 IIS = 1,500 as
31.25%

0.5 litre wine	0.3 kg cheese	Prostitute	1 kg pork	1 rabbit	1 litre oil	Gambling
1 to 4 as	2 as	2 to 8 as	6 to 8 as	8 as	12 as	plenty

* 250 denarii maximum per legionary, placed in the legion treasury, recoverable when military service ends or passed on to heirs in case of death

A legionary's equipment at the height of the Roman Empire

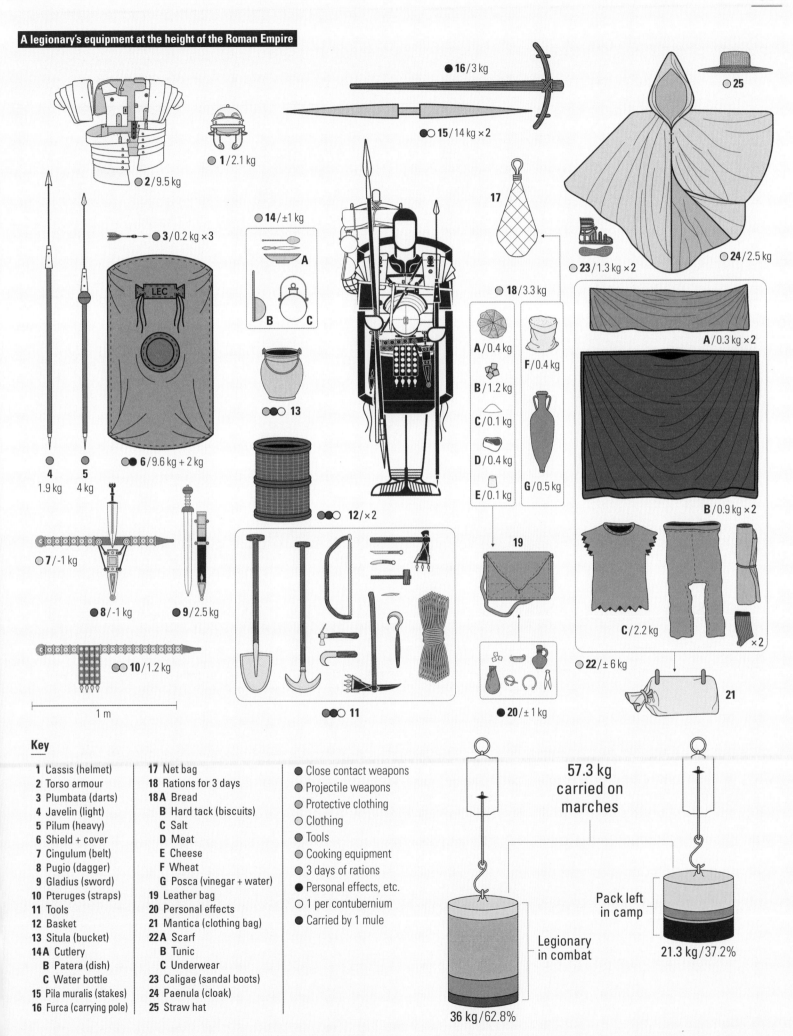

● 16 / 3 kg

○● 15 / 14 kg × 2

● 1 / 2.1 kg

● 2 / 9.5 kg

○ 25

● 3 / 0.2 kg × 3

● 14 / ±1 kg

A

B   C

17

● 18 / 3.3 kg

○ 23 / 1.3 kg × 2

○ 24 / 2.5 kg

A / 0.4 kg   F / 0.4 kg

B / 1.2 kg

C / 0.1 kg

D / 0.4 kg

E / 0.1 kg   G / 0.5 kg

LEC

● 13

A / 0.3 kg × 2

4
1.9 kg

5
4 kg

○● 6 / 9.6 kg + 2 kg

● ● 12 / × 2

B / 0.9 kg × 2

○ 7 / -1 kg

● 8 / -1 kg   ● 9 / 2.5 kg

C / 2.2 kg   × 2

○ 22 / ± 6 kg

● ● 10 / 1.2 kg

19

21

1 m

● ● ○ 11   ● 20 / ± 1 kg

Key

1 Cassis (helmet)
2 Torso armour
3 Plumbata (darts)
4 Javelin (light)
5 Pilum (heavy)
6 Shield + cover
7 Cingulum (belt)
8 Pugio (dagger)
9 Gladius (sword)
10 Pteruges (straps)
11 Tools
12 Basket
13 Situla (bucket)
14A Cutlery
  B Patera (dish)
  C Water bottle
15 Pila muralis (stakes)
16 Furca (carrying pole)

17 Net bag
18 Rations for 3 days
18A Bread
  B Hard tack (biscuits)
  C Salt
  D Meat
  E Cheese
  F Wheat
  G Posca (vinegar + water)
19 Leather bag
20 Personal effects
21 Mantica (clothing bag)
22A Scarf
  B Tunic
  C Underwear
23 Caligae (sandal boots)
24 Paenula (cloak)
25 Straw hat

● Close contact weapons
○ Projectile weapons
○ Protective clothing
○ Clothing
● Tools
○ Cooking equipment
● 3 days of rations
● Personal effects, etc.
○ 1 per contubernium
● Carried by 1 mule

57.3 kg
carried on
marches

Pack left
in camp

Legionary
in combat   21.3 kg / 37.2%

36 kg / 62.8%

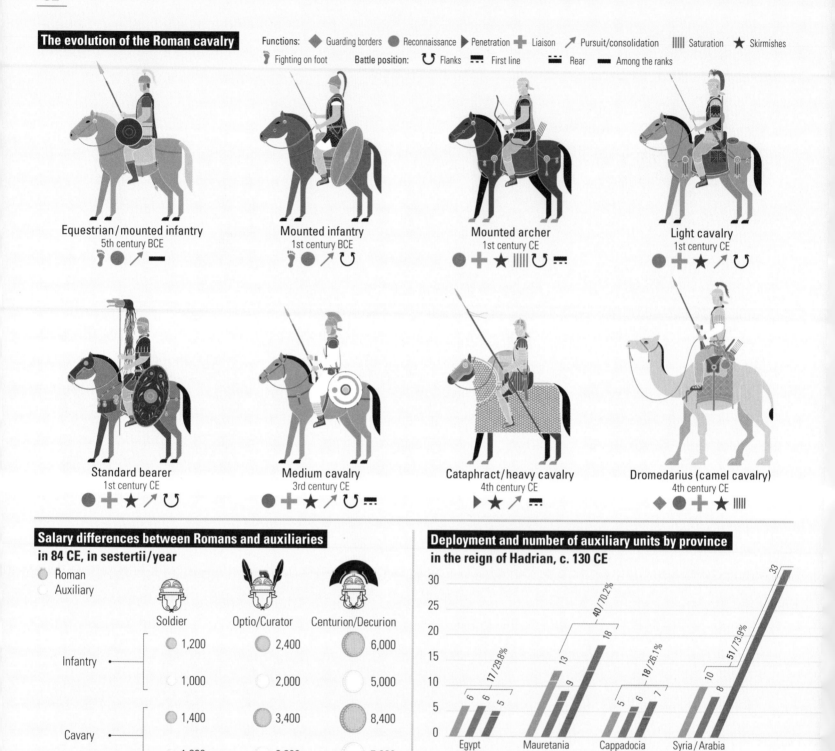

The evolution of the Roman cavalry

Functions: ◆ Guarding borders ● Reconnaissance ▶ Penetration ✚ Liaison ↗ Pursuit/consolidation ||||| Saturation ★ Skirmishes
👣 Fighting on foot Battle position: ∪ Flanks ▬ First line ▦ Rear ▬ Among the ranks

Equestrian/mounted infantry
5th century BCE
👣 ● ↗ ▬

Mounted infantry
1st century BCE
👣 ● ↗ ∪

Mounted archer
1st century CE
● ✚ ★ ||||| ∪ ▬

Light cavalry
1st century CE
● ✚ ★ ↗ ∪

Standard bearer
1st century CE
● ✚ ★ ↗ ∪

Medium cavalry
3rd century CE
● ✚ ★ ↗ ∪ ▬

Cataphract/heavy cavalry
4th century CE
▶ ★ ↗ ▬

Dromedarius (camel cavalry)
4th century CE
◆ ● ✚ ★ |||||

Salary differences between Romans and auxiliaries
in 84 CE, in sestertii/year

● Roman
○ Auxiliary

		Soldier	Optio/Curator	Centurion/Decurion
Infantry	Roman	1,200	2,400	6,000
	Auxiliary	1,000	2,000	5,000
Cavary	Roman	1,400	3,400	8,400
	Auxiliary	1,200	2,800	7,000

Deployment and number of auxiliary units by province
in the reign of Hadrian, c. 130 CE

Egypt: 6, 6, 5 — 17/29.8%
Mauretania: 13, 9, 18 — 40/70.2%
Fossatum Africae (57/14.8%)
Cappadocia: 5, 6, 7 — 18/26.1%
Syria/Arabia: 10, 8, 33 — 51/73.9%
Limes Arabicus (69/18%)

VI. CAVALRY AND AUXILIARIES

At the start of the Republic, the Roman army had few cavalry soldiers. It soon recognized their potential, however, when it was battered by the charges of Hispanic and Gallic heavy cavalry in the Second Punic War. By the end of the 2nd century, Rome could also boast its own contingents of cavalry, recruited from its allies in Hispania and Gaul. The legions, meanwhile, were still accompanied by 120 mounted legionaries, but these were restricted to tactical missions, as combat was entrusted to allied cavalry soldiers, sometimes fighting in mixed units.

Mounted legionaries were originally young members of the upper classes, and came from the senatorial or equestrian classes (the latter were given a 'public horse', granted through a state subsidy). These horsemen had to serve the Republic for ten years, after which the censors examined their service records and the condition of their horse. A successful inspection could lead to a command post in the army as a military tribune (elected by the people for a consular legion), appointment to a military campaign by a consul or praetor and candidature for elections for the highest magistracy, the quaestorship.

After the Marian reforms, service on horseback was no longer obligatory for members of the equestrian class. The tradition of ten years of military service endured, however, but this now entailed positions of command, and the work of the cavalry was taken on by contingents of mounted auxiliaries (albeit commanded by equestrians or young members of the senatorial order) and cohorts combining 120 cavalrymen and 680 foot soldiers. This strategy gave the Roman army an effective mounted force that

Different types of auxiliaries

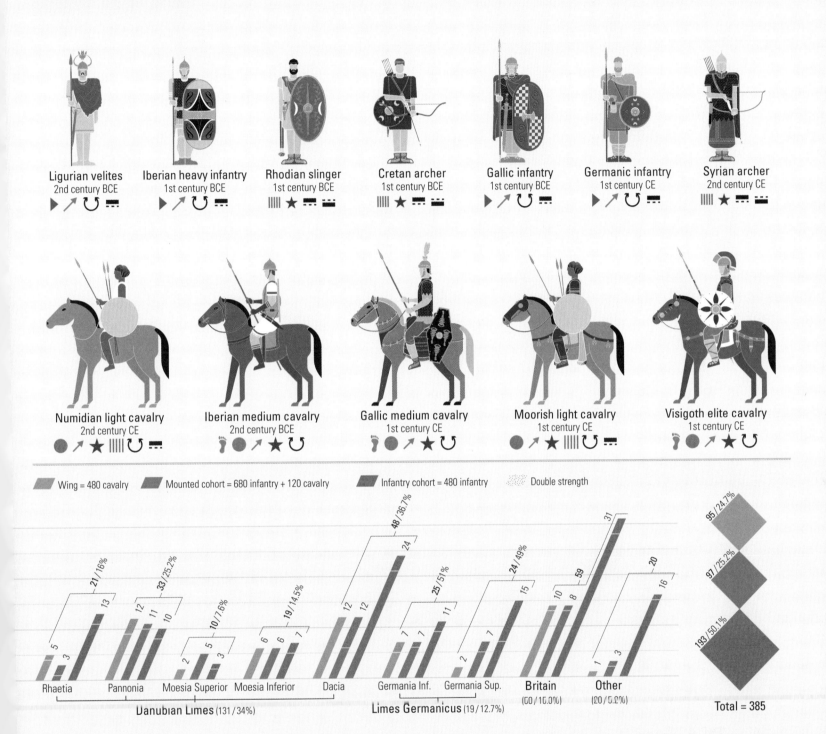

Ligurian velites
2nd century BCE

Iberian heavy infantry
1st century BCE

Rhodian slinger
1st century BCE

Cretan archer
1st century BCE

Gallic infantry
1st century BCE

Germanic infantry
1st century CE

Syrian archer
2nd century CE

Numidian light cavalry
2nd century CE

Iberian medium cavalry
2nd century BCE

Gallic medium cavalry
1st century CE

Moorish light cavalry
1st century CE

Visigoth elite cavalry
1st century CE

Wing = 480 cavalry   Mounted cohort = 680 infantry + 120 cavalry   Infantry cohort = 480 infantry   Double strength

Rhaetia   Pannonia   Moesia Superior   Moesia Inferior   Dacia   Germania Inf.   Germania Sup.   Britain   Other

Danubian Limes (131 / 34%)   Limes Germanicus (19 / 12.7%)

Total = 385

was well integrated into its tactical planning. The auxiliaries and their families were granted Roman citizenship (if they did not already have it) once they completed their military service.

In the 4th century, reforms implemented by Diocletian and his successors reacted to developments in their enemies' armies – now highly mobile due to their extensive use of horses – and reduced the number of foot soldiers in favour of cavalrymen. Severus Alexander later incorporated cataphracts (horsemen with heavy armour made of overlapping metal plates) into the Roman cavalry. The legionary cavalry unit was similarly reinforced, for in the middle of the 3rd century it grew from 120 to 726 men, divided into 22 turmae. These new horse soldiers were probably drawn from the legionaries, and it seems that, at that time, the proportion of horsemen to foot soldiers

was 1:3, compared to 1:10 prior to the Marian reforms. When the Emperor Gallienus, for example, deployed an army on the Rhine, its detachments included legions, auxiliary cavalrymen and *numeri*, back-up troops that were increasingly recruited on the far reaches of the Empire and allowed to fight according to their own traditions. He then stationed this army in Milan, where it was primed to make rapid interventions, in conjunction with detachments of infantry.

By the mid-3rd century, horses played an ever more significant role in the first line of battle. Even cavalry officers and sub-officers could be found there, largely drawn from the growing number of Germanic recruits to the Roman army. These developments also affected the evolution of the infantry, which now served to resist the charges of heavy cavalry.

VII. SIEGE WARFARE

Sieges were complex operations for the armies of the ancient world. They required the concentration of a substantial number of troops (three legions plus auxiliaries in Jerusalem, for example) in one particular place for a relatively long period of time. This situation would put a strain on food supplies, and so sieges were often used as a tactic intended to force an enemy into submission and negotiation. Hannibal, for instance, would never risk prolonged sieges as his lines of supply were too vulnerable.

Several sieges have been recorded in Roman military history, starting with the legendary siege of the Etruscan city of Veii (15 km to the north of Rome). Veii is said to have held out for a full ten years, until 396 BCE, but it was probably subjected to a regular series of attacks rather than a sustained siege of the kind later seen in Syracuse (213–212 BCE), Carthage (146 BCE), Alesia (52 BCE), Perusia (41–40 BCE) and Jerusalem (70 CE). These sieges were massive undertakings which, despite the use of artillery and elaborate siege engines, predominantly consisted of starving the besieged population by cutting off its food supply and access to water until it was forced to surrender or became so debilitated that it could no longer put up any effective resistance. In the meantime, the attacking army set about building large access ramps that would allow its soldiers to scale the walls.

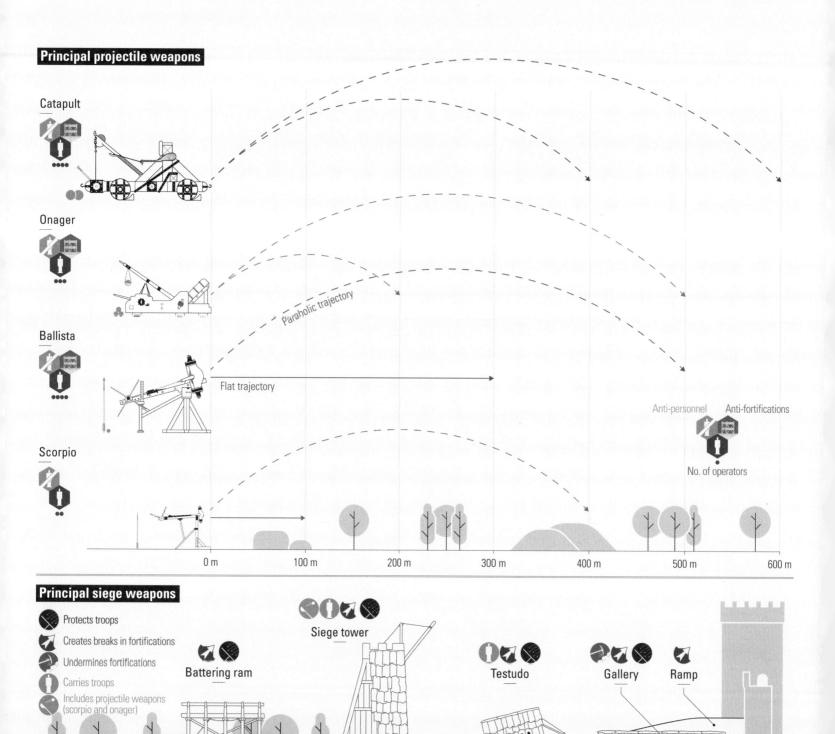

Principal projectile weapons

Catapult

Onager

Ballista

Scorpio

Parabolic trajectory

Flat trajectory

Anti-personnel   Anti-fortifications

No. of operators

0 m   100 m   200 m   300 m   400 m   500 m   600 m

Principal siege weapons

Protects troops

Creates breaks in fortifications

Undermines fortifications

Carries troops

Includes projectile weapons (scorpio and onager)

Battering ram

Siege tower

Testudo   Gallery   Ramp

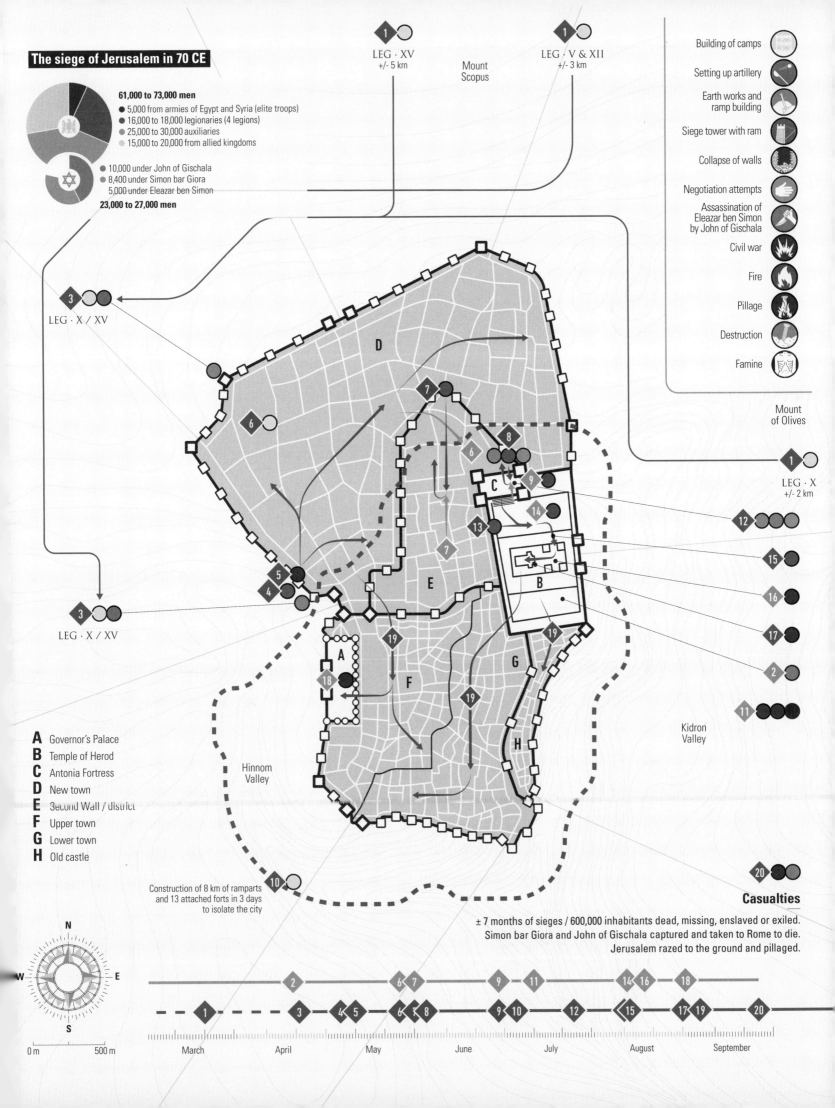

The siege of Jerusalem in 70 CE

61,000 to 73,000 men
- 5,000 from armies of Egypt and Syria (elite troops)
- 16,000 to 18,000 legionaries (4 legions)
- 25,000 to 30,000 auxiliaries
- 15,000 to 20,000 from allied kingdoms

- 10,000 under John of Gischala
- 8,400 under Simon bar Giora
- 5,000 under Eleazar ben Simon

23,000 to 27,000 men

Legend (right):
- Building of camps
- Setting up artillery
- Earth works and ramp building
- Siege tower with ram
- Collapse of walls
- Negotiation attempts
- Assassination of Eleazar ben Simon by John of Gischala
- Civil war
- Fire
- Pillage
- Destruction
- Famine

LEG · XV +/- 5 km

LEG · V & XII +/- 3 km

Mount Scopus

LEG · X / XV

LEG · X / XV

LEG · X +/- 2 km

Mount of Olives

Kidron Valley

Hinnom Valley

Construction of 8 km of ramparts and 13 attached forts in 3 days to isolate the city

Casualties

± 7 months of sieges / 600,000 inhabitants dead, missing, enslaved or exiled. Simon bar Giora and John of Gischala captured and taken to Rome to die. Jerusalem razed to the ground and pillaged.

A Governor's Palace
B Temple of Herod
C Antonia Fortress
D New town
E Second Wall / district
F Upper town
G Lower town
H Old castle

N
W   E
S

0 m   500 m

March   April   May   June   July   August   September

VIII. THE LEGIONS AND THE EMPIRE

Under the Roman Republic, the legions conducted campaigns every year, but the army was dissolved in the winter and then reconvened the following year in a particular location. Over the course of the 3rd century BCE, and most particularly during the Second Punic War, the four consular legions were too fully stretched to satisfy all the army's needs. Moreover, soldiers usually found themselves too far away from Italy to come home for the winter, and so they stayed put and any new commanding officers would travel to join them. By the 2nd century BCE, this procedure had become standardized, and the increasing number of provinces obliged Rome to establish many permanent garrisons. In the 1st century BCE, civil wars, which added to the demands of the wars of repression and conquest, resulted in the professionalization of the legions, as well as their rising number. In 42 BCE, the young Octavian was commissioned by his fellow Triumvirate members, Lepidus and Mark Antony, to dissolve the Caesarean legions and post many of their veterans in Roman colonies. There was a similar overhaul in 30 BCE, when the number of legions had swelled to 60 as a result of frequent wars. The restoration of peace sparked the dissolution of most of the legions, because of the high cost of maintaining them and the political danger that they represented. Augustus slimmed down the number of legions to 18, but this cut proved too drastic and by the end of the Principate period there were 25 in all. Some legions were subsequently wiped out in battle (most notably, three in 9 CE) or dissolved (eight in 69 CE), but 16 new ones were also created. Their number increased steadily in the 2nd century to stabilize at 30, although three more were added at the beginning of the 3rd century.

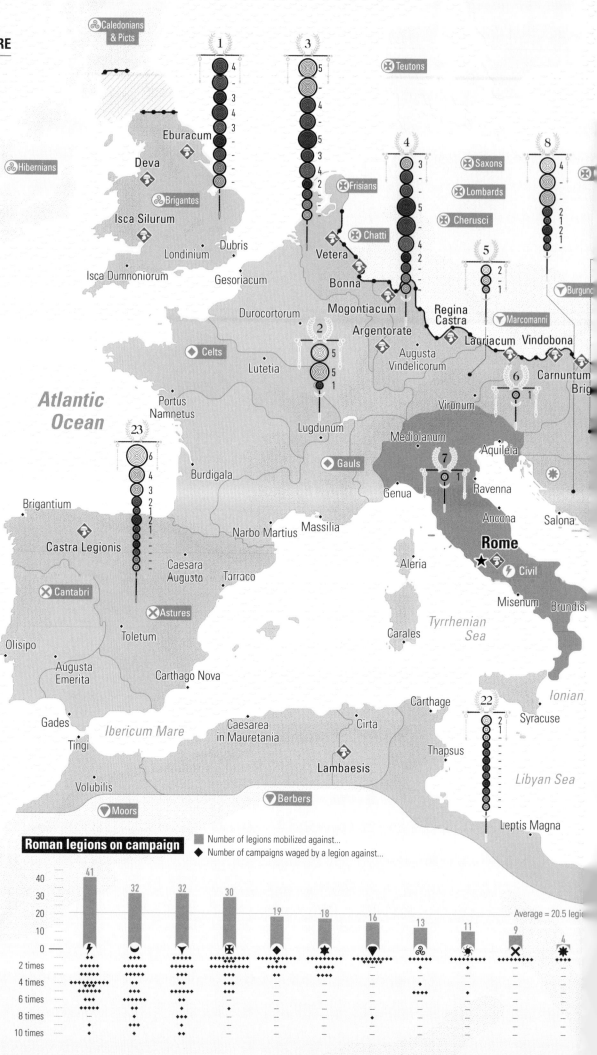

Roman legions on campaign

Number of legions mobilized against...

◆ Number of campaigns waged by a legion against...

Average = 20.5 legions

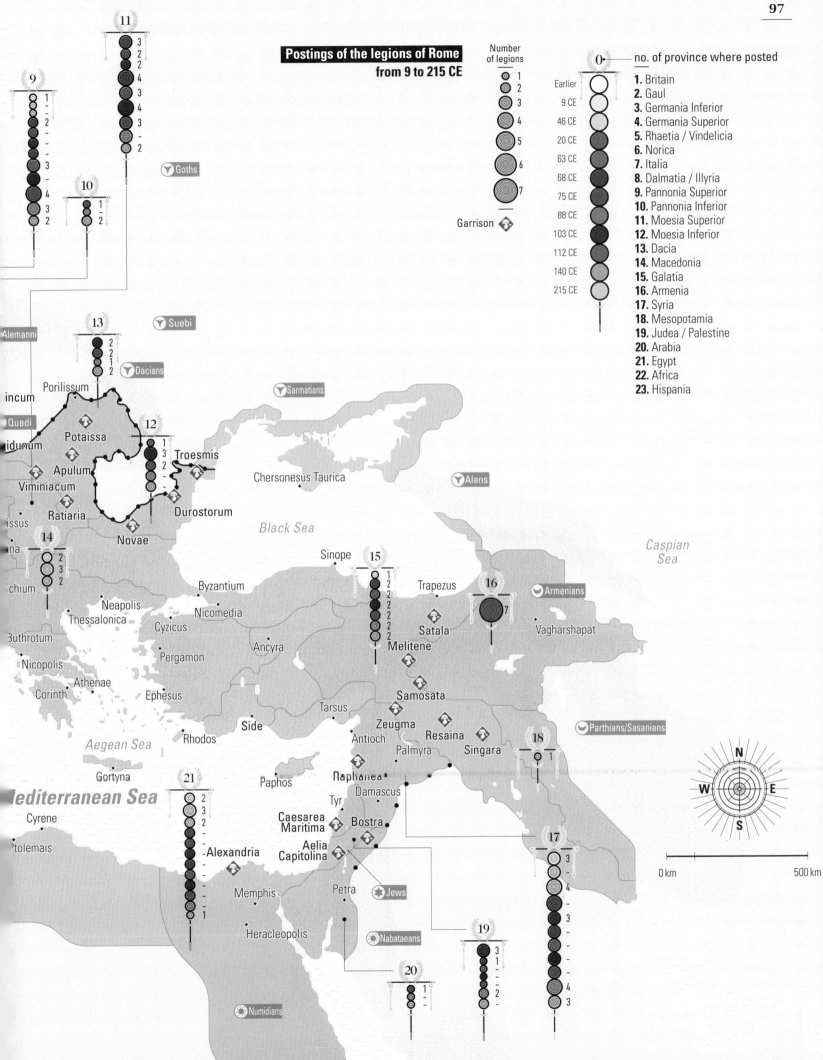

Postings of the legions of Rome from 9 to 215 CE

Number of legions

1
2
3
4
5
6
7

Garrison

no. of province where posted

Earlier
9 CE
46 CE
20 CE
63 CE
68 CE
75 CE
88 CE
103 CE
112 CE
140 CE
215 CE

1. Britain
2. Gaul
3. Germania Inferior
4. Germania Superior
5. Rhaetia / Vindelicia
6. Norica
7. Italia
8. Dalmatia / Illyria
9. Pannonia Superior
10. Pannonia Inferior
11. Moesia Superior
12. Moesia Inferior
13. Dacia
14. Macedonia
15. Galatia
16. Armenia
17. Syria
18. Mesopotamia
19. Judea / Palestine
20. Arabia
21. Egypt
22. Africa
23. Hispania

Goths
Suebi
Dacians
Sarmatians
Alemanni
Quadi
Alans
Armenians
Parthians/Sasanians
Jews
Nabataeans
Numidians

Porolissum
Potaissa
Apulum
Viminiacum
Ratiaria
Troesmis
Novae
Durostorum
Chersonesus Taurica
Black Sea
Caspian Sea
Sinope
Byzantium
Nicomedia
Cyzicus
Ancyra
Trapezus
Satala
Melitene
Vagharshapat
Neapolis
Thessalonica
Pergamon
Buthrotum
Nicopolis
Corinth
Athenae
Ephesus
Side
Tarsus
Samosata
Zeugma
Antioch
Palmyra
Resaina
Singara
Rhodos
Aegean Sea
Gortyna
Paphos
Naphanea
Tyr
Damascus
Caesarea Maritima
Bostra
Aelia Capitolina
Petra
Mediterranean Sea
Cyrene
Ptolemais
Alexandria
Memphis
Heracleopolis

0 km   500 km

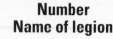

History of the legions of the Roman Empire

⚡	Civil wars & wars of succession
✳	Thracians / Dalmatians
✖	Cantabrians / Astures
◇	Gauls
✠	Germans / Franks / Chatti / Batavians...
⋎	Dacians / Marcomanni / Sarmatians / Goths...
▽	Moors / Berbers

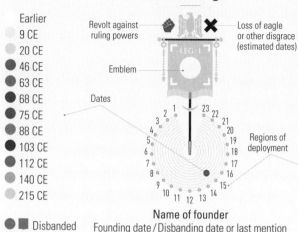

Number / Name of legion

Earlier
9 CE
20 CE
46 CE
63 CE
68 CE
75 CE
88 CE
103 CE
112 CE
140 CE
215 CE

Disbanded
Annihilated

Revolt against ruling powers
Emblem
Dates
Name of founder
Founding date / Disbanding date or last mention
Number of known campaigns (from founding to disbanding)

Loss of eagle or other disgrace (estimated dates)

Regions of deployment

Base locations
1. Britain
2. Gaul
3. Germania Inferior
4. Germania Superior
5. Rhaetia / Vindelicia
6. Norica
7. Italia
8. Dalmatia / Illyria
9. Pannonia Superior
10. Pannonia Inferior
11. Moesia Superior
12. Moesia Inferior
13. Dacia
14. Macedonia
15. Galicia
16. Armenia
17. Syria
18. Mesopotamia
19. Judea / Palestine
20. Arabia
21. Egypt
22. Africa
23. Hispania

Legio I Adiutrix
Nero
68 CE / 440 CE
24 campaigns

Legio I Germanica
14 / 69 CE   25 BCE
Julius Caesar
48 BCE / 69 CE
10 campaigns

Legio I Italica
69 CE
Nero
66 CE / 5th cent.
18 campaigns

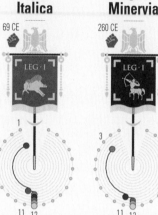

Legio I Minervia
260 CE
Domitian
82–83 CE / 360 CE
20 campaigns

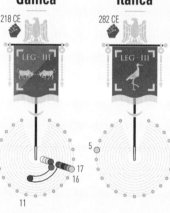

Legio III Gallica
218 CE
Julius Caesar
48 BCE / 4th cent.
23 campaigns

Legio III Italica
282 CE
Marcus Aurelius
165 CE / 4th cent.
16 campaigns

Legio III Parthica
Septimius Severus
197 CE / 5th cent.
6 campaigns

Legio IV Flavia Felix
Vespasian
70 CE / 5th cent.
16 campaigns

Legio IV Macedonica
68 CE
Julius Caesar
48 BCE / 70 CE
6 campaigns

Legio IV Scythica
219 CE   62–63 CE
Mark Antony
40–31 BCE / 4th cent.
18 campaigns

Legio V Alaudae
14 CE   16 BCE / 70 CE
Julius Caesar
56 BCE / 70 CE
15 campaigns

Legio V Macedonica
Pansa / Octavian
43 BCE / 5th cent.
17 campaigns

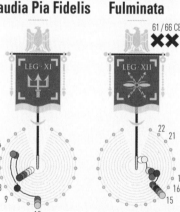

Legio XI Claudia Pia Fidelis
Julius Caesar / Octavian
58–42 BCE / 4th cent.
22 campaigns

Legio XII Fulminata
61 / 66 CE
Julius Caesar / Lepidus
58–44 BCE / 3rd cent. CE
18 campaigns

Legio XIII Gemina
14 CE
Julius Caesar
58 BCE / 4th cent. CE
27 campaigns

Legio XIV Gemina Martia Victrix
14 / 69 CE
Julius Caesar / Octavian
57–44 BCE / 258 CE
31 campaigns

Legio XV Apollinaris
14 CE
Julius Caesar / Octavian
53–44 BCE / 5th cent. CE
21 campaigns

Legio XV Primigenia
70 CE
Caligula
39 CE / 70 CE
3 campaigns

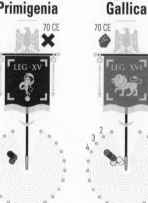

Legio XVI Gallica → Legio XVI Flavia Firma
70 CE
Octavian
43 BCE / 70 CE
7 campaigns

Vespasian
70 CE / 4th cent.
7 campaigns

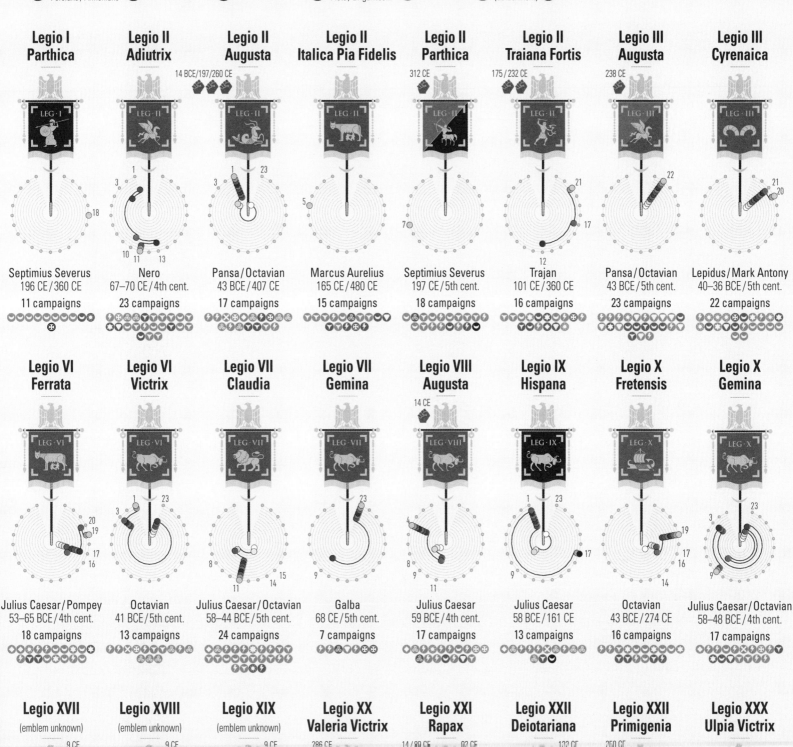

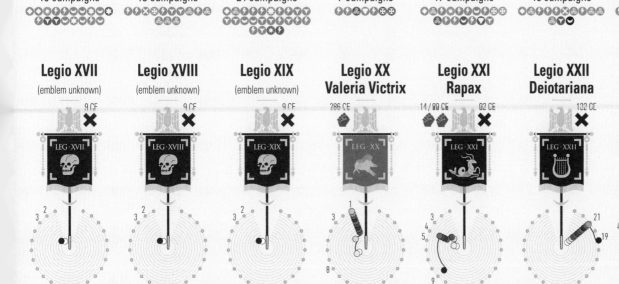

SEAFARING ROME

Although Rome was not initially a sea power, circumstances forced it to become one. In 311 BCE, Rome began to annually appoint two magistrates with responsibility for the navy (*duoviri navales*); each was head of a small fleet of ten warships equipped to combat piracy in the Tyrrhenian Sea. Rome's naval interests were strengthened in 306–302 BCE, the period ascribed by Polybius to an alliance between Rome and Rhodes (which was famous for its prowess at sea). In 306 BCE, Rome signed its third treaty with Carthage, which established each party's respective sphere of influence in the Mediterranean. By the start of the First Punic War in 264 BCE, however, Rome no longer had a navy and was forced to turn to allies such as Tarentum, Locris, Velia and Naples for triremes and penteconters. Rome subsequently built its own fleet, comprising 100 quinqueremes and 20 triremes. Roman pragmatism is well illustrated by its decision to fight the Carthaginians in their preferred element, and with their own vessel of choice – the quinquereme, which Rome had now mastered. Nevertheless, despite Lutatius Catulus's victory over a poorly armed and badly trained Punic fleet in 241 BCE, Rome remained primarily a land power.

From 200 BCE onwards, Rome depended on the naval strength of its Greek allies, especially Rhodes. Allied cities in Ionia, Phoenicia, Pamphylia and Syria provided most of the ships in the Roman fleets. Rome also built its own ships but they were manned by crews from allied cities. Rome gradually began to adopt Greek and Eastern naval practices during the Social War (90–88 BCE) and, after the war against King Mithridates (89–85 BCE), the idea of a permanent Roman navy was finally mooted. In 67 BCE, Pompey overcame the pirates who had ruled the Mediterranean. In the civil war between Caesar and Pompey, the allied maritime cities still played a major role, and it was only after the final civil war in 30 BCE that Rome assembled its own permanent sea and river fleets. These were often manned by foreigners or slaves, although over time more citizens and freed men were enlisted.

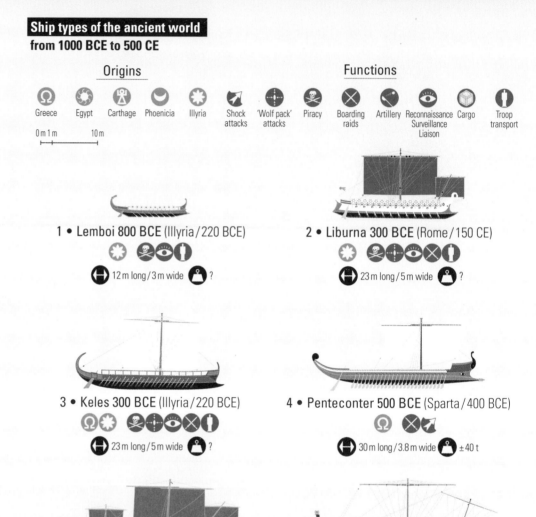

Ship types of the ancient world from 1000 BCE to 500 CE

Origins: Greece, Egypt, Carthage, Phoenicia, Illyria

Functions: Shock attacks, 'Wolf pack' attacks, Piracy, Boarding raids, Artillery, Reconnaissance Surveillance Liaison, Cargo, Troop transport

0 m 1 m — 10 m

1 • **Lemboi 800 BCE** (Illyria / 220 BCE)
12 m long / 3 m wide ?

2 • **Liburna 300 BCE** (Rome / 150 CE)
23 m long / 5 m wide ?

3 • **Keles 300 BCE** (Illyria / 220 BCE)
23 m long / 5 m wide ?

4 • **Penteconter 500 BCE** (Sparta / 400 BCE)
30 m long / 3.8 m wide ± 40 t

5 • **Navis actuaria 300 BCE** (Rome / 20 CE)
31 m long / 6.5 m wide ± 50 t

6 • **Bireme 300 BCE** (Rome / 50 CE)
32 m long / 4.3 m wide ± 50 t

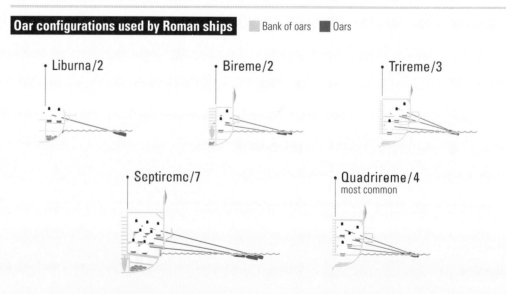

Oar configurations used by Roman ships ▮ Bank of oars ▮ Oars

• Liburna / 2

• Bireme / 2

• Trireme / 3

• Septireme / 7

• Quadrireme / 4
most common

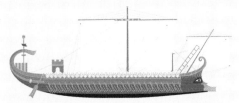

7 • Diere / Trireme 300 BCE (Rome / 260 BCE)

   38 m long / 6 m wide   ±60 t

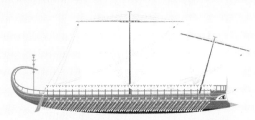

8 • Triere 704 BCE (Carthage / 250 BCE)

    40 m long / 6 m wide   ±70 t

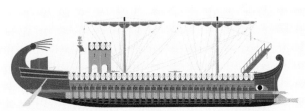

9 • Quadrireme 350 BCE (Rome / 260 BCE)

   50 m long / 7 m wide   ±80 t

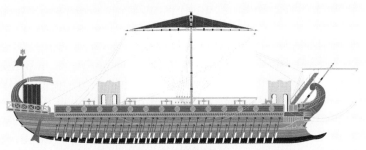

10 • Quinquereme 400 BCE (Rome / 68 BCE)

    58 m long / 7 m wide   100 t

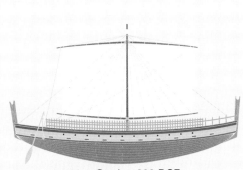

11 • Gaulos 200 BCE

    ±40 m long / 10 m wide   ?

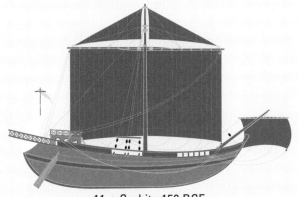

11 • Corbita 150 BCE

   55 m long / 13 m wide   ?

Power and speed   ～ Cruising speed   ～ Maximum speed   ▶ Ram   ● Catapult   ■ Archer's tower   ✖ Scorpio / Ballista   ╱ Corvus   ❬ War dolphin   ★ Continuous deck

Lemboi •1	16 rowers / soldiers ▶		7–14 knots
Liburna •2	44 rowers / 10 seamen / ±10 soldiers ▶		
Keles •3	23 rowers / 3 seamen / ±10 soldiers ▶		
Penteconter •4	50 rowers / 3 seamen / ±10 soldiers ▶		6–10 knots
Navis actuaria •5	50 rowers / 3 seamen / ±30 soldiers ▶✖✖		±5–8 knots
Bireme •6	50 rowers / ±10 seamen / ±30 soldiers ▶✖✖❬		
Trireme •7	170 rowers / 25 seamen / 50 soldiers ▶■✖✖╱❬★		
Triere •8	240 rowers / ±10 seamen / ±50 soldiers ▶✖✖╱★		±3–8 knots
Quadrireme •9	230 rowers / 40 seamen / 75 soldiers ▶▶✖✖╱❬★		±3–8 knots
Quinquereme •10	300 rowers / 50 seamen / 130 soldiers ▶▶●●●●●●●●●●●■✖✖╱❬★		

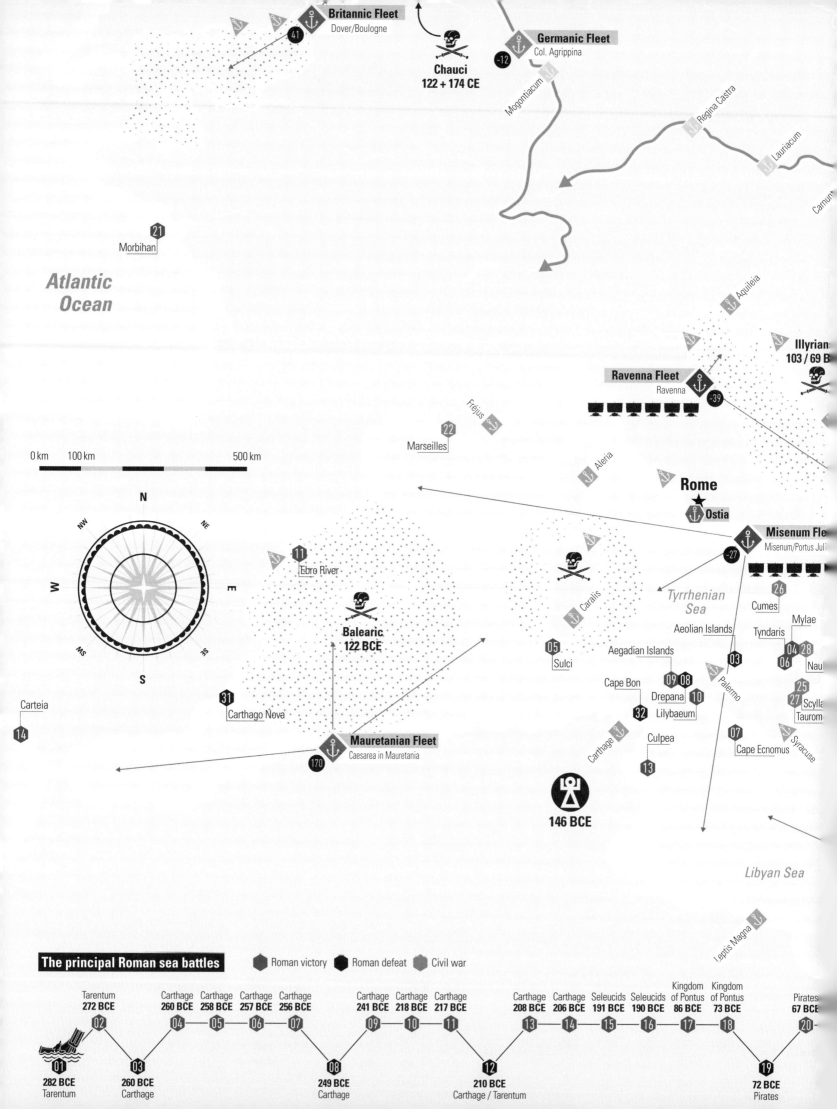

Britannic Fleet
Dover/Boulogne
41

Chauci
122 + 174 CE

Germanic Fleet
Col. Agrippina
-12

Mogontiacum

Regina Castra

Lauriacum

Carnun

Atlantic Ocean

Morbihan
21

Aquileia

Illyrian
103 / 69 B

Ravenna Fleet
Ravenna
-39

Fréjus

Marseilles
22

Aleria

Rome ★

Ostia

Misenum Fle
Misenum/Portus Jul
-27

26

Cumes

Tyrrhenian Sea

0 km	100 km			500 km

N
NW N NE
W E
SW SE
S

Ebro River
11

Balearic
122 BCE

Caralis

Sulci
05

Aegadian Islands

Aeolian Islands

Tyndaris

Mylae
04 28

06 Nau

Cape Bon
09 08

Drepana 10

32 Lilybaeum

Palermo
03

25
27 Scylla
Taurom

Carteia

Carthago Nova
31

Mauretanian Fleet
Caesarea in Mauretania
170

14

Carthage

Culpea

13

Cape Ecnomus
07

Syracuse

146 BCE

Libyan Sea

Leptis Magna

The principal Roman sea battles
⬡ Roman victory ⬤ Roman defeat ⬢ Civil war

	Tarentum **272 BCE**		Carthage **260 BCE**	Carthage **258 BCE**	Carthage **257 BCE**	Carthage **256 BCE**		Carthage **241 BCE**	Carthage **218 BCE**	Carthage **217 BCE**		Carthage **208 BCE**	Carthage **206 BCE**	Seleucids **191 BCE**	Seleucids **190 BCE**	Kingdom of Pontus **86 BCE**	Kingdom of Pontus **73 BCE**		Pirates **67 BCE**
	02		04	05	06	07		09	10	11		13	14	15	16	17	18		20
01		03					08				12							19	

282 BCE
Tarentum

260 BCE
Carthage

249 BCE
Carthage

210 BCE
Carthage / Tarentum

72 BCE
Pirates

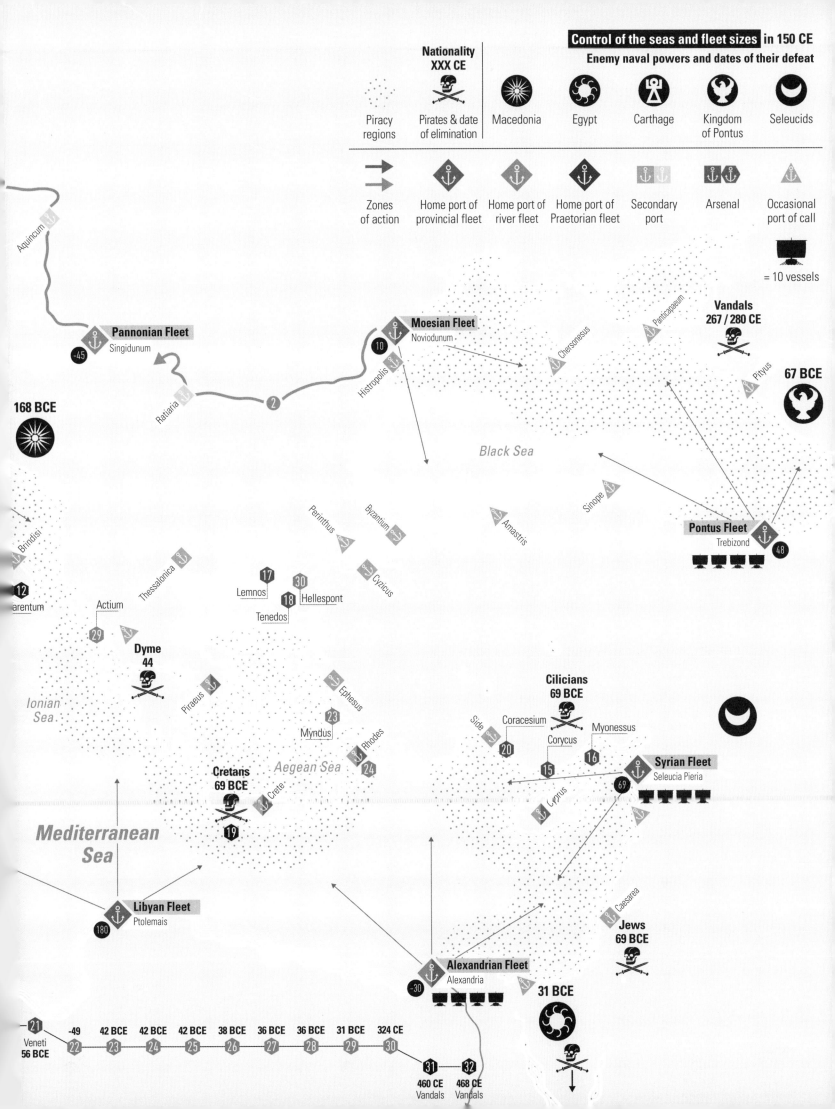

Control of the seas and fleet sizes in 150 CE
Enemy naval powers and dates of their defeat

Nationality
XXX CE

Piracy regions

Pirates & date of elimination

Macedonia

Egypt

Carthage

Kingdom of Pontus

Seleucids

Zones of action

Home port of provincial fleet

Home port of river fleet

Home port of Praetorian fleet

Secondary port

Arsenal

Occasional port of call

= 10 vessels

Aquincum

Pannonian Fleet
Singidunum
-45

Moesian Fleet
Noviodunum
10

Histropolis

Panticapaeum

Vandals
267 / 280 CE

Chersonesus

Pityus

67 BCE

168 BCE

Ratiaria

2

Black Sea

Sinope

Amastris

Pontus Fleet
Trebizond
48

Brindisi

Perinthus

Byzantium

Cyzicus

12

Tarentum

Thessalonica

Lemnos
17

Hellespont
30

Tenedos
18

Actium
29

Dyme
44

Piraeus

Ephesus

Myndus
23

Rhodes
24

Ionian Sea

Cilicians
69 BCE

Side

Coracesium
20

Corycus
15

Myonessus
16

Syrian Fleet
Seleucia Pieria
69

Aegean Sea

Cretans
69 BCE

Crete
19

Mediterranean Sea

Cyprus

Libyan Fleet
Ptolemais
180

Caesarea

Jews
69 BCE

Alexandrian Fleet
Alexandria
-30

31 BCE

21
Veneti
56 BCE

-49
22

42 BCE
23

42 BCE
24

42 BCE
25

38 BCE
26

36 BCE
27

36 BCE
28

31 BCE
29

324 CE
30

31

32

460 CE
Vandals

468 CE
Vandals

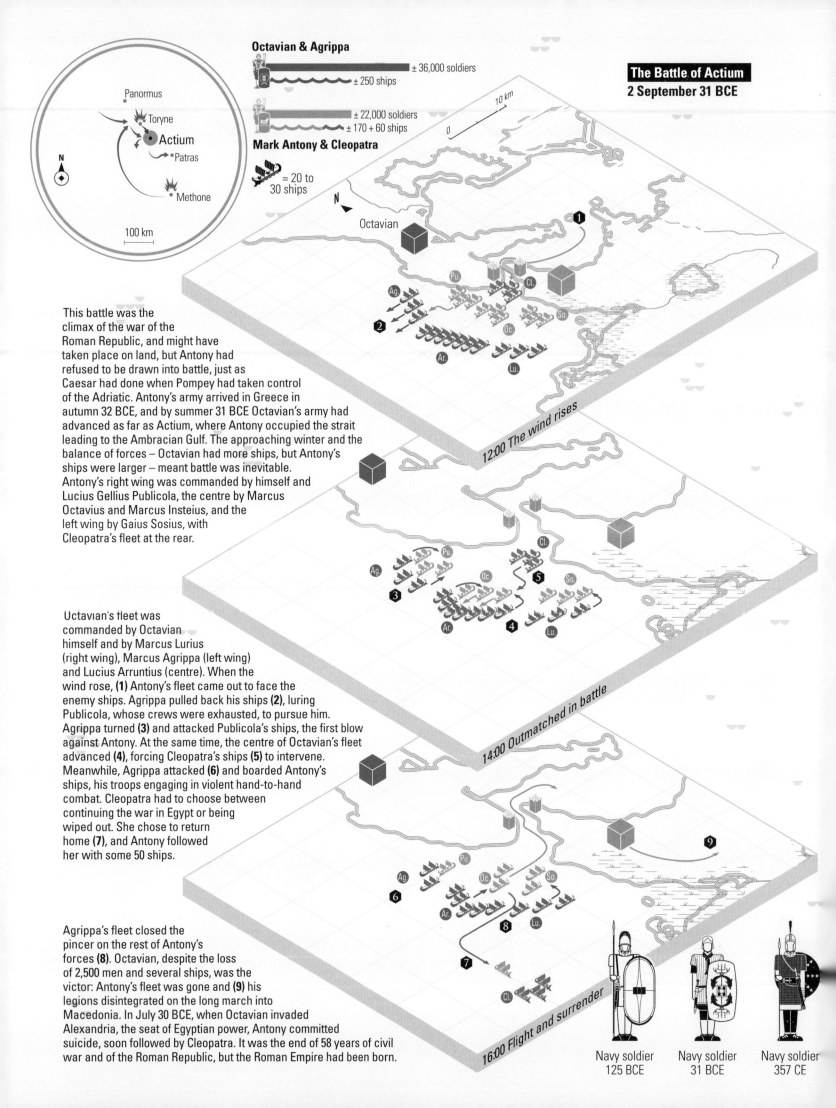

Octavian & Agrippa

± 36,000 soldiers
± 250 ships

± 22,000 soldiers
± 170 + 60 ships

Mark Antony & Cleopatra

= 20 to 30 ships

The Battle of Actium
2 September 31 BCE

Panormus
Toryne
Actium
Patras
Methone

N

100 km

0 — 10 km

Octavian

1
2
3
4
5
6
7
8
9

Ag.
Pu.
Cl.
Oc.
So.
Ar.
Lu.

12:00 The wind rises

14:00 Outmatched in battle

16:00 Flight and surrender

This battle was the climax of the war of the Roman Republic, and might have taken place on land, but Antony had refused to be drawn into battle, just as Caesar had done when Pompey had taken control of the Adriatic. Antony's army arrived in Greece in autumn 32 BCE, and by summer 31 BCE Octavian's army had advanced as far as Actium, where Antony occupied the strait leading to the Ambracian Gulf. The approaching winter and the balance of forces – Octavian had more ships, but Antony's ships were larger – meant battle was inevitable. Antony's right wing was commanded by himself and Lucius Gellius Publicola, the centre by Marcus Octavius and Marcus Insteius, and the left wing by Gaius Sosius, with Cleopatra's fleet at the rear.

Octavian's fleet was commanded by Octavian himself and by Marcus Lurius (right wing), Marcus Agrippa (left wing) and Lucius Arruntius (centre). When the wind rose, **(1)** Antony's fleet came out to face the enemy ships. Agrippa pulled back his ships **(2)**, luring Publicola, whose crews were exhausted, to pursue him. Agrippa turned **(3)** and attacked Publicola's ships, the first blow against Antony. At the same time, the centre of Octavian's fleet advanced **(4)**, forcing Cleopatra's ships **(5)** to intervene. Meanwhile, Agrippa attacked **(6)** and boarded Antony's ships, his troops engaging in violent hand-to-hand combat. Cleopatra had to choose between continuing the war in Egypt or being wiped out. She chose to return home **(7)**, and Antony followed her with some 50 ships.

Agrippa's fleet closed the pincer on the rest of Antony's forces **(8)**. Octavian, despite the loss of 2,500 men and several ships, was the victor: Antony's fleet was gone and **(9)** his legions disintegrated on the long march into Macedonia. In July 30 BCE, when Octavian invaded Alexandria, the seat of Egyptian power, Antony committed suicide, soon followed by Cleopatra. It was the end of 58 years of civil war and of the Roman Republic, but the Roman Empire had been born.

Navy soldier 125 BCE

Navy soldier 31 BCE

Navy soldier 357 CE

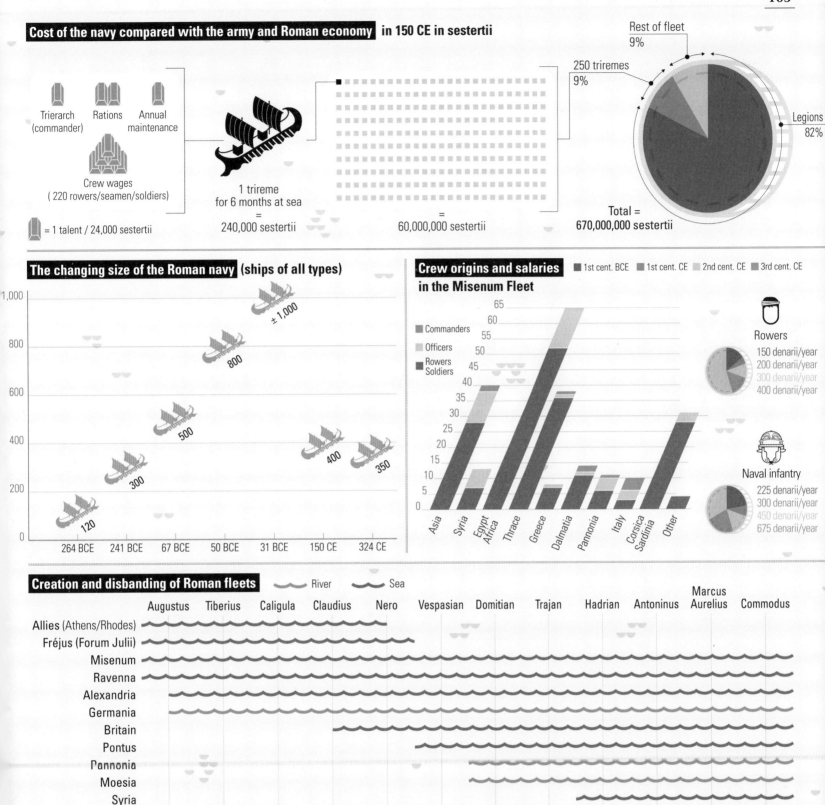

Cost of the navy compared with the army and Roman economy in 150 CE in sestertii

Trierarch (commander)
Rations
Annual maintenance
Crew wages (220 rowers/seamen/soldiers)

= 1 talent / 24,000 sestertii

1 trireme for 6 months at sea
=
240,000 sestertii

=
60,000,000 sestertii

Total = 670,000,000 sestertii

Rest of fleet 9%
250 triremes 9%
Legions 82%

The changing size of the Roman navy (ships of all types)

1,000
800
600
400
200
0

± 1,000
800
500
400
350
300
120

264 BCE   241 BCE   67 BCE   50 BCE   31 BCE   150 CE   324 CE

Crew origins and salaries in the Misenum Fleet

■ 1st cent. BCE ■ 1st cent. CE ■ 2nd cent. CE ■ 3rd cent. CE

■ Commanders
■ Officers
■ Rowers Soldiers

65 60 55 50 45 40 35 30 25 20 15 10 5 0

Asia Syria Egypt Africa Thrace Greece Dalmatia Pannonia Italy Corsica Sardinia Other

Rowers
150 denarii/year
200 denarii/year
300 denarii/year
400 denarii/year

Naval infantry
225 denarii/year
300 denarii/year
450 denarii/year
675 denarii/year

Creation and disbanding of Roman fleets   River   Sea

Augustus Tiberius Caligula Claudius Nero Vespasian Domitian Trajan Hadrian Antoninus Marcus Aurelius Commodus

Allies (Athens/Rhodes)
Fréjus (Forum Julii)
Misenum
Ravenna
Alexandria
Germania
Britain
Pontus
Pannonia
Moesia
Syria
Libya

After the restoration of peace in Rome and the Mediterranean, the navy was consolidated as an integral part of the armed forces, but it was only under Nero that the Roman fleet became truly autonomous, with no assistance from long-time seafaring allies (although many crew members still originated from Rome's maritime provinces). The navy's principal ports were Misenum and Ravenna. Over time, secondary fleets were created and dispatched as needed to Britain or to the regions of the Mediterranean, such as Syria, Egypt or other parts of Africa. Some detachments were also given permanent postings in a particular port, including Caesarea in Mauretania and Ptolemais in Libya, and, later on, ports on the Rhine and the Danube, and on the Black Sea. There was never any permanent naval presence on the Euphrates, although it would have been extremely useful to the army. Unfortunately, it proved impossible to navigate this river against the current, and towing would have taken too much time and overstretched the resources available. The Roman army did, however, include detachments of sailors in its campaigns against the Parthians, and it sometimes built boats in situ to transport troops and equipment.

WARS AND CAMPAIGNS

I. CIVIL WARS

The history of Rome is punctuated by civil wars, which were too numerous to describe here in full. The earliest conflicts were basically fought within the city and its surrounds: 494 BCE, for example, saw the first *secessio plebis*, in which the plebeians of the city assembled on the Mons Sacer (Sacred Mountain), 4.5 km from Rome, to demand more political rights; this led to the foundation of the Plebeian Council. Uprisings of this kind reflected the slow evolution of Roman institutions, although advances were triggered by key events such as the publication in 451–449 BCE of the Twelve Tables, which outlined legal principles and paved the way for the gradual concession of equal political rights for all citizens.

After the centuries of external wars to safeguard Rome's future, internal political conflicts emerged again in the late 2nd century BCE within the city itself, as a result of opposition to the reforms proposed by the Gracchus brothers. Thirty years later, Italian allies living under Latin law, who had substantial weight inside the armed forces, demanded rights as full Roman citizens. This confrontation escalated into the bloody Social War (so named because the word for allies was *socii*), which raged from 90 to 88 BCE. In 89 BCE, the Plautia Papiria became law, granting the right of citizenship to all Italians living to the south of the River Po and eventually bringing this devastating civil war to an end. Some of the main actors in the conflict, such as Gaius Marius (who was fairly sympathetic to the insurgents), took advantage of their military rank to establish themselves on the political stage in Rome. After the Marian reforms of 107 BCE, however, legionaries were at odds with the Roman State for 25 years, as their allegiance shifted between different charismatic generals, both during their service and afterwards. This state of affairs had such significant political repercussions that it was directly responsible for the many military engagements that ensued in the first half of the 1st century BCE. Political opportunists, including major figures of the time – Gaius Marius and Sulla, followed by Crassus, Pompey and Caesar – took advantage of Rome's military difficulties in Italy and the provinces to appoint themselves to positions of command, thereby hoping to achieve victories that would not only strengthen their hand in Rome but also fill their coffers with spoils. Gaius Marius and Sulla, for example, came into dispute over the command in the East against Mithridates VI, who had conquered part of Greece in 88 BCE. Their rivalry was eventually resolved when Sulla marched on Rome and claimed leadership of the army that had been sent to fight this war. He succeeded in driving Mithridates out of Greece and Ionia before confining him to the Black Sea region. The war was rekindled, however, in 74 BCE, when Nicomedus IV bequeathed the kingdom of Bithynia to Rome. Various commanders were dispatched to fight against Mithridates, notably Lucullus, but, despite some successes, the Romans became bogged down in around 69 BCE. In 73–72 BCE, during the final throes of the conflicts in the East and the disorder stirred up in the south of the Italian peninsula by the Social War, a Thracian gladiator called Spartacus led a successful uprising of slaves in the latter region. As for Pompey, who had been outstanding in the Social War, he was dispatched in 67 BCE to put an end to the pirates who were terrorizing the Dalmatian coast. The following year, he was sent to fight against Mithridates, whom he defeated for once and for all, and went on to quell unrest in Syria and Asia Minor. Shortly afterwards, the consul Julius Caesar went to war against the Gauls, under the pretext of a Germanic threat to Gallia Narbonensis.

A struggle for supreme power was inevitable. Crassus, a member of an informal group known as the First Triumvirate alongside Pompey and Caesar, also wanted to strengthen his position. He launched an attack on the kingdom of Parthia, but his expedition proved a disaster and was brought to a halt in 63 BCE. The enmity between Pompey and Caesar intensified in 50 BCE, when Caesar sought a second term as consul. Eventually, on 11 January 49 BCE, after the proposals put forward by Caesar's supporters, including Mark Antony, were rejected out of hand by the Senate (which was in thrall to Pompey), Caesar entered Italy and marched on Rome. Pompey fled with a group of senators to Greece and Macedonia. Caesar settled matters in Rome before turning towards Hispania, where he neutralized the legions loyal to Pompey. After being re-elected as a consul for the year 48 BCE, he crossed the Adriatic, taking Pompey by surprise, but he was unable to gain a decisive victory. Caesar then lured Pompey to Thessalia and finally managed to defeat him in Pharsalus in August 48 BCE. Pompey was assassinated shortly afterwards, on 28 September 48 BCE, at the orders of Ptolemy XIII, king of Egypt, where he had taken refuge.

War returned to Rome after Caesar's assassination on 15 March 44 BCE. Caesar's assassins (the Liberators) and Caesar's former supporters (the Caesarians) formed opposing sides, and the Caesarians also battled amongst themselves. The strong and popular Mark Antony, and the adopted son of Caesar, Octavian, joined forces with Lepidus to defend Caesar's legacy, while the Liberators tried to divide the Caesarians. On 1 January 43 BCE, the Senate granted Octavian the right of *propraetor imperium* (power to command), as well as other privileges, particularly that of being able to stand for election as a consul ten years earlier than the required legal age. In April 43 BCE, Antony was defeated at the Battle of Mutina by an opposing force whose numbers now included Octavian, who marched on Rome and was subsequently elected as a consul on 19 August 43 BCE. He soon made his peace with Antony and Lepidus, and in November of that year, the Roman State officially instated them as joint rulers, known as the Second Triumvirate. This trio shared the Roman provinces between them and published proscriptive denunciations of their enemies in order to seize their wealth.

The first task facing the Second Triumvirate was to rid themselves of Caesar's assassins, some of whom had taken refuge in Egypt and the East. The two sides met in two battles in Philippi (Macedonia) in September and October 42 BCE, with the Triumvirate coming out on top. This victory quickly ushered in a second wave of conflicts, however, driven by quarrels between Octavian and Antony. The latter had acquired enormous wealth in the East, while Octavian controlled Rome and Italy, with its symbolic importance. By 34 BCE, their relationship had deteriorated badly, and things came to a head on 2 September 31 BCE at the Battle of Actium, a naval confrontation between Octavian's fleets and those of Mark Antony and Cleopatra. Octavian emerged victorious, and the following year, on 30 August, he further underlined his superiority at the Battle of Alexandria, thus bringing an end to this civil war.

The imperial regime that was now ushered in by Octavian, who became Emperor Augustus, was not immune to the problem of civil conflict, but it nevertheless enjoyed relative stability until 235 CE, when the Empire succumbed to some thirty years of wars between various pretenders to the imperial throne.

OPTIMATES	Emergence of factions 133 BCE	POPULARES

OPTIMATES

'The best men'

Conservatives

POPULARES

'Favouring the people'

Reformers

| Senate | Magistrates | | Tribunes | Magistrates | Assemblies |

Political representatives

- Supporting the authority of the Senate
- Maintaining the oligarchy
- Reserving magistrate posts for the elite

Political goals

- Protecting and extending the freedoms of the common people (plebeians)
- Improving the living conditions of the plebeians

Political reforms

Nothing should change **0**

1 **Agrarian laws** (redistribution of public land, foundation of colonies, limits on the size of properties on public land)

2 **Grain laws** (controlling the price of grain in Rome, and eventually making it free to the poorest residents)

3 **Reduction of debts**

4 **Opening Roman citizenship to Italian allies**

5 **Control of courts passed to equestrian class**

Principal members

GNAEUS & MARCUS
OCTAVIUS

MARCUS LICINIUS
CRASSUS

GAIUS SEMPRONIUS
GRACCHUS

TIBERIUS
GRACCHUS

LUCIUS CORNELIUS
SULLA

GAIUS
MARIUS

MARCUS PORCIUS
CATO

LUCIUS CORNELIUS
CINNA

CATILINE

GAIUS CASSIUS
LONGINUS

PUBLIUS CLODIUS
PULCHER

GAIUS PAPIRIUS
CARBO

MARCUS TULLIUS
CICERO

GNAEUS MAGNUS
POMPEY

GAIUS JULIUS
CAESAR

MARCUS AEMILIUS
LEPIDUS

LUCIUS LICINIUS
LUCULLUS

LUCIUS
OPIMIUS

MARCUS JUNIUS
BRUTUS

MARK
ANTONY

GAIUS JULIUS CAESAR
(OCTAVIAN)

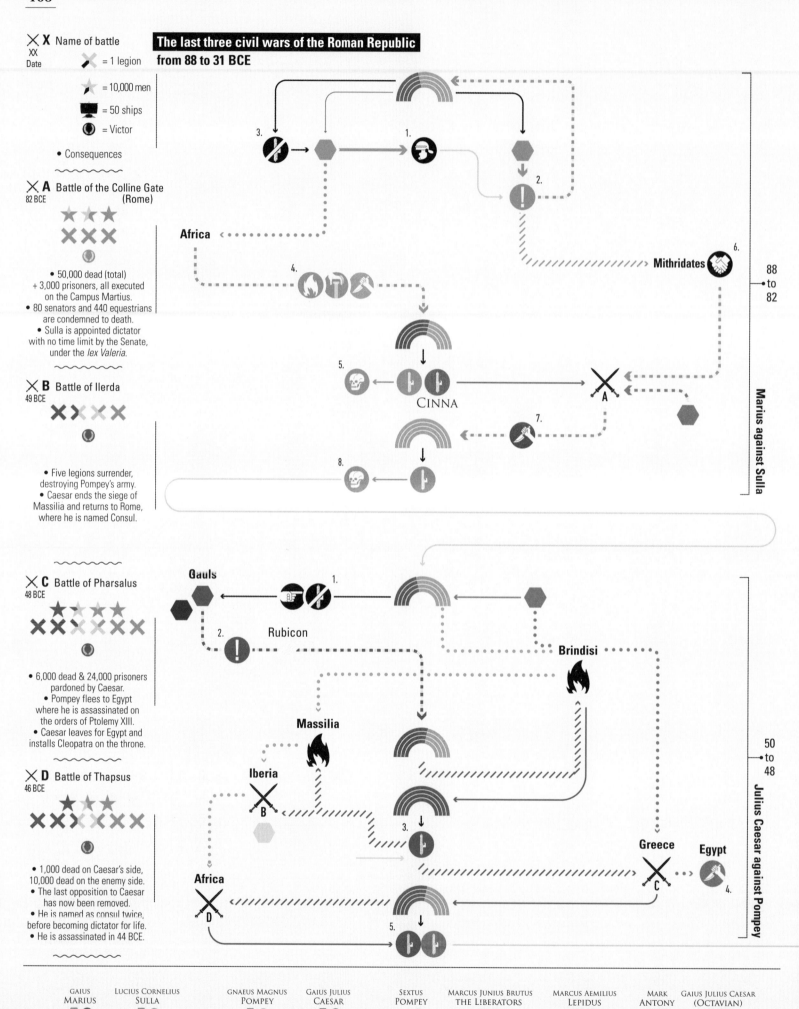

The last three civil wars of the Roman Republic from 88 to 31 BCE

X Name of battle
XX Date

= 1 legion

★ = 10,000 men

= 50 ships

= Victor

• Consequences

A Battle of the Colline Gate (Rome)
82 BCE

★ ★ ★
✗ ✗ ✗

• 50,000 dead (total) + 3,000 prisoners, all executed on the Campus Martius.
• 80 senators and 440 equestrians are condemned to death.
• Sulla is appointed dictator with no time limit by the Senate, under the *lex Valeria*.

B Battle of Ilerda
49 BCE

✗ ✗ ✗ ✗

• Five legions surrender, destroying Pompey's army.
• Caesar ends the siege of Massilia and returns to Rome, where he is named Consul.

C Battle of Pharsalus
48 BCE

★ ★ ★ ★
✗ ✗ ✗ ✗ ✗

• 6,000 dead & 24,000 prisoners pardoned by Caesar.
• Pompey flees to Egypt where he is assassinated on the orders of Ptolemy XIII.
• Caesar leaves for Egypt and installs Cleopatra on the throne.

D Battle of Thapsus
46 BCE

★ ★ ★
✗ ✗ ✗ ✗ ✗ ✗

• 1,000 dead on Caesar's side, 10,000 dead on the enemy side.
• The last opposition to Caesar has now been removed.
• He is named as consul twice, before becoming dictator for life.
• He is assassinated in 44 BCE.

Africa

Mithridates

CINNA

Gauls

Rubicon

Brindisi

Massilia

Iberia

Africa

Greece

Egypt

88 to 82

Marius against Sulla

50 to 48

Julius Caesar against Pompey

GAIUS **MARIUS**

LUCIUS CORNELIUS **SULLA**

GNAEUS MAGNUS **POMPEY**

GAIUS JULIUS **CAESAR**

SEXTUS **POMPEY**

MARCUS JUNIUS BRUTUS **THE LIBERATORS**

MARCUS AEMILIUS **LEPIDUS**

MARK **ANTONY**

GAIUS JULIUS CAESAR **(OCTAVIAN)**

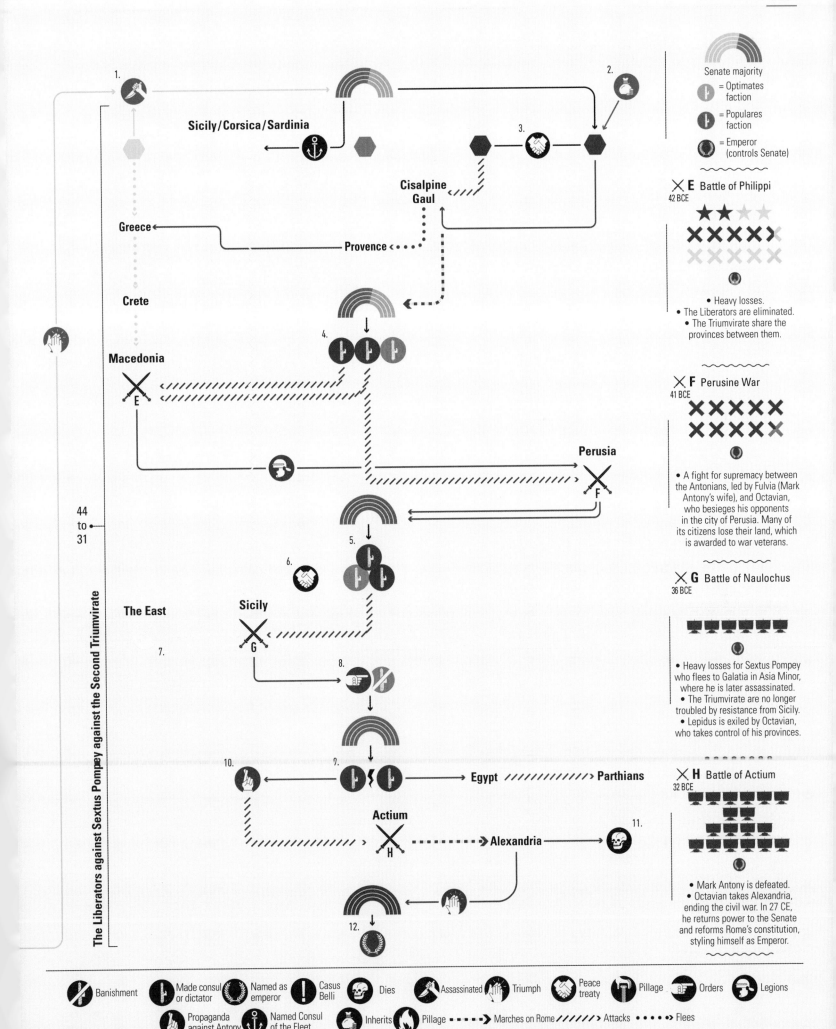

The Liberators against Sextus Pompey against the Second Triumvirate

44 to 31

Sicily/Corsica/Sardinia

Cisalpine Gaul

Greece

Provence

Crete

Macedonia

Perusia

The East

Sicily

Egypt ⟶ Parthians

Actium

Alexandria

Senate majority

= Optimates faction

= Populares faction

= Emperor (controls Senate)

✕ E Battle of Philippi
42 BCE

• Heavy losses.
• The Liberators are eliminated.
• The Triumvirate share the provinces between them.

✕ F Perusine War
41 BCE

• A fight for supremacy between the Antonians, led by Fulvia (Mark Antony's wife), and Octavian, who besieges his opponents in the city of Perusia. Many of its citizens lose their land, which is awarded to war veterans.

✕ G Battle of Naulochus
36 BCE

• Heavy losses for Sextus Pompey who flees to Galatia in Asia Minor, where he is later assassinated.
• The Triumvirate are no longer troubled by resistance from Sicily.
• Lepidus is exiled by Octavian, who takes control of his provinces.

✕ H Battle of Actium
32 BCE

• Mark Antony is defeated.
• Octavian takes Alexandria, ending the civil war. In 27 CE, he returns power to the Senate and reforms Rome's constitution, styling himself as Emperor.

Banishment | Made consul or dictator | Named as emperor | Casus Belli | Dies | Assassinated | Triumph | Peace treaty | Pillage | Orders | Legions

Propaganda against Antony | Named Consul of the Fleet | Inherits | Pillage | - - -▶ Marches on Rome | ////▶ Attacks | • • •▶ Flees

II. CARTHAGE

Carthage was founded in 814 BCE and it had long looked to the sea to extend its influence. It started by competing with the Phoenicians and the Greeks for control over the Mediterranean trade routes. It was set on a peninsula, enclosed to the rear by a defensive wall running for almost 33 km. Its population is difficult to ascertain. According to the historian Strabo, it had 700,000 inhabitants in 149 BCE, but this figure is far higher than those found elsewhere. It seems that in 146 BCE the Carthaginian army had a total of 30,000 men, and the city's last line of defence, men and women, numbered no more than 50,000. The population could not, therefore, have exceeded these figures, although they were complemented by the population of the city's outlying territory, between Susa and Annaba. By the 3rd century BCE, Carthage ruled over an empire that stretched along the North African coastline from Tlemcen to Tripoli, while also embracing islands – the Balearics, Sardinia, Sicily and, more marginally, Malta – and the coast and hinterlands of Iberia, which were endowed with mines and other resources.

The supremely well-organized state of Carthage undoubtedly perpetuated the aristocratic traditions that marked its origins, but its constitution nevertheless found room for some democratic principles. Relatively little is known about Punic society, but it was apparently controlled by an aristocracy of ship owners, merchants and landlords who monopolized political and religious posts. Rightful male citizens formed a middle class that could vote in the people's assembly, but the status of Carthaginian women remains unclear. As in Rome, there was a class of freed slaves, some of whom rose to wealth, as well as public and private slaves, who could also be prosperous and relatively independent (they even had the right to marry legally). Archaeological discoveries have demonstrated – refuting the claims of ancient writers – that Carthaginian society also played host to numerous foreigners originating from an array of different places.

Carthage's political regime managed to avoid both tyranny and dictatorship through its combination of aristocracy and democracy. In the 3rd–2nd centuries BCE, two *sufetes* were elected every year, largely on the basis of their wealth. Although they were elected and their name means 'judges', contemporary sources often call them 'kings', since they were the heads of state. The sufetes exercised power, and they retained their titles even after they retired from service. They also administered justice, possibly in public, with former sufetes serving as judges. Alongside them was a council of elders, whose members were probably appointed for life by their peers. This council exercised strict control over the sufetes and negotiated the passage of laws, declarations of war and peace treaties with them, as well as receiving foreign ambassadors and dispatching delegations to other lands. The council also included several smaller panels, each with thirty members; these were responsible for overseeing various political issues. In addition, a judicial tribunal called the Council of 104 would judge and debrief generals after a war and also kept watch over Carthage's ruling families, to prevent political manoeuvring. A popular assembly, convened by the sufetes, possessed the right to discuss specific issues such as state budgets, public works projects and the freeing of public slaves. The assembly also nominated Carthage's military leaders and, in peacetime, its governors.

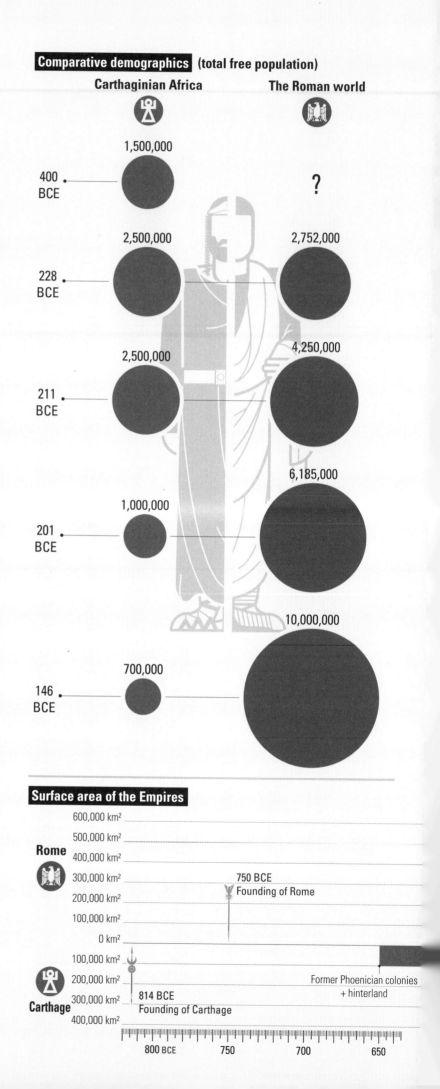

Comparative demographics (total free population)

Carthaginian Africa   The Roman world

400 BCE — 1,500,000   ?

228 BCE — 2,500,000   2,752,000

211 BCE — 2,500,000   4,250,000

201 BCE — 1,000,000   6,185,000

146 BCE — 700,000   10,000,000

Surface area of the Empires

Rome
600,000 km²
500,000 km²
400,000 km²
300,000 km²
200,000 km²
100,000 km²
0 km²

750 BCE
Founding of Rome

Carthage
100,000 km²
200,000 km²
300,000 km²
400,000 km²

814 BCE
Founding of Carthage

Former Phoenician colonies + hinterland

800 BCE   750   700   650

Diplomacy and resources of the Punic Empire

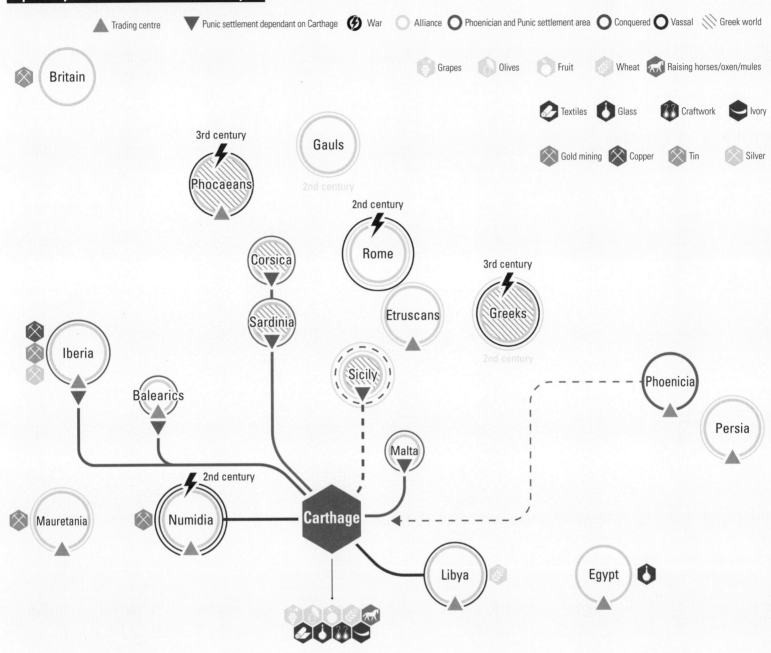

▲ Trading centre ▼ Punic settlement dependant on Carthage ⚡ War ◯ Alliance ◉ Phoenician and Punic settlement area ◯ Conquered ◯ Vassal ⧅ Greek world

Grapes   Olives   Fruit   Wheat   Raising horses/oxen/mules

Textiles   Glass   Craftwork   Ivory

Gold mining   Copper   Tin   Silver

Britain

Gauls
2nd century

3rd century
Phocaeans

Corsica

Sardinia

2nd century
Rome

Etruscans

3rd century
Greeks
2nd century

Iberia

Balearics

Sicily

Phoenicia

Persia

Malta

2nd century
Mauretania   Numidia   Carthage

Libya

Egypt

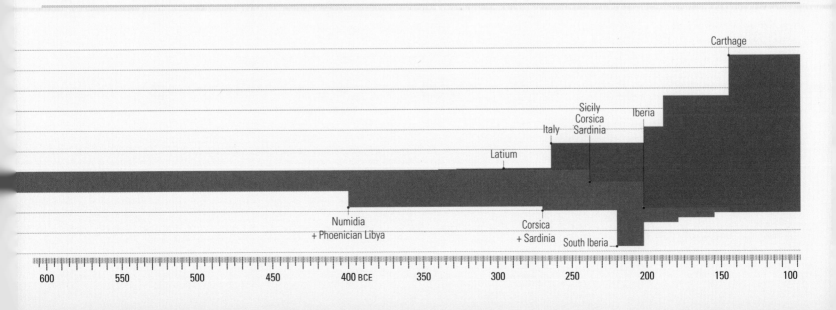

Carthage

Sicily
Corsica
Sardinia

Iberia

Italy

Latium

Numidia
+ Phoenician Libya

Corsica
+ Sardinia

South Iberia

600   550   500   450   400 BCE   350   300   250   200   150   100

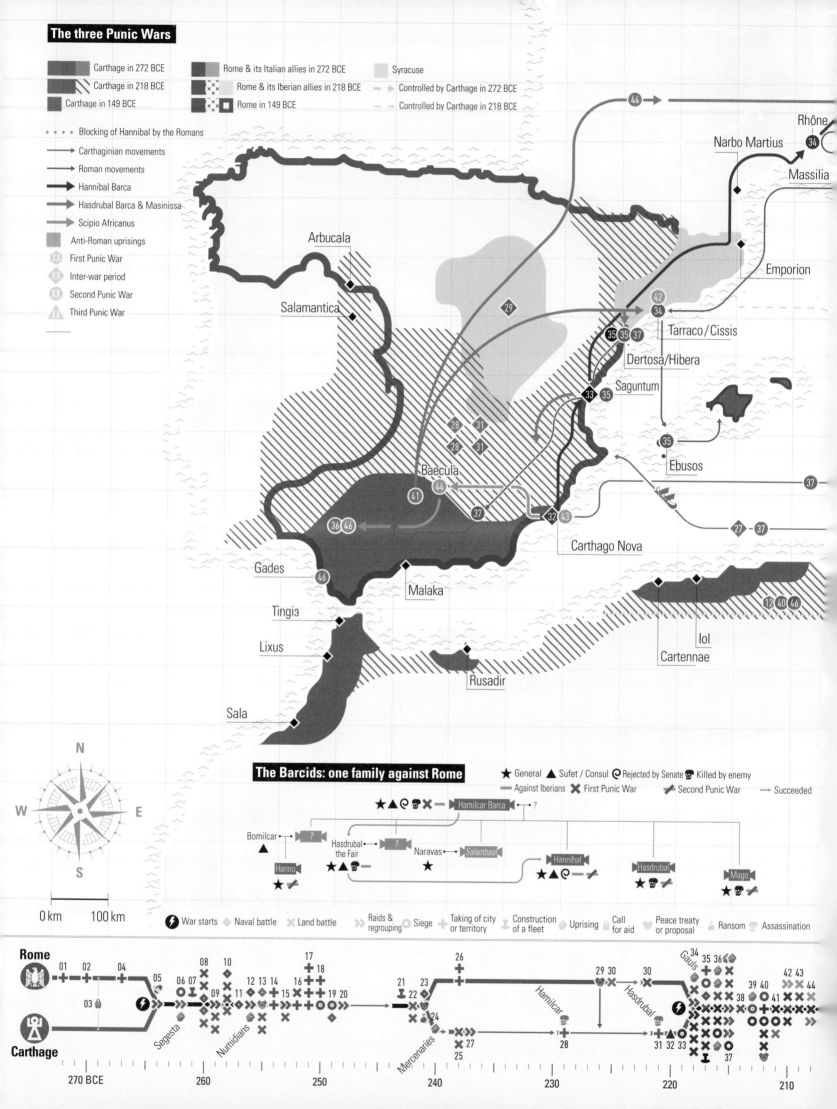

The three Punic Wars

- Carthage in 272 BCE
- Carthage in 218 BCE
- Carthage in 149 BCE
- Rome & its Italian allies in 272 BCE
- Rome & its Iberian allies in 218 BCE
- Rome in 149 BCE
- Syracuse
- Controlled by Carthage in 272 BCE
- Controlled by Carthage in 218 BCE

- ···· Blocking of Hannibal by the Romans
- → Carthaginian movements
- → Roman movements
- → Hannibal Barca
- → Hasdrubal Barca & Masinissa
- → Scipio Africanus
- Anti-Roman uprisings
- First Punic War
- Inter-war period
- Second Punic War
- Third Punic War

Rhône
Narbo Martius
Massilia
Emporion
Tarraco / Cissis
Dertosa/Hibera
Saguntum
Arbucala
Salamantica
Ebusos
Baecula
Carthago Nova
Gades
Malaka
Iol
Cartennae
Tingis
Lixus
Rusadir
Sala

N W E S
0 km   100 km

The Barcids: one family against Rome

★ General ▲ Sufet / Consul ☺ Rejected by Senate ☠ Killed by enemy
— Against Iberians ✗ First Punic War ⚔ Second Punic War → Succeeded

Hamilcar Barca   ?
Bomilcar ?
Hasdrubal the Fair   ?   Naravas   Salambaal
Hanno
Hannibal
Hasdrubal
Mago

⚡ War starts ◆ Naval battle ✗ Land battle ≫ Raids & regrouping ○ Siege ✚ Taking of city or territory ⊥ Construction of a fleet ♙ Uprising Call for aid Peace treaty or proposal Ransom ☠ Assassination

Rome
Carthage

Segesta
Numidians
Mercenaries
Hamilcar
Hasdrubal
Gauls

270 BCE   260   250   240   230   220   210

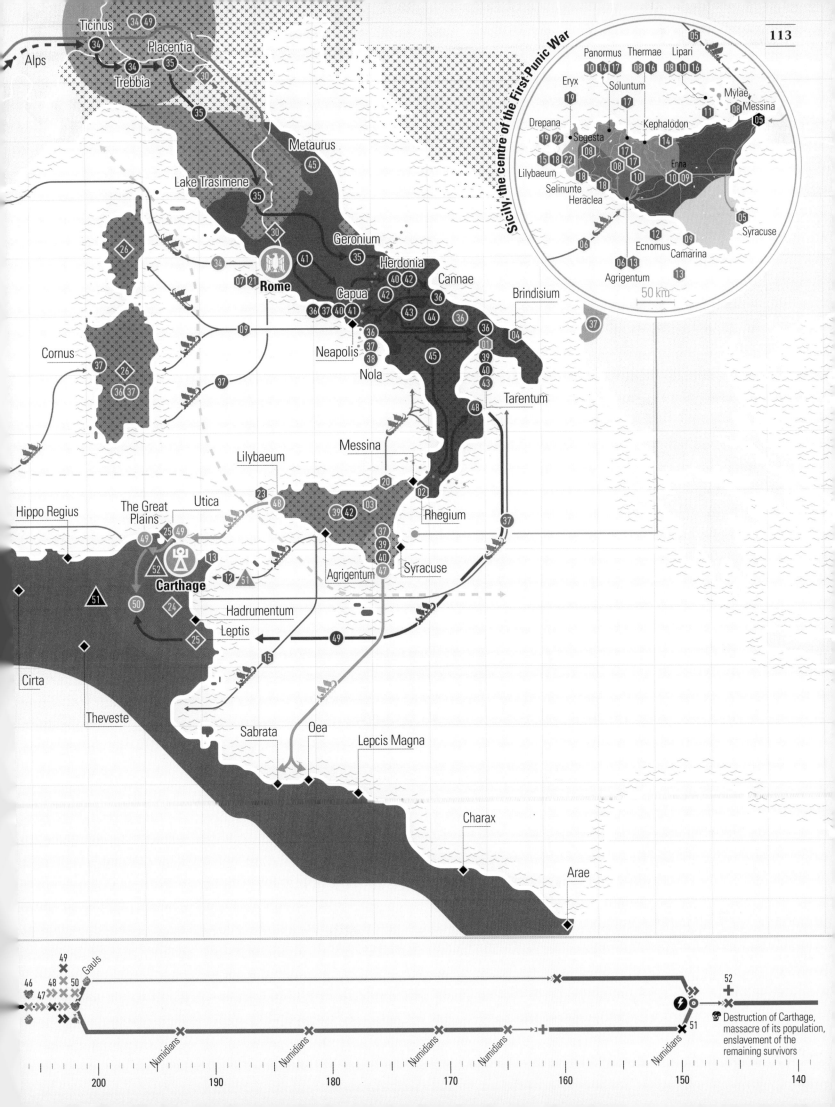

Carthaginian military roles

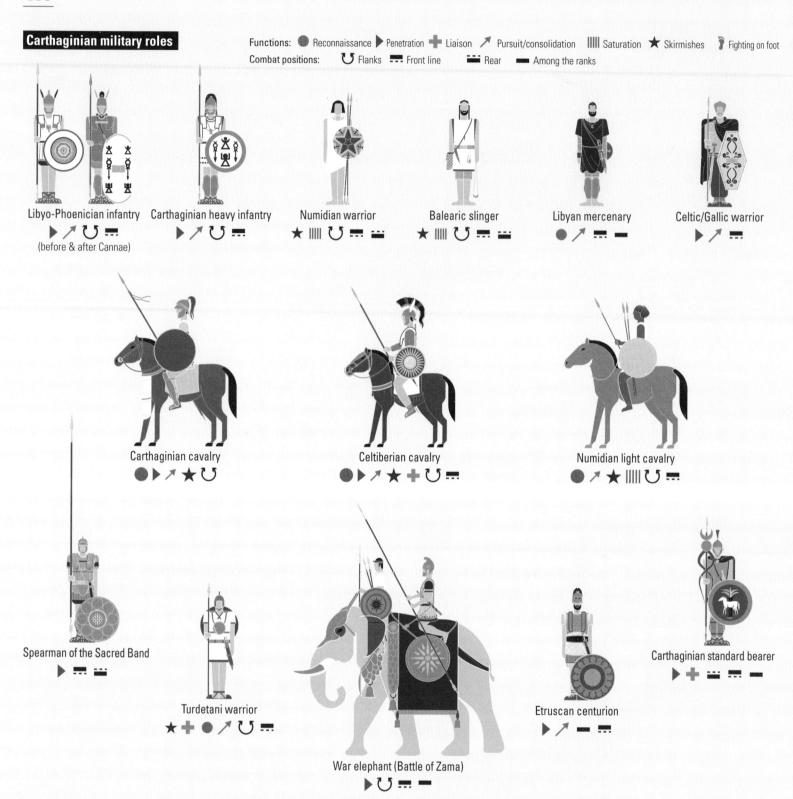

Functions: ● Reconnaissance ▶ Penetration ✚ Liaison ↗ Pursuit/consolidation ||||| Saturation ★ Skirmishes 🦶 Fighting on foot

Combat positions: � Flanks ⋯ Front line ▬▬ Rear ▬ Among the ranks

Libyo-Phoenician infantry
▶ ↗ � ⋯
(before & after Cannae)

Carthaginian heavy infantry
▶ ↗ � ⋯

Numidian warrior
★ ||||| � ⋯ ▬▬

Balearic slinger
★ ||||| � ⋯ ▬▬

Libyan mercenary
● ↗ ▬▬ ▬

Celtic/Gallic warrior
▶ ↗ ▬▬

Carthaginian cavalry
● ▶ ↗ ★ �

Celtiberian cavalry
● ▶ ↗ ★ ✚ � ⋯

Numidian light cavalry
● ↗ ★ ||||| � ⋯

Spearman of the Sacred Band
▶ ▬▬ ▬▬

Turdetani warrior
★ ✚ ● ↗ � ▬▬

War elephant (Battle of Zama)
▶ � ▬▬ ▬

Etruscan centurion
▶ ↗ ▬▬ ⋯

Carthaginian standard bearer
▶ ✚ ▬▬ ▬▬ ▬

Carthage never established a standing army, out of distrust. The army generals were elected by the popular assembly and overseen by the council of elders; its other ranks were filled by citizens, subjects from territories controlled by Carthage, soldiers from allied forces and, finally, mercenaries. Little is known, however, about the details of its hierarchical structure, while the estimates given for its total headcount are often fanciful.

This veritable melting pot was organized into units defined along ethnic lines that provided the army's mid-ranking officers – but their superiors were always Carthaginian aristocrats. Citizens, who were in the minority, were assigned to serve in the infantry. Conscripts from territories controlled by Carthage came from Africa, Iberia and the Balearic islands. The Africans (from what is now Libya) formed a light infantry detachment armed with javelins, daggers and round shields. The Iberians, considered allies more than subjects, also served in the light infantry, while the Balearic soldiers were closer to being mercenaries. Other major sources of support for the Carthaginian army included the Numidians – highly prized for their horsemanship – as well as Transalpine and Cisalpine Gaul, Liguria, and Italian cities such as Capua.

The army largely consisted of infantry – revolving around the Sacred Band, an elite unit that could withstand heavy enemy attacks – and it generally went into battle in several lines of tightly packed phalanxes, flanked by cavalry and elephants. There is little record of archers, and perhaps surprisingly, the Carthaginian navy never played a decisive role, even though it was equipped with quinqueremes.

The major battles of the Second Punic War

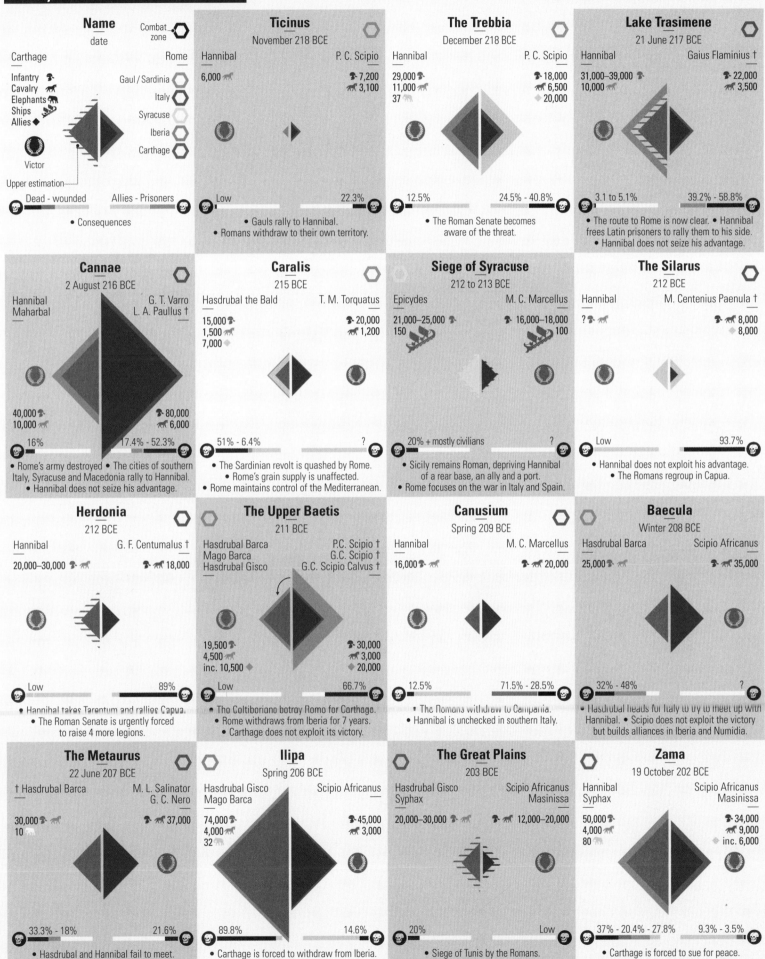

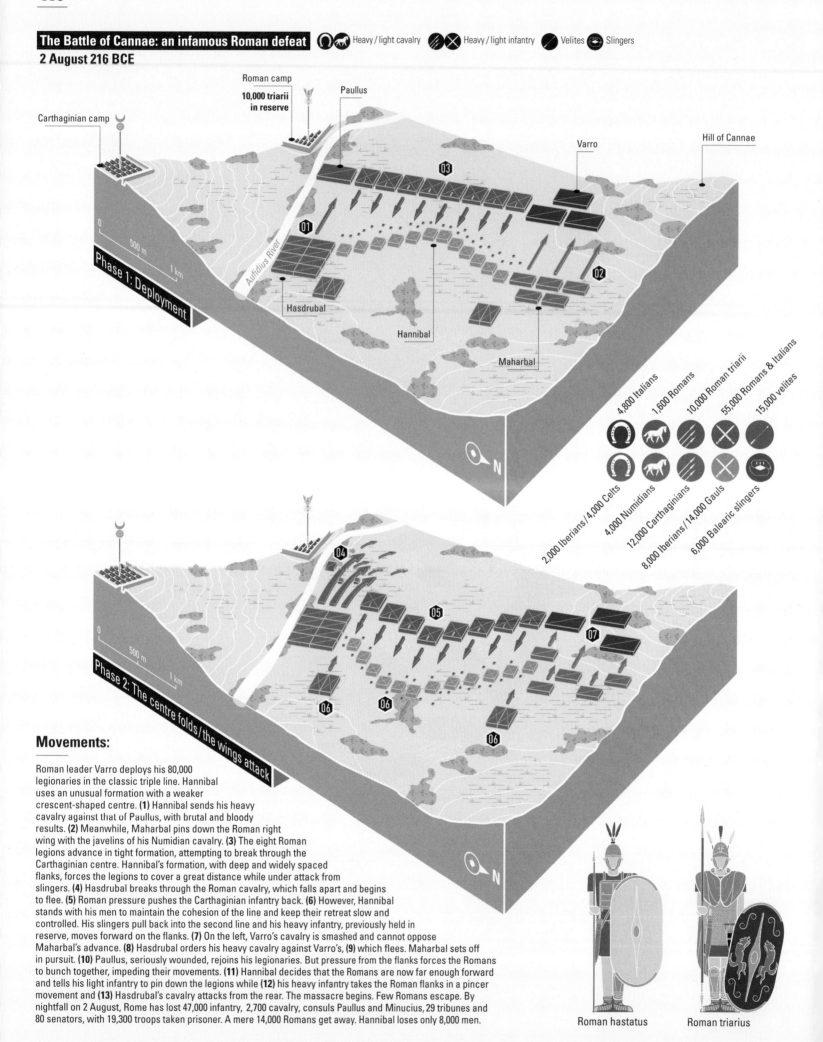

The Battle of Cannae: an infamous Roman defeat

2 August 216 BCE

Ω🐎 Heavy / light cavalry ⚔✕ Heavy / light infantry ◣ Velites 👝 Slingers

Carthaginian camp

Roman camp
10,000 triarii in reserve

Paullus

Varro

Hill of Cannae

03

01

02

Hasdrubal

Hannibal

Maharbal

Aufidius River

Phase 1: Deployment

0   500 m   1 km

N

Phase 2: The centre folds / the wings attack

0   500 m   1 km

04

05

07

06

06

06

N

4,800 Italians — 2,000 Iberians / 4,000 Celts

1,600 Romans — 4,000 Numidians

10,000 Roman triarii — 12,000 Carthaginians

55,000 Romans & Italians — 8,000 Iberians / 14,000 Gauls

15,000 velites — 6,000 Balearic slingers

Movements:

Roman leader Varro deploys his 80,000 legionaries in the classic triple line. Hannibal uses an unusual formation with a weaker crescent-shaped centre. **(1)** Hannibal sends his heavy cavalry against that of Paullus, with brutal and bloody results. **(2)** Meanwhile, Maharbal pins down the Roman right wing with the javelins of his Numidian cavalry. **(3)** The eight Roman legions advance in tight formation, attempting to break through the Carthaginian centre. Hannibal's formation, with deep and widely spaced flanks, forces the legions to cover a great distance while under attack from slingers. **(4)** Hasdrubal breaks through the Roman cavalry, which falls apart and begins to flee. **(5)** Roman pressure pushes the Carthaginian infantry back. **(6)** However, Hannibal stands with his men to maintain the cohesion of the line and keep their retreat slow and controlled. His slingers pull back into the second line and his heavy infantry, previously held in reserve, moves forward on the flanks. **(7)** On the left, Varro's cavalry is smashed and cannot oppose Maharbal's advance. **(8)** Hasdrubal orders his heavy cavalry against Varro's, **(9)** which flees. Maharbal sets off in pursuit. **(10)** Paullus, seriously wounded, rejoins his legionaries. But pressure from the flanks forces the Romans to bunch together, impeding their movements. **(11)** Hannibal decides that the Romans are now far enough forward and tells his light infantry to pin down the legions while **(12)** his heavy infantry takes the Roman flanks in a pincer movement and **(13)** Hasdrubal's cavalry attacks from the rear. The massacre begins. Few Romans escape. By nightfall on 2 August, Rome has lost 47,000 infantry, 2,700 cavalry, consuls Paullus and Minucius, 29 tribunes and 80 senators, with 19,300 troops taken prisoner. A mere 14,000 Romans get away. Hannibal loses only 8,000 men.

Roman hastatus   Roman triarius

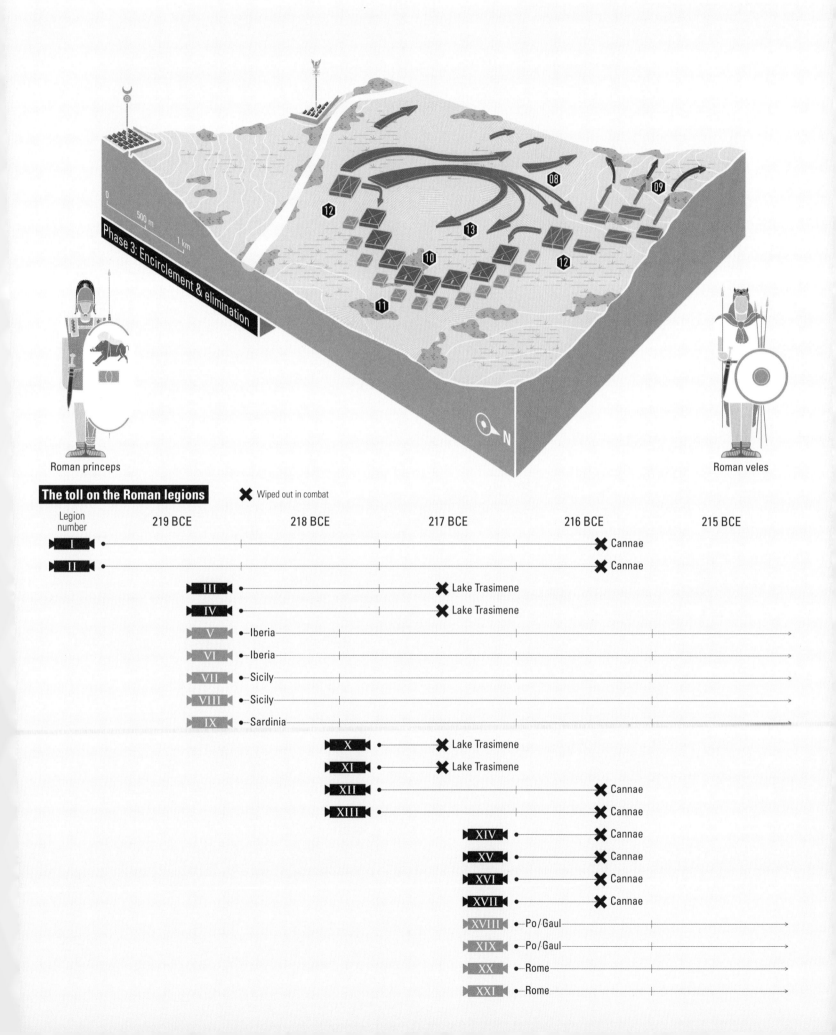

Phase 3: Encirclement & elimination

Roman princeps

Roman veles

N

The toll on the Roman legions

✖ Wiped out in combat

Legion number	219 BCE	218 BCE	217 BCE	216 BCE	215 BCE
I	●			✖ Cannae	
II	●			✖ Cannae	
III	●	✖ Lake Trasimene			
IV	●	✖ Lake Trasimene			
V	● Iberia				
VI	● Iberia				
VII	● Sicily				
VIII	● Sicily				
IX	● Sardinia				
X	●	✖ Lake Trasimene			
XI	●	✖ Lake Trasimene			
XII	●			✖ Cannae	
XIII	●			✖ Cannae	
XIV		●		✖ Cannae	
XV		●		✖ Cannae	
XVI		●		✖ Cannae	
XVII		●		✖ Cannae	
XVIII		● Po/Gaul			
XIX		● Po/Gaul			
XX		● Rome			
XXI		● Rome			

Although the First Punic War was primarily fought at sea, the second was firmly based on land. Two battles in particular were crucial: the Battle of Cannae, in Apulia, southern Italy, and the Battle of Zama, in present-day Tunisia.

The Battle of Cannae took place on 2 August 216 BCE (1 July in the Julian calendar). The consuls Lucius Aemilius Paullus and Gaius Terentius Varro reacted to the capture of a Roman base and storehouse by joining forces to confront Hannibal (consular armies usually went to war on their own). In all, their armies comprised eight legions, plus the equivalent in allied troops. The two consuls alternated the overall command on a daily basis, but they were very different men. Paullus tended towards caution but Varro arrogantly sought victory at any cost.

Hannibal astutely made his move when it was Varro's turn to lead the Roman troops. He also chose a battlefield that put the Romans at a disadvantage, as the river to their right blocked any

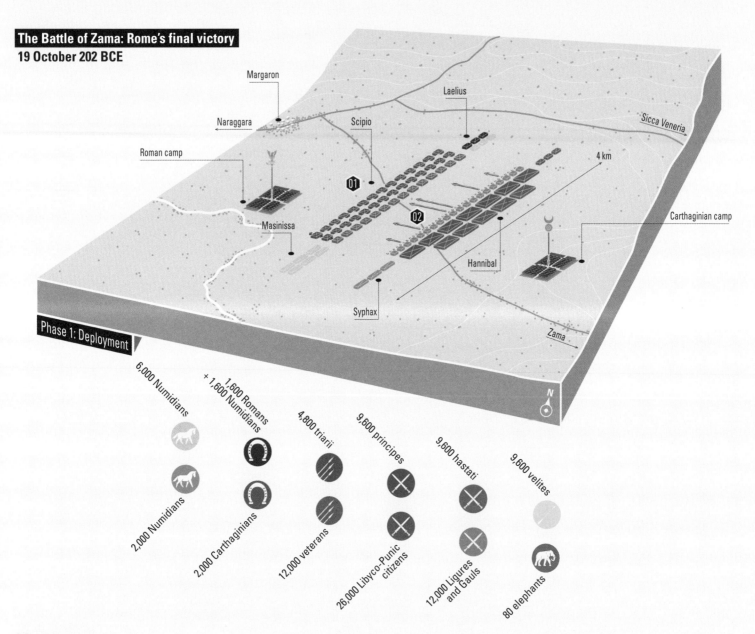

The Battle of Zama: Rome's final victory
19 October 202 BCE

Margaron

Laelius

Naraggara

Scipio

Sicca Veneria

Roman camp

01

4 km

Masinissa

02

Carthaginian camp

Hannibal

Syphax

Zama

Phase 1: Deployment

N

6,000 Numidians

1,600 Romans + 1,600 Numidians

4,800 triarii

9,600 principes

9,600 hastati

9,600 velites

2,000 Numidians

2,000 Carthaginians

12,000 veterans

26,000 Libyco-Punic citizens

12,000 Ligures and Gauls

80 elephants

Movements:

The Battle of Zama was crucial. The Romans had finally tipped the scales and set foot on Carthaginian territory after sixteen years of failure. Hannibal was forced to give up his position in Italy to come to the aid of Carthage, which had urgently recalled him. On 19 October 202 BCE, Hannibal was in a weak position, with few cavalrymen, poorly trained elephants, many newly levied soldiers and only a handful of veterans. Aware of his lack of cavalry and wanting to exhaust the Roman front line before sending in his veterans, he chose to lead with his 80 elephants, in front of a first line of mercenaries from Gaul and Liguria, with troops levied in Africa as a second line and the experienced veterans as a third line. The Punic heavy cavalry was on the right while the Numidian cavalry in the left would be facing another Numidian cavalry troop, newly allied with the Romans. **(1)** Scipio deployed a three-line infantry, but not in the usual quincunx formation. The principii stood behind the first line of hastati, with the triarii behind them. The lanes between these lines were filled by velites, creating what looked like a classic formation. **(2).** Hannibal's elephants attacked but they were scared by the Roman trumpets and charged into the Numidian left wing, **(3)** scattering Hannibal's troops. **(4)** The cavalry of

Masinissa and Laelius then put the Carthaginian cavalry to flight. The rest of the elephants passed through the Roman ranks down the lanes now cleared by the velites, and were slaughtered at the rear. **(5)** Hannibal sent in his mercenaries, but the Roman front line held fast. **(6)** In combat, the mercenaries received little support from the second line and almost came to blows with them before they engaged. **(7)** With the Carthaginian cavalry routed, there was a pause in the battle, in which Scipio called back his hastati and evacuated the wounded. **(8)** He then deployed the hastati in the centre of his line, with the principes and triarii extending the line on both sides to encircle the Carthaginians. Hannibal tried to send in his veterans but **(9)** Masinissa and Laelius returned with their cavalry and attacked the Carthaginians from the rear. The battle was over. Scipio lost between 1,500 and 2,500 men in total; Hannibal lost some 10,000 to 25,000 men, with a similar number taken prisoner. Hannibal fled home to announce the defeat to the Senate, who had to surrender. The peace treaty required Carthage to pay an indemnity of 10,000 silver talents over 50 years and led to the loss of almost all their territory and the destruction of their fleet, definitively ruining all Carthaginian ambitions in the Mediterranean. Carthage never recovered.

retreat. Furthermore, they were blinded by the sun, as well as by the sand and dust blown in their faces by strong winds. The Roman losses in the ensuing battle included Varro himself, two quaestors, 29 military tribunes, 80 senators and several future candidates for the magistrature. In all, the Roman army lost around 50,000 men, while Hannibal only lost some 8,000 of his elite soldiers. The Battle of Cannae became a turning point. It triggered the formation of more mobile fighting units, and it marked the end of the Roman legions' use of phalanx strategies. It also ushered in the appointment of a single military commander, to the detriment of the old tradition of alternating command.

The Second Punic War dragged on until the autumn of 202 BCE, when the Romans met the Carthaginians in Zama, some 30 km to the north of Maktar. This time, Hannibal had the advantage of numbers, but he was fatally hampered by the defection to the Roman side of the highly skilled Numidian cavalry led by Masinissa.

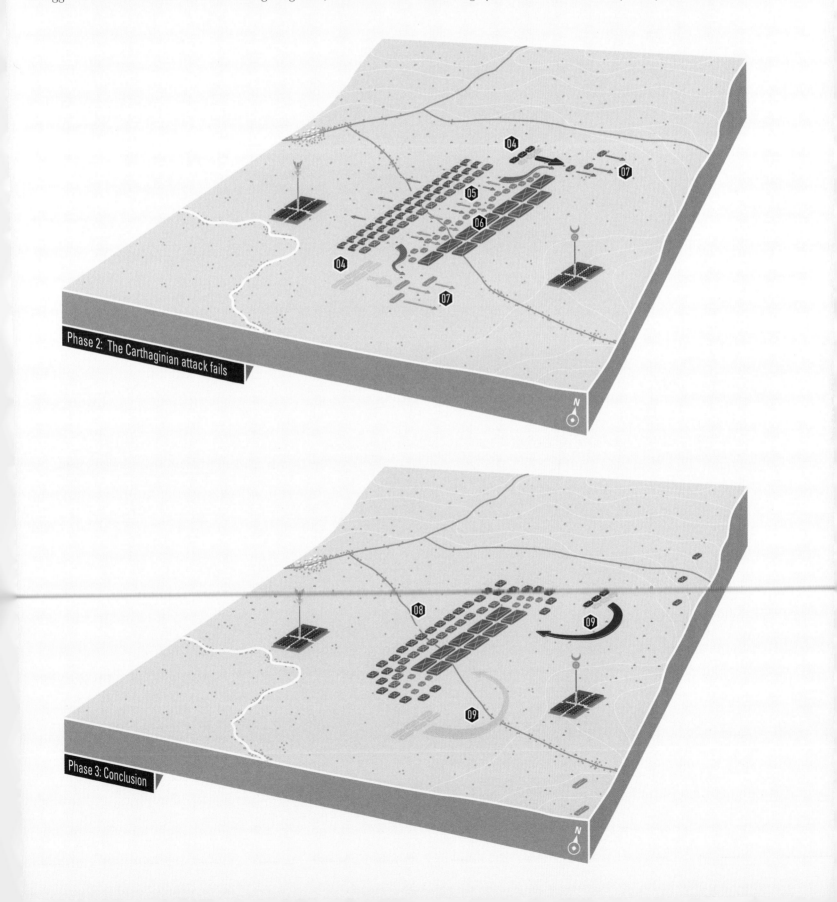

Phase 2: The Carthaginian attack fails

Phase 3: Conclusion

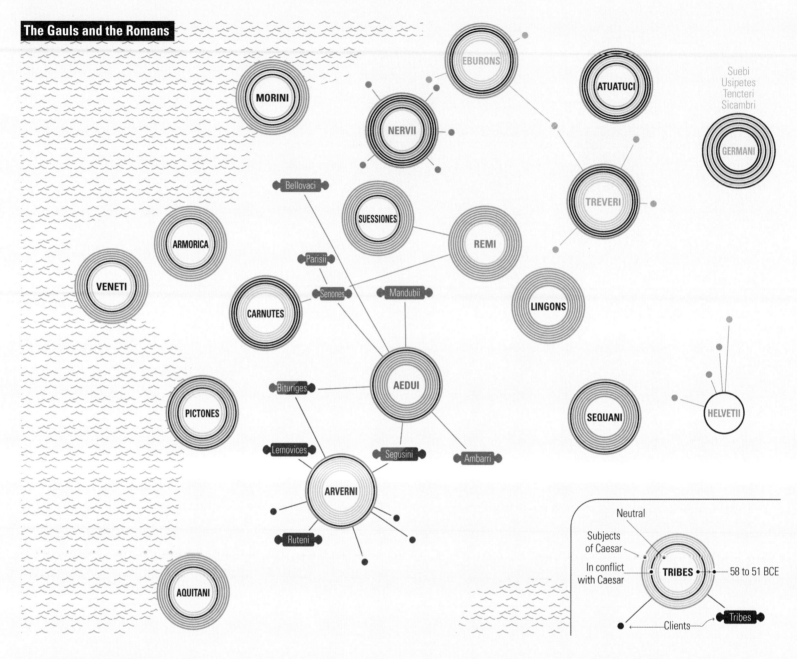

III. THE GALLIC WARS

In the middle of the 1st century BCE, the lands of Gaul found themselves in a paradoxical situation. Although the various Gallic peoples had been socially organized according to the Mediterranean-style, city-based model for around a hundred years and had established links with Gallia Narbonensis and Italy, they were nevertheless vulnerable to two outside threats. Firstly, since the early 1st century BCE, the Germanic peoples had been pushing towards the southwest and had occupied almost all the territory of the Helvetii; secondly, the Upper Rhine had been penetrated by Ariovistus, the king of the Suebi, at the head of a Germani coalition. These events had been closely observed by the Romans, who had not forgotten an earlier invasion by the Cimbri and the Teutons. Furthermore, Rome itself was being shaken at that time by the power struggles between Crassus, Pompey and Caesar. Crassus and, more particularly, Pompey were making political capital out of their recent successes, while Caesar was anxious for an opportunity to boost his own reputation and financial assets in a similar fashion – and he found it in 59 BCE when, after his consulship, he was appointed proconsul of Gaul.

The Gauls were far from united at that juncture, and they did not see themselves as a single nation – quite to the contrary, in fact, since they were continually fighting amongst themselves, at the orders of an extremely wealthy elite (knights who wielded power and patronage over a mass of 'clients'). In central Gaul, the Gallic peoples had been dominated by the Arverni, but they gradually ceded power to the Aedui, who were allies of the Romans. In 71 BCE, the Arverni and the Sequani successfully sought an alliance with the Suebi king, Ariovistus, against the Aedui. At the conclusion of ten years of fighting, it was this coalition that eventually came out on top.

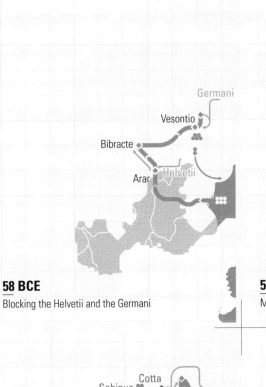

58 BCE
Blocking the Helvetii and the Germani

57 BCE
Marching against the tribes of the North

56 BCE
Campaign against the Veneti and the tribes of the West

55 BCE
First landing in Britain and operations in the East

54 BCE
Second landing in Britain and campaign against the Eburons

53 BCE
The aftermath of Ambiorix's revolt

Julius Caesar's invasion of Gaul
from 58 to 50 BCE

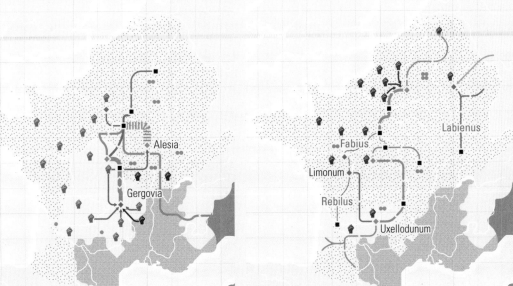

52 BCE
Gallic revolt led by Vercingetorix

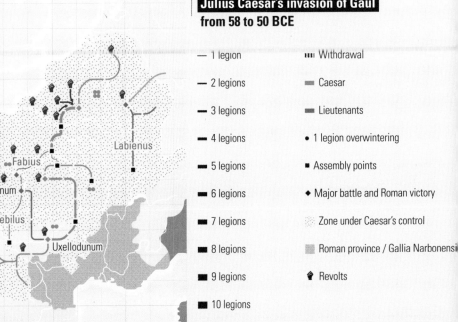

51 BCE
Pacifying the rest of the Gauls

— 1 legion	ⅢⅢ Withdrawal
— 2 legions	▬ Caesar
— 3 legions	▬ Lieutenants
— 4 legions	• 1 legion overwintering
▬ 5 legions	■ Assembly points
▬ 6 legions	◆ Major battle and Roman victory
▬ 7 legions	⠿ Zone under Caesar's control
▬ 8 legions	Roman province / Gallia Narbonensis
▬ 9 legions	⚑ Revolts
▬ 10 legions	
▬ 11 legions	

When the Helvetii decided to migrate westward to settle in Saintonge and set up a Gallic principate with the help of the Aedui, the newly appointed consul Julius Caesar was determined to intervene. Caesar sealed a pact of friendship with Ariovistus so that they could join forces against the Helvetii (the Aedui were divided into two opposing clans and could no longer be trusted). Caesar confronted the Helvetii, who were allied with the Raurici, Tulingi and Latobrigi, along with a group of Boii, and forced them to cross the territory of the Sequani. Caesar's army comprised three legions mobilized in Cisalpine Gaul, supplemented by two new, urgently levied legions and another one commanded by Labienus that was posted in the territory of the Segusini. After one successful skirmish led by Labienus, Caesar had to abandon his pursuit of the Helvetii in order restock his army's food supplies. He marched on Bibracte (on Mount Beuvray), chased by the

Helvetii, who were roundly defeated in the subsequent battle. Caesar allowed them to make their way, however, to the lands of the Lingons (between Langres and Dijon), where they could serve as a buffer against Ariovistus, with whom Caesar also opened up negotiations. These proved fruitless, and so Caesar continued to advance, first to Besançon and then on to Alsace. Ariovistus requested another meeting with Caesar but treacherously used it as an attempt to capture him. An armed confrontation was inevitable, and the resulting Battle of Mulhouse was won by the Romans.

After the winter of 71 BCE, with Caesar now clearly considering the Rhine to be the frontier of the Empire, he had to thwart an attack by the Belgae (from present-day Belgium), with the assistance of the Remi. The two sides met by the river Aisne but avoided any full-scale confrontation as both were short of food supplies. The Gallic forces dispersed and Caesar ended up conquering, one by one, the Bellovaci,

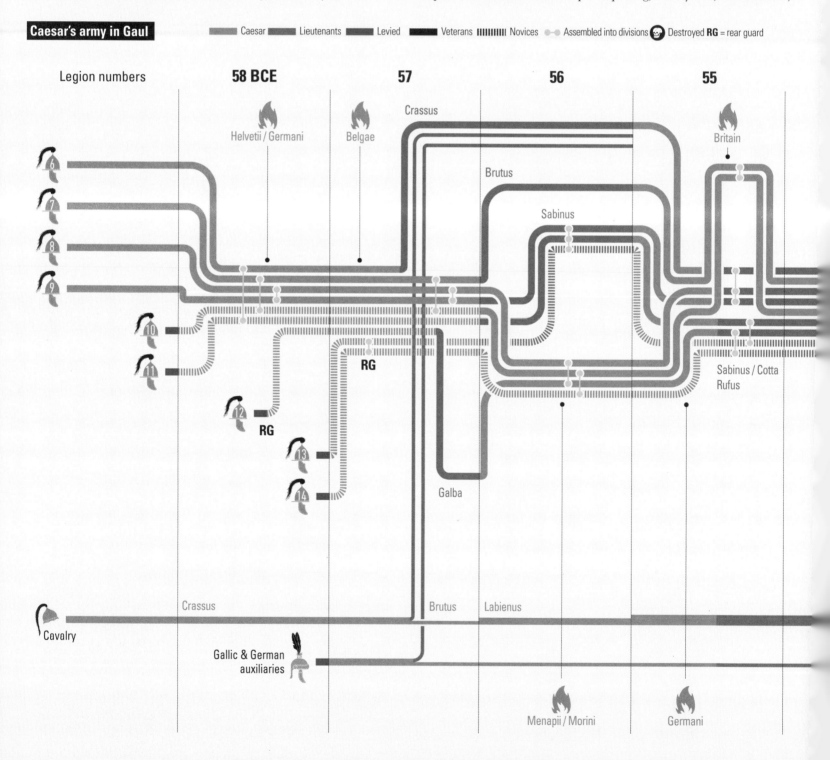

the Ambiones, the Suessiones, the Atuatuci and the Nervii. After the subsequent surrender of the peoples of Normandy, Caesar, believing that Gaul had been entirely conquered, distributed his troops in winter camps in the territories of the Carnutes (Orléans), the Turones (Tours) and the Andecavi (Anjou). The autumn of 56 BCE, however, was marked by an uprising by the Veneti in Morbihan, which forced Rome to mount a new military campaign. Caesar attacked and defeated the Veneti, while his legates brought order to Normandy and marched against the Menapii and the Morini. Nevertheless, Caesar's troops were still vulnerable because poor harvests had obliged him to establish numerous winter camps. In 54 BCE, the chief of the Eburons, Ambiorix, managed to lure Roman troops out of one of these camps, near Liège, and promptly slaughtered a whole legion and half. There followed rebellions by the Nervii, Atuatuci and Treviri, but these were repressed and severely punished the following spring.

The Eburons, meanwhile, were virtually wiped out. Undeterred, the Gallic chiefs took advantage of Caesar's trip to Rome, where he had pressing political issues to deal with, and launched further full-scale rebellions in his absence. A revolt by the Carnutes in the winter of 52 BCE was followed by a call from Vercingetorix, king of the Arverni, for a mass uprising, while, to the east, the Treviri tried to persuade the Germani to join the general insurgency.

Caesar returned to Gaul with new troops and immediately pounced on the Nervii and the Senonii. He then sent his legate, Labienus, to fight the Treviri, who were duly crushed, while Caesar meted out similar treatment to the Menapii. He moved on to the Rhine, with a view to negotiating with the Ubii, a Germanic people, but they had already beaten a retreat.

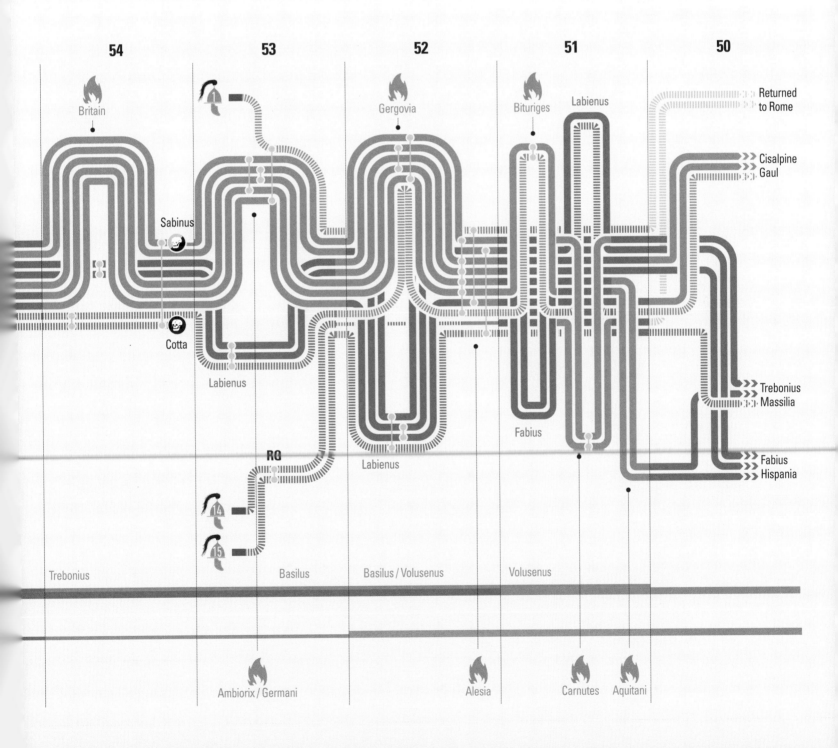

The siege of Alesia
27 September 52 BCE

246,000 (relief forces)

80,000 (army of Vercingetorix) + 8,000 cavalry

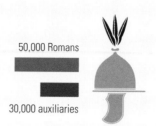

50,000 Romans

30,000 auxiliaries

Gauls

Gauls

Germani

Centurion

Legionary

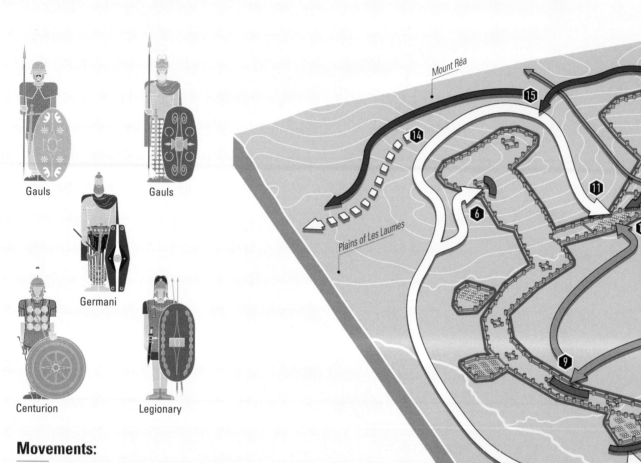

River Rabutin

Mount Réa

Plains of Les Laumes

River Brenne

Movements:

Following a series of losses, Vercingetorix withdrew to the oppidum (fortified settlement) of Alesia (1), where he had made preparations to repeat his victory at the battle of Gergovia. Caesar's twelve legions, in pursuit of the Gauls (2), realized that a trap that had been set for them. Caesar had two walls built (3), one facing the oppidum (the circumvallation), designed to stop anyone from getting out, and the other (the contravallation) facing outwards to counter external attacks. This outer fortification (24 km) included camps and fortlets. While the Romans were building their fortifications, Vercingetorix sent cavalrymen (4) to contact the relief army, a coalition of 240,000 warriors, the majority of whom were Arverni and Aedui, with the addition of tribes from Belgian and Celtic Gaul. The night before the attack, 60,000 Gauls with breaching equipment tried to attack the fortifications at an apparent weak spot (5), but with little success. The next day, the relief army arrived and began to attack the outer fortifications (6) at two points simultaneously. Vercingetorix and his warriors also attempted a sally (7–8), but the inconclusive results drove Vercingetorix to change direction and head for Mount Réa (9). The situation became dangerous for the Romans as the Gauls got past the trenches and began to breach the Roman defences. Caesar had to call for reinforcements from the legions (10). The numerous and well-coordinated Gauls threatened the Roman forces (11). However, Caesar and his generals counterattacked with fresh troops (12), and the Gauls were pushed back. At the same time, Caesar sent his Germanic cavalry to attack the relief army from the rear (13). The latter fled (14), crushing the hopes of the Gauls. They tried to return to their homelands but were pursued by the Romans and were massacred during the night (15). Vercingetorix had no choice but to withdraw (16). He surrendered and was brought before Caesar the next day.

Roman defensive fortifications facing out onto the plain of Les Laumes

Stretch of ground studded with booby traps

8 rows of ditches with stakes

Trench filled with stakes 1.5 m

Ditch filled with water

Ditch

1 tower every 24 m

Trench, 6 m wide

1 m

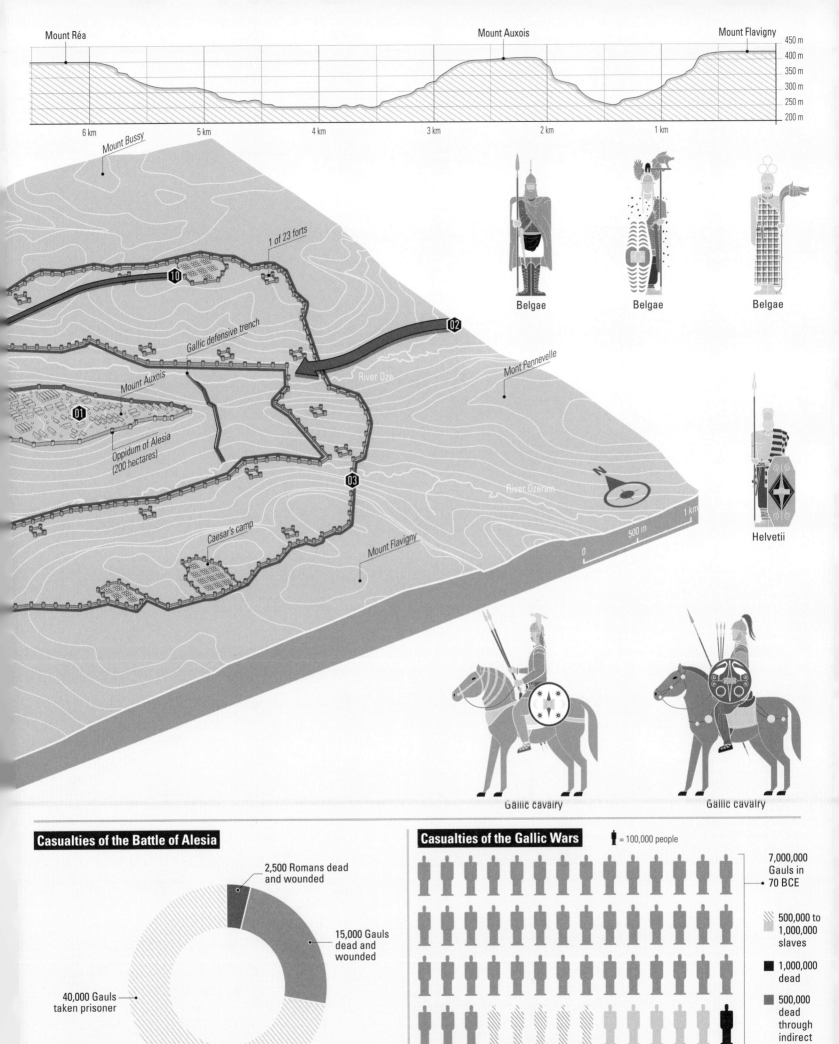

Mount Réa
Mount Auxois
Mount Flavigny

450 m
400 m
350 m
300 m
250 m
200 m

6 km   5 km   4 km   3 km   2 km   1 km

Mount Bussy

1 of 23 forts

10

02

Gallic defensive trench

River Oze

Mont Pennevelle

Mount Auxois

01

Oppidum of Alesia
(200 hectares)

03

River Ozerain

N

1 km

500 m

0

Caesar's camp

Mount Flavigny

Belgae

Belgae

Belgae

Helvetii

Gallic cavalry

Gallic cavalry

Casualties of the Battle of Alesia

2,500 Romans dead
and wounded

15,000 Gauls
dead and
wounded

40,000 Gauls
taken prisoner

Casualties of the Gallic Wars

= 100,000 people

7,000,000
Gauls in
70 BCE

500,000 to
1,000,000
slaves

1,000,000
dead

500,000
dead
through
indirect
causes
(famine &
disease)

IV. SPARTACUS

Slave uprisings were frequent under the Roman Republic, but most were of little consequence. Three of them, however, escalated into full-scale Servile Wars in which the rebels took full advantage of the Romans' vulnerability to local instability. The first two took place in Sicily: from 135–132 BCE, the slave Eunus led rural slaves to create a Hellenic-style kingdom that later served as a model, from 104–100 BCE, for a further rebellion, led by Salvius Tryphon.

It is the slave revolt led by Spartacus (73–71 BCE) that has gained the most renown, however, both at the time and today (largely thanks to Stanley Kubrick's film). This conflict unfurled on the Italian mainland, not in a distant province, and was recorded by various contemporary writers. It arose within the context of the disorganization engendered by the Social War, which was

particularly intense in southern Italy. Spartacus was a Thracian. We do not know how or why he became a slave, but we do know that he found himself in a gladiators' barracks in Capua. He led an initial rebellion of 70 to 78 Thracians, Germans and Gauls (1), who succeeded in attracting the support of shepherds and slaves from large estates. Most of this band was recruited on a march to Naples (2), where they took refuge on the slopes of Vesuvius (3). This was a wealthy area, allowing them to pillage villas and their lands.

Despite his spectacular successes, however, Spartacus never managed to completely control the situation or win over his followers with his ideas. Although Spartacus was elected leader (along with the Celts Crixus and Oenomaus), the revolt did not give rise to a hierarchical organization but rather to a warriors' assembly that was responsible for making decisions. Spartacus's troops came to number around 70,000 men, but it is wrong to imagine an army of gladiators since most were rural slaves. This army spent the winter in Campania. Rome dispatched a praetor with 3,000 men to quell the rebellion, but these troops were inexperienced (the most

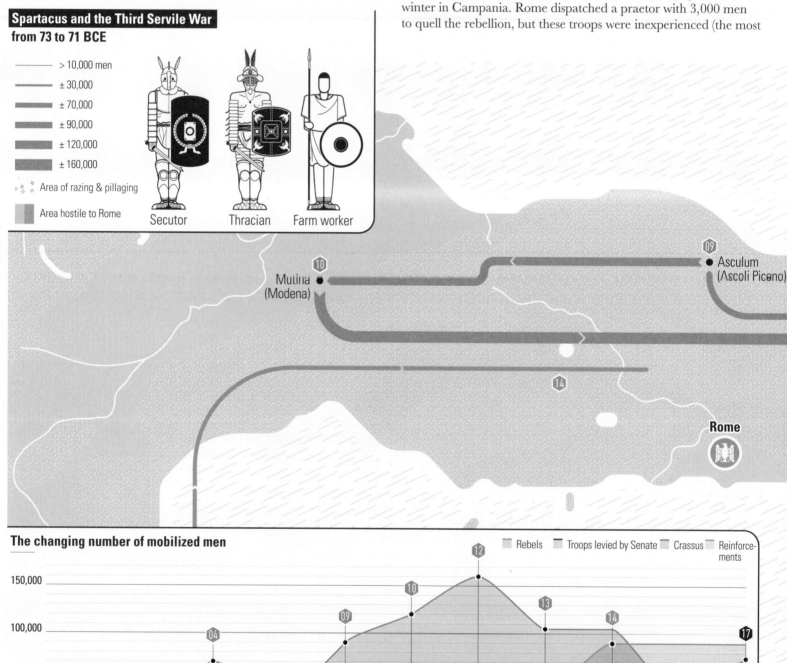

Spartacus and the Third Servile War
from 73 to 71 BCE

———	> 10,000 men
——	± 30,000
——	± 70,000
——	± 90,000
——	± 120,000
——	± 160,000

Area of razing & pillaging

Area hostile to Rome

Secutor   Thracian   Farm worker

Mutina
(Modena)

Asculum
(Ascoli Piceno)

Rome

The changing number of mobilized men

Rebels   Troops levied by Senate   Crassus   Reinforcements

150,000

100,000

50,000

0

battle-hardened legions were otherwise engaged in Spain and Asia Minor) and were easily routed. A second praetor then arrived on the scene with a further 7,000 men; it is not known whether they were soldiers or an improvised militia, but, either way, they were crushed in their turn. With the coming of spring, the army of slaves headed towards Lucania, losing Oenomaus on the way (4–6). Spartacus anticipated the mobilization of more resolute Roman troops and organized an army capable of resisting them. It is hard to ascertain his long-term objectives, but they did not include the abolition of slavery, as some modern commentators have supposed. With his army now comprising some 150,000 men, Spartacus marched towards the Alps, with the intention of escaping to Gaul, while Crixus and 30,000 Germans and Gauls went their own way to continue the fight against the Romans. Crixus led his men to Apulia, where they squared up against the army of the consul Gellius Publicola near Mount Gargano (7). The rebels were defeated and Crixus was killed.

Historical accounts diverge at this point, but it seems that Spartacus attacked and overcame the army of Gellius (8), before defeating the troops of Cornelius Lentulus, in Ascoli (9). Another Roman army, with 10,000 men led by Cassius Longinus, governor of Cisalpine Gaul, confronted Spartacus in Mutina but was also beaten (10). Finally, the hugely wealthy former praetor Licinius Crassus was dispatched to reinstill order, heading six newly raised legions augmented by consular legions: 40,000–50,000 men in all. The proconsul of Macedonia, Terentius Varro Lucullus, broke off his commitment to the Third Mithridatic War to sail to Brindisi to provide support (14). Spartacus's army then returned to Thurii (11), before heading towards Rhegium (13), in the hope of reaching Sicily. Crassus's troops blocked the way on all sides, however, and Spartacus's army began to disintegrate. He set off for Petelia (16) but ended up going towards Paestum. Spartacus engaged the Romans in battle one last time in Senerchia (17) but his forces were overwhelmed and he was killed.

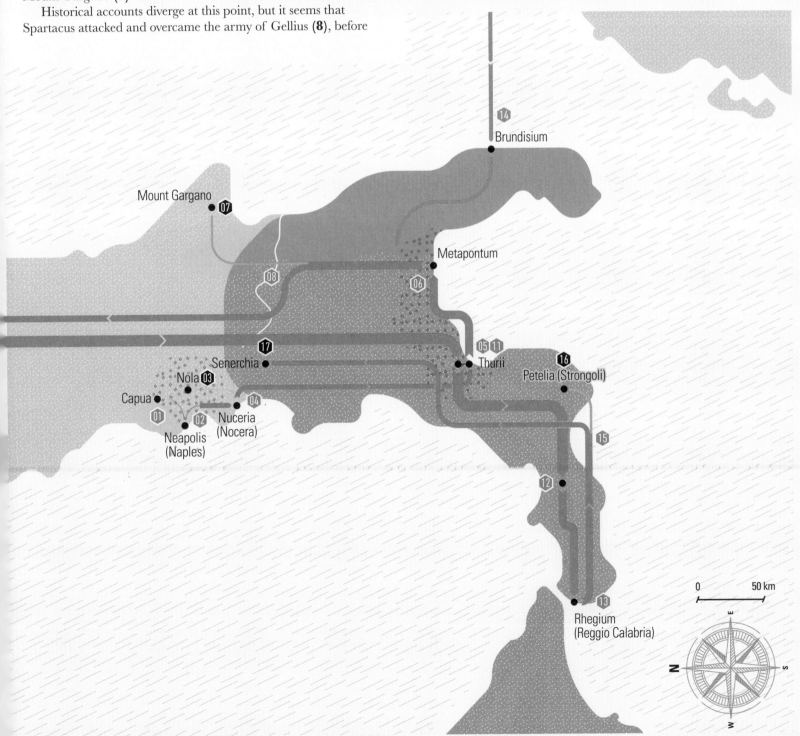

BIBLIOGRAPHY

Archaic Period

Dominique Briquel, *Le Regard des autres: les origines de Rome vues par ses ennemis (début du IVe siècle-début du Ier siècle av. J.-C.)*, Paris: Les Belles Lettres, 1997

T. J. Cornell, *The Beginnings of Rome: Italy and Rome from the Bronze Age to the Punic Wars (c. 1000–264 BC)*, London & New York: Routledge, 1995

Alexandre Grandazzi, *The Foundation of Rome: Myth and History*, Ithaca & London: Cornell University Press, 1991

Jacques Poucet, *Les Origines de Rome. Tradition et histoire*, Brussels: Facultés Universitaires Saint-Louis, 1985

—, *Les Rois de Rome: tradition et histoire*, Brussels: Académie Royale de Belgique, 2000

Christopher Smith, *Early Rome and Latium: Economy and Society c. 1000 to 500 BC*, Oxford & New York: Clarendon Press, 1996

Rome

Filippo Coarelli, *Rome and Environs: An Archaeological Guide*, Berkeley, CA: University of California Press, 2014

—, *Il Foro Romano. II. Periodo repubblicano e augusteo*, Rome: Quasar, 1985

—, *Il Foro Boario dalle origini alla fine della Repubblica*, Rome: Quasar, 1988

—, *Il Campo Marzio*, Rome: Quasar, 1997

—, *Palatium. Il Palatino dalle origini all'impero*, Rome: Quasar, 2012

Alexandre Grandazzi, *Urbs. Histoire de la ville de Rome des origines à la mort d'Auguste*, Paris: Perrin, 2017

Pierre Gros, *L'Architecture romaine du début du IIIe siècle av. J.-C. à la fin du Haut-Empire*, vol. I, *Les Monuments publics*, Paris: A. & J. Picard, 1996; vol. II, *Maisons, palais, villas et tombeaux*, Paris: A. & J. Picard, 2001

Adam Ziolkowski, *The Temples of Mid-Republican Rome and their Historical and Topographical Context*, Rome: L'Erma di Bretschneider, 1992

Institutions

Adam K. Bowman, Edward Champlin *et al.*, *The Cambridge Ancient History*, vol. 10, *The Augustan Empire, 43 BC–AD 69*, Cambridge: Cambridge University Press, 1996

Adam K. Bowman, Peter Garnsey *et al.* (eds.), *The Cambridge Ancient History*, vol. 11, *The High Empire, AD 70–192*, Cambridge: Cambridge University Press, 2000

Adam K. Bowman, Averil Cameron *et al.* (eds.), *The Cambridge Ancient History*, vol. 12, *The Crisis of Empire, AD 193–337*, Cambridge: Cambridge University Press, 2005

Averil Cameron, Peter Garnsey (eds.), *The Cambridge Ancient History*, vol. 13, *The Late Empire, AD 337–425*, Cambridge: Cambridge University Press, 1997

André Chastagnol, *L'Évolution politique sociale et économique du monde romain de Dioclétien à Julien. La mise en place du régime du Bas-Empire (284–363)*, Paris: Société d'Édition d'Enseignement Supérieur, 1995

Michel Christol, *L'Empire romain du IIIe siècle. Histoire politique: de 192, mort de Commode, à 325, concile de Nicée*, Paris: Errance, 1997

J. A. Crook, Andrew Lintott *et al.* (eds.), *The Cambridge Ancient History*, vol. 9, *The Last Age of the Roman Republic, 146–33 BC*, Cambridge: Cambridge University Press, 1994

Jean-Michel David, *La République romaine, de la deuxième guerre punique à la bataille d'Actium (218–31): crise d'une aristocratie*, Paris: Seuil, 2000

François Jacques, John Scheid, *Rome et l'intégration de l'Empire (44 av. J.-C.–260 apr. J.-C.)*, vol. I, *Les Structures de l'Empire romain*, Paris: PUF, 1990

Patrick Le Roux, *Le Haut-Empire romain en Occident d'Auguste aux Sévères*, Paris: Seuil, 1998

Claude Lepelley (ed.), *Rome et l'intégration de l'Empire*, vol. II, *Approches régionales de Haut-Empire romain*, Paris: PUF, 1998

Fergus Millar, *Rome, the Greek World, and the East*, vol. 2, *Government, Society and Culture in the Roman Empire*, Chapel Hill, NC: University of North Carolina Press, 2004

Claude Nicolet, *Space, Geography, and Politics in the Early Roman Empire*, Ann Arbor, MI: University of Michigan Press, 1990

—, *The World of the Citizen in Republican Rome*, Berkeley, CA: University of California Press, 1988

—, *Rome et la conquête du monde méditerranéen (264–27 avant J.-C.)*, vol. I, *Les structures de l'Italie romaine*, Paris: PUF, 2001 (10th ed.); vol. II, *Genèse d'un empire*, Paris: PUF, 1993 (4th ed.)

Ronald Syme, *The Roman Revolution* (1939), Oxford: OUP, 2002

F. W. Walbank, A. E. Astin *et al.* (eds.), *The Cambridge Ancient History*, vol. 7, *The Rise of Rome to 220 BC*, Cambridge: Cambridge University Press, 1990; vol. 8, *Rome and the Mediterranean to 133 BC*, Cambridge: Cambridge University Press, 1989

Cities

Michel Christol, *Une histoire provinciale. La Gaule narbonnaise de la fin du IIe siècle av. J.-C. au IIIe siècle apr. J.-C.*, Paris: Publications de la Sorbonne, 2010

Jean-Louis Ferrari, *Philhellénisme et impérialisme. Aspects idéologiques de la conquête romaine du monde hellénistique*, Rome: École française de Rome, 1988

Anna Heller, 'Domination subie, domination choisie: les cités d'Asie Mineure face au pouvoir romain, de la République à l'Empire', *Pallas, revue des études antiques*, no. 96, 2014, pp. 217–232

Frédéric Hurlet (ed.), *Rome et l'Occident. Gouverner l'Empire (IIe siècle av. J.-C.–IIe siècle apr. J.-C.)*, Rennes: Presses Universitaires de Rennes, 2009

François Jacques, *Le Privilège de liberté. Politique impériale et autonomie municipale dans les cités de l'Occident romain (161–244)*, Rome: École Française de Rome, 1984

—, *Les Cités de l'Occident romain*, Paris: Les Belles Lettres, 1990

Patrick Le Roux, *La Péninsule Ibérique aux époques romaines, 206 av. J.-C–409 apr. J.-C.*, Paris: A. Colin, 2010

—, *Romains d'Espagne. Cités et politique dans les provinces*, Paris: A. Colin, 1995

Fergus Millar, *Rome, the Greek World, and the East*, vol. I, *The Roman Republic and the Augustan Revolution*, Chapel Hill, NC: University of North Carolina Press, 2002

—, *The Roman Near East (31 BC–AD 337)*, Cambridge, MA: Harvard University Press, 1993

Society

John Andreau, Raymond Descat, *The Slave in Greece and Rome*, trans. Marion Leopold, Madison, WI: University of Wisconsin Press, 2011

Jean-Christian Dumont, *Servus. Rome et l'esclavage sous la République*, Rome: École Française de Rome, 1987

Andrea Giardina (ed.), *The Romans*, trans. Lydia G. Cochrane, Chicago & London: University of Chicago Press, 1993

Andrea Giardina, Aldo Schiavone (eds.), *Società romana e produzione schiavistica*, vol. 1, *Italia insediamenti forme economiche*; vol. 2, *Merci, mercati e scambi nel Mediterraneo*; vol. 3, *Modelli etici, diritto e trasformazioni sociali*, Rome & Bari: Editori Laterza, 1981

Danielle Gourevitch, Marie-Thérèse Raepsaet-Charlier, *La Femme dans la Rome antique*, Paris: Hachette Littératures, 2001

Paul Veyne, *Bread and Circuses: Historical Sociology and Political Pluralism*, London: Penguin, 1990

—, *La Société romaine*, Paris: Seuil, 2001

Emperors

Fergus Millar, *The Emperor in the Roman World, 31 BC– AD 337*, Ithaca, NY: Cornell University Press, 1977

Michael P. Speidel, *Riding for Caesar. The Roman Emperors' Horse Guards*, London: Batsford, 1994

Religion

Mary Beard, John North *et al.*, *Religions of Rome*, vol. 1, *A History*; vol. 2, *A Sourcebook*, Cambridge: Cambridge University Press, 1998

Yann Berthelet, *Gouverner avec les dieux. Autorité, auspices et pouvoir, sous la République romaine et sous Auguste*, Paris: Les Belles Lettres, 2015

Franz Cumont, *The Oriental Religions in Roman Paganism*, Chicago: Open Court Publishing Company, 1911

Georges Dumézil, *Archaic Roman Religion*, Chicago: Chicago University Press, 1970

Duncan Fishwick, *The Imperial Cult in the Latin West: Studies in the Ruler Cult of the Western Provinces of the Roman Empire*, vol. 1, *Part 1–2*, Leiden: Brill, 1987; vol. 2, *Part 2.2*, Leiden: Brill, 1991–92; vol. 3, *Provincial Cult. Part 1: Institutions and Evolution. Part 2: The Provincial Priesthood. Part 3: The Centre. Provincial Cult. Part 4: Bibliography, Indices, Addenda*, Leiden: Brill, 2002–5

Robin Lane Fox, *Pagans and Christians*, London: Viking; New York: Alfred J. Knopf, 1986

Augusto Fraschetti, *Roma e il principe*, Rome: Laterza, 2005

Fritz Graf, *Magic in the Ancient World*, Cambridge, MA & London: Harvard University Press, 1997

Pierre Maraval, Simon Claude Mimouni *et al.*, (eds.), *Le Christianisme des origines à Constantin*, Paris: PUF, 2006

Margaret M. Mitchell, Frances M. Young (eds.), *The Cambridge History of Christianity*, vol. 1, *Origins to Constantine*, Cambridge: Cambridge University Press, 2006

John Scheid, 'The Religious Roles of Roman Women', *in* Georges Duby, Michelle Perrot (eds.), *History of Women in the West*, vol. I, *From Ancient Goddesses to Christian Saints*, ed. Pauline Schmitt Pantel, Cambridge, MA: Harvard University Press, 1994

—, 'Les rôles religieux des femmes à Rome. Un complément', in Regula Frei-Stolba, Anne Bielman, Olivier Bianchi (eds.), *Les Femmes antiques entre sphère privée et sphère publique*, Berne: P. Lang, 2003

—, *An Introduction to Roman Religion*, Bloomington, IN: Indiana University Press, 2003

Robert Turcan, *Mithra et le mithriacisme*, Paris: Les Belles Lettres, 1993

Françoise Van Haeperen, 'Les acteurs du culte de *Magna Mater* à Rome et dans les provinces occidentales de l'Empire', in Stéphane Benoist, Anne Daguet-Gagey *et al.* (eds.), *Figures d'empire, fragments de mémoire*, Villeneuve-d'Ascq: Septentrion, 2011, pp. 467–84

Economy

Jean Andreau, *The Economy of the Roman World*, Ann Arbor, MI: Michigan Classical Press, 2015

—, *La Vie financière dans le monde romain: les métiers de manieurs d'argent: IVe siècle av. J.-C.–IIIe siècle apr. J.-C.*, Rome: École Française de Rome, 1987

Tenney Frank, *An Economic Survey of Ancient Rome*, vol. 1, *Rome and the Italy of the Republic*, Baltimore, MD: The John Hopkins Press, 1933; vol. 5, *Rome and Italy of the Empire*, Baltimore, MD: The John Hopkins Press, 1940

Claude Nicolet, *Censeurs et publicains. Économie et fiscalité dans la Rome antique*, Paris: Fayard, 2000

—, *Rendre à César. Économie et société dans la Rome antique*, Paris: Gallimard, 1988

Walter Scheidel, Ian Morris *et al.* (eds.), *The Cambridge Economic History of the Greco-Roman World*, Cambridge: Cambridge University Press, 2007

Army

Pierre Cosme, *L'Armée romaine, VIIIe siècle av. J.-C.– Ve siècle apr. J.-C.*, Paris: A. Colin, 2012

Paul Erdkamp (ed.), A *Companion to the Roman Army*, Oxford: Blackwell, 2011

Yann Le Bohec, *The Imperial Roman Army*, London: B.T. Batsford, 1994

Patrick Le Roux, *L'Armée romaine et l'organisation des provinces ibériques d'Auguste à l'invasion de 409*, Paris: De Boccard, 1982

Claude Nicolet, 'Les guerres puniques', in Claude Nicolet, *Rome et la conquête du monde méditerranéen*, Paris: PUF, 1997, pp. 594–626

Michel Reddé, Siegmar von Schnurbein (eds.), *Alésia et la bataille du Teutoburg: un parallèle critique des sources*, Ostfildern: Jan Thorbecke Verlag, 2008

—, *Alésia: fouilles et recherches franco-allemandes sur les travaux militaires romains autour du Mont-Auxois (1991–1997)*, vol. I, *Les Fouilles*; vol. II, *Le Matériel*; vol. III, *Planches hors texte*, Paris: Institut de France, 2001

Michel Reddé, *Mare nostrum. Les infrastructures, le dispositif et l'histoire de la marine militaire sous l'Empire romain*, Rome: École Française de Rome, 1986

Pat Southern, *The Roman Army: A Social and Institutional History*, Oxford: ABC-CLIO, 2007

Culture

Hervé Inglebert (ed.), *Histoire de la civilisation romaine*, Paris: PUF, 2005

Fergus Millar, *Rome, the Greek World, and the East*, vol. II, *Government, Society and Culture in the Roman Empire*, Chapel Hill, NC: University of North Carolina Press, 2004